XIIPÚKTAN

George Bryant, Fort Yuma Reservation in Winterhaven (California), 2007. Photo by Amy Miller.

World Oral Literature Series: Volume 5

Xiipúktan (First of All):
Three Views of the Origins of the Quechan People

by George Bryant

Linguistic work by Amy Miller

http://www.openbookpublishers.com

© 2013 George Bryant and Amy Miller.

Some rights are reserved. The articles of this book are licensed under a Creative Commons Attribution-NonCommercial-NoDerivs 3.0 Unported Licence (CC-BY-NC-ND 3.0). This license allows for copying any part of the work for personal and non-commercial use, providing author attribution is clearly stated. Attribution should include the following information:

Bryant, George and Miller, Amy. *Xiipúktan (First of All): Three Views of the Origins of the Quechan People*. Cambridge, UK: Open Book Publishers, 2013. DOI: 10.11647/OBP.0037

Further details about CC-BY-NC-ND licenses are available at:
http://www.creativecommons.org/licenses/by-nc-nd/3.0/

Digital material and resources associated with this volume are available on our website at: http://www.openbookpublishers.com/isbn/9781909254404

This is the fifth volume in the World Oral Literature Series, published in association with the World Oral Literature Project.

ISSN: 2050-7933 (Print)
ISSN: 2050-362X (Online)

ISBN Paperback: 978-1-909254-40-4
ISBN Hardback: 978-1-909254-64-0
ISBN Digital (PDF): 978-1-909254-41-1
ISBN Digital ebook (epub): 978-1-909254-42-8
ISBN Digital ebook (mobi): 978-1-909254-43-5
DOI: 10.11647/OBP.0037

Cover image: Taylor Lake, Lower Colorado River, California. http://bit.ly/ICwTyy, all rights reserved. Every effort has been made to contact copyright holder; any omission will be corrected if notification is made to the publisher.

All paper used by Open Book Publishers is SFI (Sustainable Forestry Initiative), and PEFC (Programme for the Endorsement of Forest Certification Schemes) Certified.

Printed in the United Kingdom and United States by Lightning Source for
Open Book Publishers (Cambridge, UK)

Contents

Authors' biographies	vi
Dedication	vii
PART I: ACKNOWLEDGEMENTS AND INTRODUCTION *by Amy Miller*	1
Acknowledgements	2
Introduction	3
A Quechan Account of Origins	5
The Quechan Legend of the Creation	6
The Migration of the Yuman Tribes	7
From English to Quechan	7
From recording to manuscript	12
Alphabet	13
Grammar	15
Conventions	16
References	17
PART II: THE QUECHAN LEGEND OF THE CREATION *Retold in the Quechan language by George Bryant*	19
PART III: A QUECHAN ACCOUNT OF ORIGINS *Retold in the Quechan language by George Bryant*	59
PART IV: THE MIGRATION OF THE YUMAN TRIBES *Told in the Quechan language by George Bryant*	171
Notes	187

Authors' biographies

George Bryant was born in 1921 and grew up in a Quechan-speaking family. He attended school on Fort Yuma Reservation and later at the Phoenix Indian School, Yuma High School, and the Sherman Institute. As a young man he enlisted in the United States Marine Corps, serving in combat in the Pacific in World War II and in Korea. Later he was elected to the Quechan Tribal Council, where he was involved in getting the federal government to restore tribal lands and in planning many of the projects that have made the tribe successful today. He is now retired and lives in Yuma, Arizona.

Bryant follows a family tradition of working to preserve the Quechan language. His grandfather, Chappo Bryant, and his father, Michael Bryant, were both involved in linguistics projects with linguist A. M. Halpern in the 1930s. George Bryant has been working with linguist Amy Miller since 1998. He is the primary contributor to the forthcoming *Quechan Dictionary*, and (along with Barbara Levy, Millie Romero, and Amy Miller) he devoted many years to translating stories for the forthcoming volume *Stories from Quechan Oral Literature from the Collection of A. M. Halpern*.

Amy Miller earned a PhD in linguistics from the University of California, San Diego, where she studied with Margaret Langdon. She is the author of *A Grammar of Jamul Tiipay* (2001), co-author of the *Barona Inter-Tribal Dictionary* (2008), and co-editor of *Kar'úk: Native Accounts of the Quechan Mourning Ceremony by A.M. Halpern* (1997). She has been studying and documenting Yuman languages since 1984.

Pa'iipáa Kwatsáan nyi'awéeyk 'awésh

PART I: ACKNOWLEDGEMENTS AND INTRODUCTION

by Amy Miller

Acknowledgements

Much of our recording and reviewing was done at the Quechan Elderly Nutrition Site in Winterhaven, California between 2003 and 2006, and we thank the staff of the Site, especially the late Betty Robles, for their hospitality.

Many people have helped to get this book published, and we are grateful to them all, including Quechan Language Preservation Program director Barbara Levy and language teachers Ila Dunzweiler, Arlie Emerson, Della Escalanti, and Judith Osborne; Marilyn Swafford, formerly of Quechan Social Services; Quechan grants writer Cliff O'Neill; the family of George Bryant; and our good friend Susan Decker. Amy Miller would also like to thank the staff of the Santa Barbara Museum of Natural History, and John R. Johnson in particular, for their assistance during the tenure of her NSF grant, and Matthew Hanser for proofreading English portions of the manuscript.

This material is based upon work supported by the National Science Foundation under Grant No. 0317783. Any opinions, findings, and conclusions or recommendations expressed in this material are those of the authors and do not necessarily reflect the views of the National Science Foundation.

Publication of this book is made possible by the Institute of Museum and Library Services Native American/Native Hawaiian Museum Services Program grant number MN-00-13-0025-13. We thank the Quechan Tribal Council for prompt approval of the grant budget. We are also grateful to Open Book Publishers and their director, Dr. Alessandra Tosi, as well as the World Oral Literature Project and its director, Dr. Mark Turin, for making the publication of this book possible.

Introduction

The Quechan people live along the lower part of the Colorado River in an area which has been their home for a very long time.[1] Traditionally, Quechan territory extended from around Needles, California, to the Gulf of California (Forde 1931:88). Today, the Quechan Indian Nation occupies Fort Yuma Indian Reservation, a portion of their original territory extending along the east side of the river from Winterhaven, California into Yuma, Arizona. Information about traditional Quechan culture may be found in Forde (1931), Bee (1983), and Halpern (1997). Aspects of Quechan history, society, and politics have been discussed by Forbes (1965) and Bee (1981).

The Quechan language, also known as Yuma or Kwatsáan, belongs to the Yuman language family. The Yuman family has three major branches, as diagrammed in Figure 1: River (the branch to which Quechan belongs), Pai, and Delta-California. Kiliwa is regarded as a language isolate within the family.

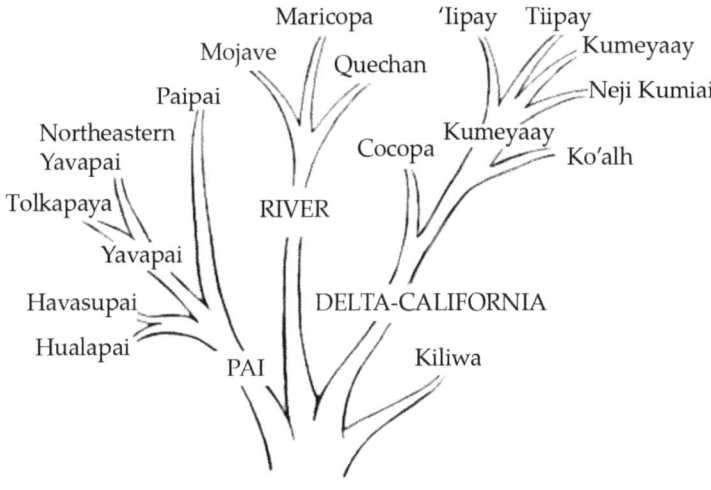

Figure 1. The Yuman language family

---

1 While Bee (1981:viii) points out that Spanish records of the late 17th century are the first to mention the Quechan by name, Stewart (1983:1) cites evidence that their ancestors have lived in the area for at least a millennium.

According to Quechan tradition, the Quechan, Maricopa, Cocopa, and Kumeyaay (whom the Quechan call Kamia) people were created together at the beginning of time.² Eventually they were taken to the sacred mountain 'Avíi Kwa'amée (more widely known as Newberry Mountain, located north of Needles, California), where they were taught the proper way to live in the world, and when they came down from this mountain the tribes went their separate ways. The name Quechan makes explicit reference to this traditional history: Quechan is an anglicized spelling of *Kwaatsáan*, which means 'those who descended'.³ As Mr. Bryant explains in Part III, it is shortened from *Xáam Kwaatsáan* 'those who descended by means of water',⁴ a name which refers either to the descent of the Quechan people from 'Avíi Kwa'amée (Bee 1983:97) or to their subsequent route down the Colorado River to their traditional territory (George Bryant, personal communication).

The creation story is central to Quechan literature and culture. It tells how the people came into existence and explains the origin of their environment and their oldest traditions. It also forms the backdrop against which much of the tribe's extensive oral literature may be understood.

There are almost as many different versions of the Quechan creation story as there are Quechan families. (Different families even have different ways of saying the name of the Creator.)⁵ Different versions reflect different family backgrounds and traditions, and no single version is more legitimate or more "correct" than any other. On the contrary, the variation in its stories adds much to the richness and vibrancy of Quechan literature. For two published views of the Creation which differ from those in this volume, see Wilson (1984) and the film *Journey from Spirit Mountain*.

This volume presents three views of the origins of the Quechan people. Two are traditional: one is based on a story recorded by anthropologist J.P. Harrington at the beginning of the twentieth century, while the other was researched and recalled by Quechan tribal member George

---

2   The Mojave and Hualapai, along with the Mexicans and whites, were created shortly thereafter; see Part III of this volume.
3   *Kwaatsáan* is based on the archaic plural form *aatsáan-k* 'they descended'; modern plural forms are *natsén-k* and *atsáan-k* (the latter with initial *a* rather than *aa*).
4   This interpretation assumes that *xáam* is composed of '*axá* 'water' plus instrumental case marker -*m*; while the loss of the initial syllable is expected, vowel lengthening is not. Under another interpretation, *xáam* is composed of *xáa* 'different way, different manner, different direction, etc.' plus instrumental case marker -*m*, and *Xáam Kwaatsáan* means 'those who descended a different way'.
5   Mr. Bryant uses two versions of the name of the Creator, *Kukwiimáatt* and *Kukumáatt*, interchangeably.

Bryant nearly a hundred years later. These two versions of the creation story complement one another and together provide a richer and more comprehensive account of the origins of the Quechan people than could either version on its own.[6] The third narrative provides a bridge between traditional creation stories and today's world. It is based loosely on the modern scientific view of a migration across the Bering Strait, yet it also describes how various Yuman tribes came to settle in their traditional locations and how they got their names, and in this way it serves as a sequel to the traditional stories in Parts II and III.

This volume does not reveal any tribal secrets; rather, it restores to its original language a story which has been in print in English for over a hundred years. It is presented here in a bilingual format which we hope will be useful to fluent speakers, language learners, and English speakers alike. The sections below explain exactly how the restoration was done.

A Quechan Account of Origins

An early account of the Quechan creation, entitled "A Yuma Account of Origins," was published in English by anthropologist John Peabody Harrington in 1908. Harrington learned the story from a Quechan man named Joe Homer. Homer was born sometime in the early 1860s and acquired his knowledge of the creation in the traditional Quechan way: through dreaming.[7]

Dreaming holds a central place in traditional Quechan culture and religion. "Every individual 'can dream vivid dreams'," writes Harrington (1908:326), "and whatever is dreamed is believed either to have once happened or to be about to happen. Only a few men, however, dream proficiently and professionally." These powerful few have the ability to visit the mythic past of the Quechan—and in particular the scene of the creation—in dreams.

Joe Homer told Harrington:

I was present from the very beginning, and saw and heard all. I dreamed a little of it at a time. I would then tell it to my friends. The old men would

---

[6] The reader is encouraged to consult the Mojave creation story (one version of which was documented in English by Kroeber 1948, 1972) and that of the Maricopa (one version of which was documented by Spier 1933:345ff). Both of these are clearly related to, yet quite different from, Quechan versions of the creation story.

[7] We infer this Homer's approximate date of birth from Harrington's (1908:326) statement that Homer was "about forty-five years old" at the time of publication.

say, "That is right! I was there and heard it myself." Or they would say, "You have dreamed poorly. That is not right." And they would tell me right. So at last I learned the whole of it right. [Joe Homer, quoted by Harrington 1908:327]

His version of the creation story has thus been corroborated and in some places amended by his contemporaries.

While the full version of the creation myth is traditionally told over the course of four nights, the English version published by Harrington is packed into twenty pages of scholarly prose, and we may conclude that it has been very tightly condensed. It was, however, "carefully revised by the narrator himself," according to Harrington (1908:326).

In June, 2003, George Bryant and I studied "A Yuma Account of Origins" and agreed that the story should be restored to its original language. Mr. Bryant began then and there the lengthy process of retelling it in Quechan. During the first two sessions, I transcribed his narration by hand. Thereafter Mr. Bryant consented to have the story recorded, and we recorded two sessions in September and two more in November, 2003. After retelling the story to its end, Mr. Bryant returned to the beginning of the story and retold it for a second time, for the purpose of recording. As a result the entire story is now recorded on tape. It is approximately six hours in duration. Mr. Bryant's retelling is entitled "A Quechan Account of Origins."

The Quechan Legend of the Creation

Mr. Bryant grew up "in between" cultures and considers himself fortunate to have experienced both traditional Quechan and modern American ways of life. As a child, he listened to tribal elders telling the creation story. No two narrations were quite the same, and he found each version to be useful for filling in gaps left by the others. As an adult, he researched English-language written versions of the story and found greater differences. "They didn't know too much English back then," he explains, and with regard to some details, "the interpreters didn't know how to put it right."

Mr. Bryant eventually synthesized his childhood memories and the results of his research in an article entitled "The Kwatsan Legend of the Creation", which appeared as a three-part series in the *Quechan Newsletter* in 1995. His work provides a different perspective and a bit more information about the early events of the Creation than does Harrington's.

Mr. Bryant retold his version of the creation story in the Quechan language on January 27, 2004, using a draft of "The Quechan Legend of the Creation" as a guide. His narration is approximately 62 minutes in duration.

The Migration of the Yuman Tribes

The modern age has a different view of how Native Americans came to populate the New World. "The Migration of the Yuman Tribes" presents Mr. Bryant's personal view of the origins of the Quechan people. Incorporating modern scientific information, it begins with the migration of people across the Bering Strait from Asia to North America. It then describes how the ancestors of the Yuman people traveled through the continent, dividing themselves into groups and eventually settling in what became their homelands. This portion of the narrative, which also explains how the tribes got their names, makes a fitting conclusion to traditional Creation stories as well as to the modern account.

"The Migration of the Tribes" is a spontaneous original narrative, notable for the ease and fluency with which it was told. George Bryant narrated "The Migration of the Yuman Tribes" in the Quechan language on April 1, 2004. This narration is approximately 15 minutes long.

From English to Quechan

We began with the intention of translating the narratives of Harrington (1908) and Bryant (1995) back into Quechan. We soon found that converting an English-language narrative into idiomatic Quechan is no simple task. It requires not just the translation of words and sentences but extensive restructuring at the levels of syntax, rhetorical structure, and local organization. It also typically involves the elaboration and expansion of material in order to express detail at the level considered appropriate in idiomatic Quechan and the re-creation of conversations that are merely summarized in the English version. In short, it amounts to retelling the story in Quechan using the English version as a guide.

Mr. Bryant has the remarkable ability to do all this simultaneously, if slowly and thoughtfully, in his head, producing idiomatic Quechan as the result. After a brief study of Harrington's "A Yuma Account of Origins", he used Harrington's English text as a guide, restructured and reorganized its ideas, and restated them in Quechan at the appropriate level of detail.

He did the same for "The Quechan Legend of the Creation". His Quechan renditions of these stories retain all the content of the English originals but differ from them in syntax, rhetorical structure, local organization, and level of detail. The reader who compares the line-by-line English versions presented here to the English versions published by Harrington (1908) and Bryant (1995) will immediately appreciate these differences. For example, where Harrington writes, "In vain the wicked besought Kwikumat to let them in. Most of them were drowned," Mr. Bryant elaborates:

Piipáa 'atsláytsəts mata'ár oov'ótsk,
nyáanyi,
Kukwiimáatt kwakyáavək:
" 'Aakxávapátəlyá!"
a'íik 'et.
"Kaváarək," a'íim,
avoonóok 'eta.
'Atáytanək,
'axály oopóoyk 'et.

We translate this as:

The bad people stood outside,
and at that point,
they asked Kukwiimáatt a favor:
"We want to come in too!"
they said, they say.
"No," he said,
and they were moving about there, they say.
There were a whole lot of them,
and they drowned, they say.

In re-telling this episode, Mr. Bryant expands and restructures the narrative to reflect the chronological order of events. He re-creates a conversation to which Harrington only alludes. And—by invention or memory—he supplies subtle details which Harrington omits but which are necessary in Quechan storytelling: what the people are doing and how they are oriented before Kukwiimáatt's decision (*mata'ár oov'ótsk*) and after the decision (*avoonóok*), and the number of people who are affected (*'atáyk*).

Where Harrington writes, "Lizard (Kwaatuly) lighted a wisp of arrow-weed. He lighted the southeast corner of the pyre first, and last of all the southwest corner," Mr. Bryant's re-telling is rich in traditional Quechan rhetorical devices including repetition, syntactic parallelism, and the iconic use of narrative time to mirror the duration of an event:

> Kwaatúuly,
> nyáanyi 'eethóo atháwk,
> awíim,
> taráat,
> 'a'áw aatapályək.
> 'A'áw aatapályəm aráak.
> Ayáak,
> nyaayáak,
> kavéely,
> kavéely athúum,
> nyáavik athúum,
> kwaaxwíirnyi,
> nyáany xiipúk aatapályk.
> Viiwáamk,
> viiwáamk,
> aakwíink,
> kwaaxwíirnyi aakwíink,
> viiwáanyək,
> kavéely,
> kavéely 'anyaaxáap kamémt.
> Awíntik,
> taráantik.

We translate this as:

> *As for Kwatúuly (Chuckwalla),*
> *at that point he got some willow,*
> *and so,*
> *he set it on fire,*
> *he lit a fire.*
> *He lit a fire and it blazed up.*
> *He went along,*
> *and as he went along,*

in the south,
it was in the south,
it was over here,
in the corner,
that was the first place he lit.
He went along,
he went along,
and he turned,
he turned the corner there,
and he went along,
and in the south,
he brought it into the southwest.
He did it again as he had done before,
he set it on fire again as he had done before.

Finally, consider the following passage from Bryant (1995): "While traveling toward the top he opened his eyes in spite of what some strange sense perception had warned him as it did previously to Kukwimat but since Asakwimat did not heed the warning he was blinded by the waters that filled his eyes." Mr. Bryant retells this passage in Quechan as:

Viiyáak,
viiyáaxaym,
'atsaayúu nyiuukanáavək 'etá.
Xiipúk Kukwiimáatt uu'ítsənya,
nyáany uukanáavəntík 'etá.
Avathúum:
nyáanya uukuunáavnya makyík a'áv aly'émk,
makyík athúu lya'émk,
athóxaym,
'atsaayúu,
'aayúu,
'axám áamk viiyáaxayk,
viiyáany,
uutstáaqtsəm athúum,
'axányts alyaxávək,
eethónyily.

Eethó kwa'ura'úur alyaxávək athúum,
nyáanyəm,
nyaanyiimánk,
'atsaayúulya'émk 'etá.
Eethóts tár 'ím.

In the retelling, Mr. Bryant once again restructures the narrative by reporting events in the order in which they occurred. He expands on the information presented in the original English version by making liberal use of repetition, paraphrase, and syntactic parallelism. As a result, the Quechan-language retelling brings to the foreground—and causes the listener or reader to spend some time considering—each of the events which make up this portion of the narrative. We translate the Quechan version as:

He went along,
he went along, and suddenly,
he was told things, they say.
Whatever had been said first to Kukwiimáatt,
that's what was said to him too, they say.
This (is what) happened:
he did not listen at all to what was said to him,
not at all,
and suddenly,
well,
well,
he was swimming along, and suddenly,
he was going along,
and he opened (his eyes),
and the water went in,
into his eyes.
It went into his eyeballs, and so,
at that point,
from then on,
he couldn't see anything, they say.
He was blind.

From recording to manuscript

I listened carefully and repeatedly to the recordings of Mr. Bryant retelling the two stories, and transcribed them verbatim. I divided the text into lines motivated by prosodic criteria, including melody, rhythm, and pauses, outlined in Miller (1997). Then, using Harringon (1908) and Bryant (1995) for reference, I gave each line of Quechan text a coherent English translation.

My primary goal in translating was to convey in English the intended meaning of each prosodic line of Quechan. In some cases it was necessary to add lexical information to an English line so that information conveyed either implicitly or grammatically in the Quechan line would not be lost. For instance, since English lacks a switch-reference system, it was sometimes necessary to add a noun phrase to the translation to help the reader keep track of reference. Since English lacks overt case markers for lexical noun phrases, it was sometimes necessary to add a verb to the translation of a line consisting solely of a postposed noun phrase in order to clarify that noun phrase's function. Added information appears in parentheses.

There are several reasons for translating at the level of the prosodic line: First, I hope to capture in the English translation as much as possible of the rhetorical structure and local organization of the Quechan version. Second, I hope to influence the reader's pace, encouraging him or her to give due attention to each idea that is expressed as the story unfolds. Finally, I hope that an English key to small units of Quechan language will be useful to the language learner.

Mr. Bryant and I spent many weeks reviewing the transcripts and translations of the tapes. Mr. Bryant considered each line carefully and pointed out ways in which it might be improved. His corrections to the English translations have been incorporated into the finished product. Of the numerous corrections to the Quechan transcript which he suggested, those which clarify the structure or meaning of the narrative, as well as those which seemed particularly important to Mr. Bryant, have been incorporated into the text. As a result, there are now minor discrepancies between the Quechan version as it appears here and that which is heard on the tape. Each such discrepancy is explained in notes at the end of the volume. Corrections involving matters of style—many of them intended to make the Quechan narrative sound appropriately formal—are documented in the endnotes, but in order to minimize discrepancies between the tape and the transcript they have not been incorporated into the text.

A few general observations are noted here, once and for all: First, like most speakers, Mr. Bryant frequently uses the short variants *'ím*, *'ét* or *'et*, and *'ityá* of suffixed forms of the auxiliary verb *a'íim* 'to say' to convey quotative mood. In formal speech these short forms would be replaced with the corresponding long forms *a'ím*, *a'ét*, and *a'ítyá*. Second, the word *'atsaayúu* (along with its variants *'aayúu* and *nyaayúu*) literally means 'thing'. In discourse, *'atsaayúu* and its variants are often used as hesitation words, holding the floor for the speaker while he decides how best to express his next idea, and under such circumstances they are translated with the English hesitation word *well*. Mr. Bryant would like the literal meaning 'thing' always to be kept in mind. Finally, certain auxiliary verbs are often used as clause-linking devices, and in this use they are best translated into English as conjunctions; for further discussion see Miller (1993).

Alphabet

The Quechan language is written phonemically, using a practical orthography:

Vowels:

á, à	like the *a* in *about*.
aa	a longer sound, like the *a* in *father*.
e	like the *e* in *pet*.
ee	the same sound, only held for a longer time. In certain contexts (for example, following *th*, *sh*, or *ny*), *ee* is lowered and sounds almost like the *a* in *mad*, only held for a longer time.
i	like the *i* in *pit*.
ii	like the *i* in *machine*, only held for a longer time.
o	like the *o* in *pot*.
oo	the same sound, only held for a longer time.
u	like the *u* in *put*.
uu	like the *u* in *rule*, only held for a longer time.

a	this *a*, written without an accent, represents "schwa," a special vowel whose pronunciation depends upon the sounds which surround it, as discussed below, and which may disappear or be relocated when prefixes are added to the word.
ə	this vowel represents schwa in post-stress position, where it sounds like the *e* in *government*.

Consonants:

k	like the *k* in *sky*.
kw	the same sound, but made with rounded lips. It sounds like the *kw* in *backward*.
ky	like the *ky* in *backyard*.
l	like the *l* in *freely*.
lly	to make this sound, put your tongue in position to say *ly*, then blow air out so that it goes around the sides of your tongue.
ly	like the *lli* in *million*. This sound is made with the tip of the tongue touching the lower teeth.
m	like the *m* in *mom*.
n	like Spanish *n*, as in *bonito*.
ng	like the *ng* in *sing*. This sound is found in few spoken words but many song words.
ny	like the *ny* in *canyon*.
p	like the *p* in *spin*.
q	a sound similar to *k* but pronounced farther back in the mouth.
qw	the same sound, but made with rounded lips.
r	a tapped or slightly trilled *r*, similar to the *r* in the Spanish pronunciation of *María*.
s	like Spanish *s*, as in *peso*.
sh	this is not like English *sh*; instead, it is a whistling sound made with the tip of the tongue at the roots of the teeth and slightly curled back.
t	like Spanish *t*, as in *bonito*. Made with the tongue touching the upper front teeth, or even between the front teeth.
th	like the *th* in *this*.
ts	like the *ts* in *lots*.

tt	like English *t*, as in *stun*. Made with the tongue touching the roots of the upper front teeth.
ty	like the *ty* in the expression *got ya!*
v	like the *v* in *very*.
w	like the *w* in *wet*.
x	like the *ch* in German *ach*, or like Spanish *j* as in *jota*.
xw	the same sound, but made with rounded lips.
y	like the *y* in *yes*.
'	this sound, known as "glottal stop", is actually a brief period of silence made by closing the vocal cords. It is found in the English expressions *uh-uh* and *uh-oh*.

Pronunciation tips: For many speakers, particularly those of the older generation, a vowel which begins a word is preceded by aspiration (a puff of air which some people think of as "a little *h*"). Aspiration disappears when the word is prefixed; for instance, while aspiration may be heard at the beginning of av'áak 'he walked', it is not heard in nyaav'áak 'when he walked'.

The vowels *á* and *à* are pronounced like the *a* in *about*. Unaccented *a*, on the other hand, represents an inorganic vowel known in the Yuman literature as "schwa," and its pronunciation depends upon the sounds that surround it. For instance, when followed by *y* or between palatal consonants, unaccented *a* may be pronounced like the *i* in *pit*; when followed by *w* it may be pronounced like the *u* in *put*. Unaccented *a* may disappear or be relocated when a prefix is added to the word. A sequence of *kw* followed by unaccented *a* may be pronounced either *kwa* or, in casual speech, *ku*.

When a stressed vowel is followed by *y* or *w*, the sounds are pronounced sequentially; they are not combined using English conventions. When pronouncing the sequence *áay*, for instance, one first pronounces the *aa* sound (like the *a* in *father*) then pronounces the *y* sound (as in *yes*). When pronouncing the sequence *éw*, one first pronounces the *e* (like the *e* in *pet*) and then the *w* (as in *wet*).

Grammar

The grammar of Quechan is highly complex. A detailed description may be found in Halpern (1946, 1947) and a brief update in Miller (1997:25-32). The reader is encouraged to consult these sources. To provide some idea of the extent to which Quechan differs from English, we mention here just a few of the most basic facts about the language.

The basic word order is SUBJECT-OBJECT-VERB. Noun phrases are frequently omitted if their referents are understood. Sometimes a noun phrase is placed at the end of a sentence as an afterthought. A case marker indicates the function of the noun phrase in the sentence.

Pronouns typically take the form of prefixes on the verb. There are also independent words for 'I', 'me', 'you', 'we', and 'us', but these are used primarily for emphasis.

Plurals and nominalizations may be formed from basic verb stems in various complicated ways which include prefixation, suffixation, and changes in the length and/or quality of the stressed vowel. Many verbs have two plural forms: a collective/dual form and a distributive/multiple form. The use of plural forms is optional, except in the case of motion verbs and auxiliaries, where it is obligatory.

While verb tenses are important in English, aspect and mood are important in Quechan. Progressive aspect is indicated by auxiliary verb constructions, and notions such as repetition, limited or interrupted duration, and sequentiality may be marked by suffixes on the verb. Irrealis mood (which indicates that an event has never or not yet taken place) is marked by means of a suffix on the verb, as are most other moods including optative, interrogative, and dubitative. Quotative mood is indicated by an auxiliary verb construction and imperative mood by a verbal prefix which fits into the same paradigm as the personal pronominal prefixes.

Clauses are often linked together in long chains. A switch reference marker which follows the verb tells whether its subject is the same as or different from the subject of the following verb.

Conventions

The following conventions are used in this volume:

- The text is divided into lines based on the prosodic characteristics (such as melody, rhythm, and pause) of the Quechan version. Where narration was halting or interrupted, syntactic criteria and Mr. Bryant's judgment were used to determine line breaks.
- If a prosodic line is too long to fit within a single graphic line, it is continued on a second graphic line. The second graphic line is

indented slightly. The translation of a prosodic line may also be spread over two graphic lines.
- Each prosodic line of Quechan is given a coherent translation in the facing column. To use the English translation as a key to the meaning of its Quechan counterpart, compare a complete English line (which begins flush with the center margin and may wrap onto a second, indented graphic line) with a complete Quechan prosodic line (which begins flush with the left margin and may wrap onto a second, indented graphic line).
- The text is divided into paragraphs on the basis of prosodic characteristics (such as melody and pause) of the Quechan version. Where narration was halting or interrupted, thematic criteria and Mr. Bryant's judgment were used to determine paragraph breaks. Prosodic paragraphs (and some thematic paragraphs) are separated by blank lines.
- A series of three asterisks indicates that an interruption has taken place or material has been omitted.
- When t or tt (each of which represents a distinct sound, as described above) is followed by *t*, *th*, *ts*, *tt*, or *ty*, a hyphen is used to separate the relevant symbols.

References

Bee, Robert L., *Crosscurrents Along the Colorado: The Impact of Government Policy on the Quechan Indians* (Tucson: University of Arizona Press, 1981).
—, Quechan. *Handbook of North American Indians, vol. 10: Southwest*, ed. by Alfonso Ortiz (Washington, D.C.: Smithsonian Institution, 1983).
Bryant, George, 'The Kwatsaan Legend of the Creation', in *Quechan Newsletter* (Winterhaven: Quechan Tribe, 1995).
Forbes, Jack D., *Warriors of the Colorado: The Yumas of the Quechan Nation and Their Neighbors* (Norman: University of Oklahoma Press, 1965).
Forde, C. Daryll, *Ethnography of the Yuma Indians* (University of California Publications in American Archaeology and Ethnology 28.4, 1931).
Halpern, A.M., 'Yuma I: Phonemics', *International Journal of American Linguistics* 12.1 (1946).
—, 'Yuma II: Morphophonemics', *International Journal of American Linguistics* 12.3 (1946).
—, 'Yuma III: Grammatical Processes and the Noun', *International Journal of American Linguistics* 12.4 (1946).
—, 'Yuma IV: Verb Themes', *International Journal of American Linguistics* 13.1 (1947).
—, 'Yuma V: Conjugation of the Verb Theme', *International Journal of American Linguistics* 13.2 (1947).
—, 'Yuma VI: Miscellaneous Morphemes', *International Journal of American*

Linguistics 13.3 (1947).

—, *Kar'úk: Native Accounts of the Quechan Mourning Ceremony*, ed. by Amy Miller and Margaret Langdon (Berkeley and Los Angeles: University of California Publications in Linguistics 128, 1997).

Harrington, John Peabody, 'A Yuma Account of Origins'. *Journal of American Folk-Lore* 21.82 (1908).

Journey from Spirit Mountain, Dir. Daniel Golding, perf. Preston J. Arrow-weed (Ahmut Pipa Foundation and Hokan Media Productions, 2010).

Kroeber, A.L. 'Seven Mohave Myths', *Anthropological Records* 11.1 (Berkeley and Los Angeles: University of California Press, 1948).

—, 'More Mojave Myths', *Anthropological Records* 27 (Berkeley, Los Angeles, and London: University of California Press, 1972).

Miller, Amy, 'Conjunctions and Reference Tracking in Yuma', *Proceedings of the Meeting of the Society for the Study of the Indigenous Languages of the Americas and the Hokan-Penutian Workshop* (Berkeley: Survey of California and Other Indian Languages Report 8, 1993).

—, 'Introduction' in *Kar'úk: Native Accounts of the Quechan Mourning Ceremony*, by M. Halpern (Berkeley and Los Angeles: University of California Publications in Linguistics 128, 1997).

Spier, Leslie, *Yuman Tribes of the Gila River* (Chicago: University of Chicago Press, 1933, reprinted by Dover Publications, Inc., New York, 1978).

Stewart, Kenneth M., 'Yumans: Introduction' in *Handbook of the Indians of North America, Volume 10: Southwest*, ed. by Alfonso Ortiz (Washington, D.C.: Smithsonian Institution, 1983).

Wilson, William, 'Excerpts from the *Lightning Song*' in *Spirit Mountain*, ed. by Leanne Hinton and Lucille Watahomigie (Tucson: University of Arizona Press, 1984).

PART II:
THE QUECHAN LEGEND OF THE CREATION

*Retold in the Quechan Language
by George Bryant*

DOI: 10.11647/OBP.0037.02

The Quechan Legend of the Creation

'Amattáam nyakór,[1]	Many years ago,
Pa'iipáa Nyiikwanáam 'amáy kuuváatsənyts	the Great Person who was in the sky
'amáttva vikavátsnya atséwk.	made this earth that is here.
'Atsaayúu ashtúum —	He gathered things —
vathí atháwətk vathí atháwətk athúm,	they were here and there, and so,
ashtúum,	he gathered them,
nyáanyəm atséwk.	and with those (things) he made it.
'Amáttnya atséwəm athum,	He made the earth, and so,
'axányənyts 'amáttnya aamáarək,	water covered the earth,
maxáknyi,	and under it,
'aayúu,	well,
'amátt akúp vatáyts siivám,	there was a big cave,
pa'iipáats xavík nyatsuuváayk.	and two people lived there.
'Ashéntits Kukwiimáatt a'ét.	One was Kukwiimáatt (Body of Flesh), they say.
Nyáanyts avuuváatk athúum,	There he was, and so,
'ashéntəntínyənyts 'Asákwiimáatt 'et.	the other one was 'Asákwiimáatt (Body of Fog), they say.
Nyáanyəny,	That one,
iimáatt-ts thómayúuv aly'ém,[2]	his body was not visible,
'atsaayúu,	well,
xaly'aatsxánəm lyavíik,	he was like a ghost,
athúuk 'ét.	he was, they say.
Athúm,	So,
viitháwk,	here they were,
'akór alynyaayém,	and after a long time,
Kukwiimáattányts,	Kukwiimáatt (said),
" 'Ashútsáa!"[3]	"Little brother!"
" 'Antsénáa!"[4]	or "Older brother!"
kaa'íts nyáany a'íim.[5]	he said something like that.
" 'Anyáats vi'ayáak,	"I will go,
'axám 'áamk vi'ayáanyək,	I will go swimming along,
kaawíts makyí atháwəm 'ayúuxa.	and I will see whatever is there.
Nya'ayáam,	When I have gone,

máanyts aaíim nyáavi mavák
　'anyshuutháwk.
Av'uuváanyək,
xaméer 'atkavékxá.⁶
Nya'váak,
nya'váak 'athúm,
nyáany nyakanáavxa,
kaawíts 'uuyúunya."

Vanyaa'íim,
Kukwiimáatt-ts
'amátt uukúpənya atspámək.
'Axáts mattapéek viitháwm athúm,

'axám áamk viiyáanyək,
'amáyəny nyaaváamk,
athót.

Viiyáaxayk,
eethóny shatpíittk,
viithíinyk,
viithíinyk,
llyóq a'ím atspák.

Avuuváaxaym,
kaawíts a'ávək;
kaawíts makyík thomayúuv
　aly'émtəsáa,
'atsuukanáavək uuváak 'etá,

viiyáaxáym.

Viiyáanyək —
viiyáanyək,
nyaaváamk.
'Amáy nyaaváamk,
eethónyəm uutstáaq ayúuk,
a'étá.

you just sit here and wait for me.
I will stay there,
and later on I will come back.
When I arrive,
when I arrive, then
I will tell you about that,
(about) what I have seen."

Having said this,
Kukwiimáatt
came out of the cave.
There was a tremendous amount of
　water, and so,
he went swimming along,
and he got to the surface,
he did.

He went along,
he had his eyes closed,
and he came,
and he came,
he popped up (out of the water) and
　appeared.

There he was, and suddenly,
he heard something;
he couldn't see anything, but⁷

things had been explained to him,
　they say,⁸
as he had gone along.

He went along,
he went along,
and he got there.
When he got to the surface,
he opened his eyes and looked,
they say.

Nyáany,	As for that,
nyáany a'íim kanáav 'etá.	he had been told about that, they say.[9]
A'étəm athúm,	And so,
'atsayúuk uuváak;	he sat looking at things;
tsáaməly ayúuk.	he looked at everything.
Athótəsáa,	However,
kaawíts makyí avá aly'émk,	there was nothing there,
'atsaayúu,	well,
'anyáanyənyts 'anyáaytank uuvám,	the sun was really bright,
ayúuk;	and he saw it;
'axáts aaíim makyí atháw aaly'íim,	water was just everywhere, it was all over the place,
aamáarək viitháwəm,	it had flooded (the land) and there it was,
ayúuk.	and he saw it.
Alynyiithúutsk viiv'óowxayk athúm,	He stood here thinking, and so,
"Kaawíts nyatséwəm athúm	"Something made me, so that
'amatt vathí	here on earth
'atsaayúu 'uuxúuttk viitháwm;[10]	there would be good things;
nyáanya 'atséw 'ím,	I am going to make them,
'awíi 'ím,	I am going to do it,
va'oonóom,	here I am,
pa'iipáa kwanyatsamíits nyáavi voonóontixá [11]	and there will be different kinds of people here
'atséwk nya'aavíirəm."[12]	when I have finished making them."
Nyáanyənyts,	That (person),
'atsaayúu ootséwənya alyuuváak.[13]	there he was, among the things he had made.
"Pa'iipáyxá,"	"They will be alive,"
a'étk,	he said,
kanáavək viiwáat.	and he went on talking.
Alynyiithúutsk viitháwk,	He sat here thinking about it,
iisháaly nyamshoo'órnya 'axály shathúunk,	and he put his index finger into the water,

shaakwíink vaawée vaawée
  awétk.¹⁴
Voonóonyək,
aashváarək nyamaatsítsk awíntik:

" 'Axá vathány¹⁵
'ashawáamk av'oonóok
'ashawáamk av'oonóok.
Kuur a'ím
'amátt-ts atspákxa.
Kúur a'ím
'amátt-ts atspákxa."

A'íim voonóot.

'Atsaayúu,
mas'éets athúum,
nyaathúum;
maxák atháwətk athúm,
awíim avoonóoxaym,
'amáynyi kayáamk vaayáa,
nyáany,
kúur a'ím,
'amátt-ts nyiitháwt.¹⁶

Athúm,
viitháwnyək,
arúvək 'et.
'Atsaayúu,
'anyáanyányts
'amáy nyiivák athúum,
arúvəm aviivák 'eta.

Kukwiimáatt-ts 'atsaayúu 'a'íi
  'antaqór ashtúum,
mas'éenyily shtav'ótsk,

and he stirred it, he went like this and
  like this.
He went on doing it,
he sang and accompanied (his song)
  with movement:

"This water,
I am moving it around,
I am moving it around.
In a little while,
land will appear.
In a little while,
land will appear."

He went on saying it.

Well,
there was mud,
there was;
it had been at the bottom, and so,
he went on doing this, and suddenly,
it went straight up to the surface,
that (mud),
and in a little while,
land was there.

So,
there it was,
and it dried out, they say.
Well,
that sun
was in the sky, and so,
(the mud) dried and there it was,
  they say.

Kukwimáatt got little sticks and
  things,
and he stood them upright in the mud,

awíim,	and so,
voonóoxaym,	there they were, and suddenly,
'atsaayúu 'a'íits aatspáatsk athúm.[17]	trees and things emerged from them.
'Eethóots athótk,	There were willows,
'ax'áats athótk awím,[18]	there were cottonwoods, and so,
'atsaayúu nyikamáanəntínyts,	(there were other) things that came from there as well,
nyáany nyiitséwəntík 'et.	he made those too, they say.
'Atsaayúu,	Well,
'aanáaly,	mesquite,
'aanáaly atséwəntik awim.	he made mesquite too.
Avuuváaxaym,	There he was, and suddenly,
'ashéntəntíts uuváak:[19]	someone else was there too:
'Asákwiimáatt a'íim,[20]	he was called 'Asákwiimáatt,
nyáanyts,[21]	that one,
thomayúuv alya'ém,	he was not visible,
iimáattənyts thomayúuv alya'émk,[22]	his body was not visible,
'asá lyavíik.	it was like fog.
Nyáanyts	That (person)
shuutháwk uuváanyk;	had been waiting;
'akórtan lyavíim nyaa'ávək,[23]	it seemed like a long time to him,[24]
iiwáanyts kaa'émtan avathúum.	and he felt uneasy about it.
Viiyáak,	(Kukwiimáatt) had gone,
'akóortan viiyáak,	he had gone a very long time ago,
'amáy kayáamk viiyáam,	he had gone straight up,
nyáanyi,	and at that point,
shuutháwk uuváanyk,	('Asákwiimáatt) had been waiting for him,
nyiirísh a'ím,	but there was nothing,
nyaayúum,	and when he saw this,
iiwáanyts apúyəm,	he was alarmed,[25]
avuuváak 'etá.	there he was, they say.
Ayáanypátxa lyavíik a'ét,[26]	He was eager to go too,
'amáyəly.	up above.

'Amáy axávək ayúunypat a'ím,

avuuváak a'etəma.
Kukwiimáatt-ts makyí ooyémənya.

Nyaa'íim,
aaíimk muuvílyk viiyáak 'etəmá.

'Axám áamk,[27]
makyí ooyémxanya shamathíis athótk,
aaíimk viiyáak 'étəma.

Viiyáak,
viiyáaxaym,
'atsaayúu nyiuukanáavək 'etá.
Xiipúk Kukwiimáatt uu'ítsənya,

nyáany uukanáavəntík 'etá.

Avathúum:
nyáanya uukuunáavnya makyík a'áv aly'émk,
makyík athúu lya'émk,
athóxaym,
'atsaayúu,
'aayúu,
'axám áamk viiyáaxayk,
viiyáany,
uutstáaqtsəm athúum,
'axányts alyaxávək,
eethónyily.[30]
Eethó kwa'ura'úur alyaxávək athúum,
nyáanyəm,
nyaanyiimánk,

He wanted to go up above and look around too,
there he was, they say.
(He wanted to go) the way Kukwiimáatt had gone.

So,
he hurried off without a thought, they say.

He swam,
he did not know where he was going,

he went along without a thought, they say.
He went along,
he went along, and suddenly,
he was told things, they say.[28]
Whatever had been said first to Kukwiimáatt,
that (same thing) was told to him too, they say.[29]

This (is what) happened:
he did not listen at all to what was said to him,
not at all,
and suddenly,
well,
well,
he was swimming along, and suddenly,
he was going along,
and he opened (his eyes),
and the water went in,
into his eyes.
It went into his eyeballs, and so,

at that point,
from then on,

'atsaayúulya'émk 'etá.	he couldn't see anything, they say.
Eethóts tár 'ím.[31]	He was blind.

Nyáanyi,	At that point,
athúum,	it happened,
avuuváak 'éta.	and there he was, they say.
Athúm,	It happened,
uuváatəsáa,	and there he was, but
'Asákwiimáatt 'atsaayúu tsáaməly alykwaskyíitanəny athúuk a'ét.[32]	all of 'Asákwiimáatt's other senses still remained, they say.[33]
Viitháwxáyk,[34]	There they were,
makyík tsáaməly 'aláay lya'émk 'et.	they had not all gone bad, they say.
Eethónyts athótk athót.	It was just his eyes.

Viiyáak,	He went along,
'amáttəny ayúunypat a'ím,	intending to look at the land in his turn,
viiyáak.	he went along.
Kukwiimáatt ootséwəts,	It was what Kukwiimáatt had made,
nyáanya.	that (land).
'Amáttəny apáask viiyáak viiyáak,	He went and went, feeling his way along the ground,
kaathómk siiyáak athúm,	he went along somehow, and so,
" 'Amáttənyts tsapéev eekwéevək!"	"The land is too small!"
a'íim siiyáat.[35]	he said, going along.
"Pa'iipáa —	"People —
xalyavímtəm	it might be the case
pa'iipáa 'atáyk nyáavi nyatsuuváay nyaa'íim,	that many people are going to live here,
makyí,	and where,
makyí atíivxa'ənká?"	where will they settle?"
aaly'íim viiyáak.	he thought, going along.

'Atsaayúu 'ashéntits —	One being —
xaly'aatsxánəm kwalyavíintinyts avuuváak awím,	the one who resembled also a ghost was there, and so,
nyáanyts kanáavəm a'íik 'etəma.	that one talked to him, they say.
Kukwiimáatt-ts a'íim,[36]	Kukwiimáatt said,
"Wàkatsavák!	"Be patient!

Máam,	Now,
'atsaamánxayk va'oonóom,	we are just beginning,
mayúumək," 'eta.	as you can see," he said.
Pa'iipáa Eethó Kwatáarənyts a'íim,[37]	('Asákwiimáatt) was called the Blind Person,
nyáany a'íim ashétəmá.	that's what he was called, they say.
Eethó Táar a'íim.	He was called the Blind One.
'Atsayúu lya'émk a'ím.	He couldn't see things, they say.
Nyáanyi,	At that point,
'amátt nyiinák,	he sat down there on the ground,
nyiinák,	he sat there,
kaawíts ashtúum,	and he picked something up,
mas'ée kaawíts ashtúum,	he picked up some kind of mud,
nyáanyəm,	and with that,
'atsaayúu kaawíts atséw aaly'íim voonóok 'etá,	he went about making various kinds of things, they say,
pa'iipáa kwalyavíinya.	(things) that resembled people.
Nyaayúu kwapa'iipáynya.	Living things.
Nyáanyts	Those (things)
'amáttnyi nyatsuuváay a'ím.	intended to live on the land.
Kukumáatt,[38]	As for Kukwiimáatt,
Kukumáattənyts 'amátt atséwəntik avoonóo lyaskyíik 'eta.	Kukwiimáatt was still making more land, they say.
Láw 'ím ayúuk;	He turned his head quickly and looked;
Piipáa Eethó Kwatáarny kaawíts kaawémem ayúu 'ím,	he wanted to see what the Blind Person was doing,
athúuk 'et.	he did, they say.
Pa'iipáa Eethó Kwatáarənts a'ím,	The Blind Person said,
"Mayúu alyma'émtək ma'íiva?	"Can't you see?
Pa'iipáa 'atséwk av'uuváak 'awitya.	I am making people.
Nyáavəts 'amátt vathí nyatsuuváayəxá,"	They will live here on the land,"
a'íik 'et.	he said, they say.
Kukwiimáatt-ts	Kukwiimáatt
iiwáam xiipúk atséw 'ím,	had intended to make them himself first,

pa'iipáanyənyts nyáanyi atíiv 'ím,[39]	and he had intended the people to settle there,
'amáttnya,	(on) the land,
'amátt 'ootséwnyá.	(on) the land he had made.
Nyáanyəm,	At that point,
makyík aváts awíilya'ém a'éxaym,	he had not made any yet,
'akór awíim avuuváat.	but ('Asákwiimáatt) was already doing it.
Uuváantixaym,	As he was there,
Pa'iipáa Eethó Kwatáarənyts[40]	the Blind Person
'atsaayúu atséwk,	made things,
awím,	and so,
kaawíts atséwk,	he made something,
pa'iipáats nyiitséwk,	he made people,
a'étk,	they say,
uuváatəsá,	there he was, but
Kukwiimáatt-ts uuváam	Kukwiimáatt was there,
nyáany aatsooyóoyk 'eta.	and (the Blind One) showed him those (people), they say.
Iisháalyányts,	The hands,
eeményənyts,	and the feet,
'atsaayúu lyavéek 'etəmá:	they resembled something, they say:
xanamóo.	a duck.
Iimáattənyts kaawíts pa'iipáa lyavíi lya'émk;	Their bodies were not like people's (bodies);
pa'iipáa mashoopóownya,	the people you know about,
nyáany lyavée lya'émk.	they weren't like them.
Kúur 'ím,	Soon,
kuutsanyúuv mattapéek voonóoxáym,	they were having a terrible argument, and suddenly
Kukwiimáatt-ts athúum:	Kukwiimáatt did it:
ka'ak ka'ák awíim,	he went kick! kick!,
'axály aatspáxk.	and he cast them into the water.
Athúunyək,	This happened,
xáak uuthúutsk 'étəma.[41]	and they became something different, they say.

'Axály kwanytsuuváayányts
uuthúutsk 'im.

They became water dwellers, they
say.

Pa'iipáa Eethó Kwatáarənyts
masharáyk mattapéek 'ím,
mashuuráyəny nyamathótk ayáak
'axály atáqshk,
nyáany nyiaatooqwérək siiyáak 'etá.

The Blind Person
was terribly angry, and so,
in his anger he went
and he jumped in the water,
he went following them, they say.

'Atsaayúu,
'axám shuukwíin athúuk a'ét.[42]
Athúm,
nyáany,
nyaanyiivák athúuk 'etəmá.
'Axám shuukwíints.[43]
Nyáany athúum,
nyiivák athúum.

Well,
he became a whirlpool, they say.
So,
as for that,
there he was, they say.
A whirlpool.
That's what he became,
and there he was.

Matxáts viithíik 'etá.
Nyáanyənyts,
'atsaayúu 'atsiiráav apáyk
vuuthíik 'et.

A wind came, they say.
That (wind),
it came carrying sicknesses and
things, they say.

Nyaathúum,
nyaayúuk,
Kukwiimáatt-ts athúum,
eeménya,
'atsaayúu,
'axám shuukwíin nyáanya sharéq
a'íinyək,[44]
nyeekwévək,
tsáaməly awíi lya'émtəm athúm,
kaa'íts aatspáatsk,
'atsaayúu,
'atsiiráav,
awíim,
nyáany,
nyáanyənyts athúum,

So,
when he saw this,
Kukwiimáatt did it,
(with) his foot,
or something,
he tried to stop up that whirlpool,

but he didn't succeed,
he didn't do all of it, and so,
some escaped,
(some) things,
sicknesses,
and so,
as for that,
that's what happened,

nyiimánk,	and because of that,
pa'iipáa 'atsuuráav av'áarək athópk 'eta.	people have gotten sick, they say.
Viiyáantik 'ím,	It goes on, they say,
'atsaayúu kaanáaványts.	the story.
Kukwiimáatt-ts tsaamánk,	Kukwiimáatt got started,
'atsaayúu,	well,
xaly'ánya atséwk 'etəmá.	he made the moon, they say.
'Atsaayúu,	Well,
iisháaly nyamooshoo'óora nyáanyəm awíim:	he did it with his index finger:
'amáyk tsayóq awím,	he spat on it,
nyáany awíim;	and that's what he used;
'amáynyi,	in the sky,
'anyaaxáap avány,	that place where the sun sets,
'amáy nyiivák,	it was there in the sky,
nyáanyi,[45]	in that (place),
tsasvék avoonóoxáym,	he went about wiping it, and suddenly,
nyáanyiivák,	there it was,
'anyáayk uuvák 'et.	and it was bright, they say.
Nyáanya	That
xaly'áts athúuk 'eta.	was the moon, they say.
'Atsaayúu 'anóqəm,	There were small pieces of things,[46]
'amáy kwatháwənya 'anóqəm,	there were small pieces of the sky,[47]
shalóxk oonóok,	he went about gouging them out,
nyáany awíim,	that's what he did,
'atsaayúuts athúuk 'etəma.	and they became things, they say.
Xamshéts.	(They became) stars.
Nyaanyəm,	With that,
tiinyáaməm,	at night,
'anyáayk athúuk 'et.	they shine, they say.
Viitháwət.	There they are.
'Aayúu 'antaqór avkwatháwənya,	As for the small things that are there,
asílyk athúm,	they fall in showers,
'atsaayúu,	well,
athúum,	they do,

ayáak,	they go along,
'amátt asílyək,[48]	they fall in showers to earth,
'amáttnyi asílyək.	they fall in showers to the earth.
Mattapéek athúm,	There are a whole lot of them, and so,
shíiq shíiq a'íim viiyáanyək,	they leave streaks as they go,
nyáany,	and as for that,
'amátt aváamək 'eta.	they reach the earth, they say.
Nyaa'íim,	Then,
Kukwiimáatt-ts,	Kukwiimáatt (said),
"Vatháts,	"This,
xaly'á vatháts	this moon
makyík 'ashénti nyiivá alya'emxá.	will not stay in one place.
Viiyáak,	It will travel,
vuu'áats lyavíik viiyáanyək,	it will travel as if (taking) steps,
kwanyamék atspámk aváamxá."	and it will come out at the other side."
Pa'iipáa Eethó Kwatáarəny a'íim,[49]	He said to the Blind Person,
"Xaly'ányts viiyáanyək,	"The moon goes along,
amákəly nyaaváamk,	it goes behind,
takavék viithíik;	and it comes back;
'atsaayúu,	well,
'amátt nyamathíik,	it comes to that place,
viithíinyək,	it comes this way,
takavék nyiuumáni aváaməntixá.	and it will return to its starting point.
Nyáavəts athóxá.	This will happen.
'Atsaayúu tsáaməly 'atsakwíintəm kwathútsəny,[50]	Because I make everything turn,
'amáy kwatháwənya 'atsakwíinəm athúm kwathútsəny,[51]	because I make the things in the sky turn,
nyáavəts athóxá."	this will happen."
Pa'iipáa Eethó Kwatáarənyts a'étk a'íim,	The Blind Person said,
"Nyáany 'ashoopóow aly'a'émtəká.[52]	"I don't believe that.
Nyáany makyík athúulya'émxá,	That will never happen,
'aaly'étka'e,"	I think,"
a'íik 'et.	he said, they say.

Nya'íim oonóok.

Nyáaviimánk 'et:[53]
'atsaayúu,
Kukwiimáattənyts,
xiipúk,
pa'iipáa ootséwənya kats'ák,

'axály aatspáxəm,
nyaanyiimánk,
masharáyk uuváak athúuk 'etá.

Amák uuthíik athúm,
Kukwiimáatt-ts,
'aayúu,
'amátt ootséwənya shaaxwérək,
shaaxwérəm athúum,
xwérər 'ím viivák.

Awíim uuváanyək,
'atsaayúu,
viitháwəntim,
oowéxats viitháwəntim,

nyáany alynyiithúutsk viivát.

Kukwiimáattányts,
'atsaayúu,
pa'iipáa nyiitséw 'ím,
avuuváaxáym,
aváts awíi awétəsáa,
nyáanya aatspáxk,
alyaatspáxəmk awítya.
A'íim,
uuváak athúm,

He went on saying it.

It started here, they say:
well,
Kukwiimáatt,
first,
he kicked the people that (the Blind
 Person) had made,
he cast them into the water,
and from then on,
(the Blind Person) was angry with
 him, they say.

After that,
Kukwiimáatt,
well,
he caused the earth he had made to spin,
he caused it to spin, and so,
here it is spinning.

When he had done this,
well,
there were (other things) too,
there were (other things) for him to
 do too,[54]
and those (things) are what he was
 thinking about.

Kukwiimáatt,
well,
he intended to make people,
there he was, and right away,
that (Blind One) did it (too), but
(Kukwiimáatt) threw those out,
he threw them away.
So,
there he was, and so,

'amáttnyi anák,	he sat on the ground,
mas'ée ashtúum,	and he picked up some mud,
awíim:	and he did it:
pa'iipáa nyiitséwk 'etəma.	he made people, they say.
'Aayúu,	Well,
mattaxavík aatsuumpáp;[55]	there were couples in four places;
nyáanyts 'amáttnyi nyatsuuváay a'ím.	he intended them to live on the land.
'Atsaayúu xiipúk atséwk 'etá.	They were the first things he made, they say.
Kwatsáants athúuk 'ím.	They were Quechans.
Nyáany 'iipáats athúuk 'etá.	That one was a man, they say.
Sanya'ák atséwəntik 'etá.	He also made a woman, they say.
Kukwiimáatt-ts nyaawíntik athúm,	When Kukwiimáatt had done this,
Kwa'aapá 'iipáa atséwk,	he made a Cocopa man,
'iipáa atséwk,	he made a man,
sanya'ák atséwəntik awíik 'etəmá.	and he also made a woman, they say.
Nyaawíim,	Then,
Kamayáa nyáany nyiiuutsáawəntík 'etá.	he made those Kamias in the same way, they say.[56]
'Iipáa atséwk,	He made a man,
sanya'ák atséwk.	and he made a woman.
Nyaawíntik awíim,	When he had done this,
'atsaayúu,	well,
Xattpáa 'Anyáa 'iipáa atséwk,	he made a Maricopa man,
a'ím,	and so,
sanya'ák atséwəntik 'etá.	he made a woman too, they say.
Nyáavəts avoonóom,	These (people) were around here,
***[57]	***
iiyáam oo'éevənya,	and as for the languages that they spoke,
nyáany nyiioo'éeyk 'et.	he taught these to them, they say.
Athúum,	So,
viitháwtəsáa,	there they were, but
Kwatsáan,	as for the Quechan,
sanya'ákənyts,	the woman,
"Makyík 'axóttk athúulya'émk,"	"It's not good at all,"
a'íim avuuváak 'etá.	she said as she was there, they say.

Nyaa'íim,	Then,
xavíkəm ootséwənya,[58]	(each) pair that he had made,
nyáanya	that (pair)
mattxavík nyaathúum,	became a couple,
xáak atháwk athúts a'éxayk—	and (the couples) were supposed to be in different places—
nyáany makyík áar aly'émk,[59]	and she did not want that at all,
sanya'ákənyts.	the woman.
Nyáany,	As for that,
sany'ákənyts avuuváanyək,	the woman was there,
makyík nyáava áar aly'émtək athúm,	and she did not want this at all, and so,
viiyáak,	she went off,
makyí avák,	and she stayed somewhere,
kaathómk siivák.	she stayed over there doing something.
Pa'iipáa Eethó Kwatáarənyts	The Blind Person
makyík 'akór alyavá alya'émtəsa,[60]	was never very far away,
nyáanyi,	and at that point,
viithíik,	he came,
viithíik a'ím,	he came, they say,
'axám athíik atspák a'ím;	he came up out of the water, they say;
sanya'áknya,	and as for the woman,
ayúuk,	he saw her,
siithíik,	and he came,
aváamk a'im.[61]	and he got there, they say.
Nyáany a'íim,	That's what he said,
kanáavək,[62]	he told her,
"Kukwiimáatt-ts 'atsaayúu 'atáyəm atséwk,[63]	"Kukwiimáatt makes many things,
kanáavtəsáa,	and he tells about them, but
makyík ma'áv alyma'émtəxá.	you must never listen to him.
Makyík kaawíts mawéeyəntiyúm,"	He can never do anything for you,"
a'íim,	he said,
a'íik 'etəma.	he said it, they say.

" 'Anyép 'anyka'ávək,
'anyáa 'uu'ítsəny kathúum,
nyaanyiimánək,⁶⁴
'atsaayúu 'atáyəm manyuuwítsxá.
'Atsaayúu 'atáyəm mamáam
   avmuuváaxá
'anyáa kwashíintənyám."⁶⁵

Nyaamák,
Kukwiimáatt-ts shoopóowk 'etá.⁶⁶
Shoopóow;
"Makyík 'anyáa nya'áv aly'émk⁶⁷
nyaa'uuváam," a'íim,
uukanáavək 'etá.
"Máanyts makyík 'anyép 'uu'ítsəny
   ma'áv alyma'émk,
***⁶⁸
nyáany,
nyaanyiimánk,
máanyts mathúum!
'Anyakamáanənyts mathúm,
nyiinyatatpóoyxá!"
'íik 'eta.

Nyaa'íim,
matxávik shathómpk,
uuráwk,
tsaqwérək viiv'óowk a'im.

'Atsaayúu,
kwas'eethéets,⁶⁹
'atsaayúu kwas'iitsthíts
   viikwatháwnya,⁷⁰
nyáany nyiikwakyáavək a'ím,
'atsaayúu,
avuuváaxaym,
avkoov'óowənyts mattapéek 'etá.⁷¹
Oov'óowk mattapéem,

"Listen to me,
and do what I say,
and from now on,
you will have many things.
You will eat many things

each day."

After that,
Kukwimáatt knew about it, they say.
He knew about it;
"She never listens to me
when I am there," he said,
and he explained it to her, they say.
"You never listen to what I say,

***

and as for that,
for that reason,
it is you!
Even though you are my offspring,
I will kill you!"
he said, they say.

Then,
he faced the north,
and he did it fast,
he stood there talking.

Well,
a doctor,
the doctors that were there,

he asked them for something,
and, well,
there he was, and suddenly,
the rain was terrible, they say.
It rained terribly,

The Quechan Legend of the Creation

viitháwnyək,	it continued,
viitháwnyək,	and it continued,
'anyáa tsuumpápəm kayáamk 'eta.	it went on for four days, they say.
Nyáanyəm,[72]	At that point,
'amáttəny aamáarəm'áshk,	once again (water) flooded the land,
'étəma.	they say.
Aamárəntík a'íim 'itya.[73]	It flooded it again, they say.
Uuváxáyk,[74]	There he was, and suddenly,
Kwatsáan 'iipáany nyáanyi aatsoonóoy aly'émk 'etá.[75]	he decided not to abandon the Quechan man there.
Nyáanyi xáak uuváam athúm,[76]	He was there on one side, and so,
nyaathúum,[77]	then,
nyáanyi,	at that point,
amúlyk a'ím,[78]	he decided to name him,
Marxókavék a'ím.	and he called him Marxókavék.
'Íis,	But,
nyiikamáanənyá —	as for the others —
pa'iipáats athúulya'émtəsáa,	they weren't people (any more), but
kaawíts 'iipáyk viithíkəntím —	they were other kinds of living things[79] —
nyáany awíim uuthúutsk 'etəma.[80]	he did that and they became (animals), they say.
Xáak athúum,	They were different,
awíim,	and so,
vanyoonóom;	there they were;
aváts xáak avám,[81]	and this one was different from them,
nyáanya,	and as for him,
makyík awíi lya'émtəm;	(Kukwiimáatt) didn't do anything to him;
Marxókavék a'ím amúly.	Marxókavék was his name.
Nyáany Kwatsáan xiipúkts athúum 'ityá.[82]	He was the first Quechan, they say.
Nyáanyiimánk,	Starting there,
kaawíts atséwəntík avoonóok 'etá.	(Marxókavék) went about making other things, they say.
'Atsaayúu,	Well,
'Ashpáa atséwk,	he made Eagle,

Xatalawé atséwk,	he made Coyote,
Xatakúly awiim,	he did Mountain Lion,
'Aqáaq awíim,	he did Raven,
Namás,	Raccoon,
Maxwét,	Bear,
'Amó,	Sheep,
'Apén,	Beaver,
Maxwáa,	Badger,
'Atsa'ór,	Hawk,
'Aqáaq,	and Raven,
awíim siiwáak 'etá.[83]	he went about doing them, they say.
Xiipúk,	At first,
'atsaayúu ootséwənyts tsáaməly takyéevək,	the things he had made were all together,
'axóttk avoonóok 'etəma.	and they were fine, they say.
'Axóttk avatíivk athúm,	They were fine, and so,
nyatsuuváayk avatíivəm.	they were living (together).
Avoonóoxaym,	They were there for some time, and suddenly,
iiwáanyts sàqasáq a'íi kaa'émk viitháwəm athúm,	they must have gotten restless, and so,
matta'íim,	they were talking about each other,
nyiixúu 'etk;	and they were making a ruckus;
mattanyúuv 'etk,	they were going to fight with each other,
voonóok 'etəmá.	there they were, they say.
Nyáava ayúuk athúm,	Seeing this,
Kukwiimáatt-ts masharáyk.	Kukwiimáatt got angry.
Kaawíts aqásəm'áshəm;	Once again he summoned something;
tsáaməly íim,	they would all come to an end,
shaaíiməntixá.	he would destroy them again.
Nyaa'étk awíim athúm,	When he decided to do it he did it, and so,
'axány kwiixáalyts viithíik,[84]	a flood of water came,
'amáttnya aamáarək 'et.	and it flooded the land, they say.
Viiyáak viiyáaxaym —	It went on and on —
'atsaayúuts viiyáanyək,	there was something there,
'Aqáaqts siivám,[85]	Raven was sitting there,
nyáanya,	and at that point,

makyík nyáany tapúy lya'émxá,
a'íim awíim,
kaa'émk avoonóom,

nyáanyi asáttk 'etəma.
'Axányts asáttk.

Nyaa'íim,[86]
"Nyaanyamáam,
nyáanyi amánəm,
pa'iipáa xáam uuthúutsxá.
Makyík matsakyéevək
  manytsuuváay lya'émxá.
Makyím xáak moonóok mathúm,
nyáanyi,
malyavíik avmoonóotiya."

***[87]
Athúum,
viitháwxáym,
Kukwiimáattənyts,
nyaa'íntik
kaawíts atséw 'ím avuuváak,
a'étəntiva.
Pa'iipáats,
pa'iipáa uu'ítsənya,[88]
nyiitséwəntík.[89]
Nyáanyts aaíimk avoonóok,
'atsaayúu xiipúk oowéxanyá,

makyík awíts aly'émtúm,
nyáanyiimánk awítsxá.[90]
A'íim a'íik 'etá.
Athúm,
pa'iipáats,[91]
pa'iipáa nyáanyányts —
'iitspátsəts,
mashtxáats —

(the flood) would not kill any of them,
he decided, and so,
he went about saying something (to
  end the flood),
and the water receded, they say.
The water receded.

Then,
"Finally,
from now on,
people will be different.
You won't live together any more.

You will be in different places, and so,
there,
you will do things in your own way."

***
So,
they were there, and suddenly,
Kukwiimáatt,
when he said it again,
he was intending to make something,
he must have been intending (to do so).
People,
the ones he called people,
he made more of them.
They went about doing as they pleased,
and the things they should have done
  the first time,
but never did,
starting now they would do them.
He said so, they say.
So,
people,
those people —
men,
girls —

sanyts'áakts athúum,	there were women,
xuumáarts nyaathúum.	and there were children.
Nyáavəm kwaatspáatsənyts,	The (people) who appeared at this point,
avoonóom athúm,	there they were, and so,
'atsaayúu nyiioo'éeyk 'etəma.	he taught them things, they say.
Nyáanyəm,	At that point,
nyaanyiimánk,	starting there,
nyiioo'éeyəm,	he taught them
kaawíts shoopóowk athúm;	(so that) they would know something;
iiwáam uuthúuts a'ím.	he intended them to do things for themselves.
Pa'iipáanyənyts,	Those people,
katsuukyáavək a'ét,[92]	they asked for things, they say,
viikwatháwənyts.	the ones who were there.
Nyáany,	In that way,
'atsaayúu shoopóowk athúm.	they came to know things.
'Atsaayúu,	Well,
uushíit tsáaməly shoopóowəntik athúum,	they came to know all of their names, and so,
Kukwiimáatt-ts	Kukwiimáatt
iiwáam athúum:	did it himself:
pa'iipáa 'ashénti,	one person,
sanya'ák 'ashént xo	one woman, or
áa,	yes,
pa'iipáats —	it was a person —
sanya'ák 'ashénti,	one woman,
uutháavək 'etá.	(Kukwiimáatt) got together with her, they say.
Uutháavəxáym,	He got together with her, and right away,
maxáyts nyiivák 'etá.	there was a boy, they say.
Sanya'ákənyts as'áwəm,	The woman had given birth,
'ashéntits avuuváantik 'etá.	and soon another child was there too, they say.
Nyáanya	That one
vatsíits athúuk 'et.	was a daughter, they say.
Kumastamxó,	Kumastamxó,
Kumastamxó a'ím,	(the boy) was called Kumastamxó,

shiimúlyts a'ityá.	that was his clan name, they say.
'Atsaayúu,	Well,
Xaanyé uu'íts,	what they called (the girl) was Xaanyé (Frog),
nyáanya shiimúlyts.	that was her clan name.
Nyáanyənyts,	That one,
avuuváak 'et.	there he was, they say.
Nyáanyts xiipúk alytanák athúuk 'et.	He was the first leader, they say.[93]
Avoonóontik 'etá.	(Others) were there too, they say.
Shiimúlyts avoonóok athúm,[94]	The clans were there, and so,
Xiipáa 'etk,	Xiipáa, they say,
'atsaayúu xatalwényа a'ím 'etá.	that means coyote or something, they say.
Mat'á a'íim,[95]	Mat'á, they say,
talypó uu'íits,	what it means is roadrunner,
Maavé,	and Maavé,
'aavé taaxán nyáany a'íim 'íikəta.	that means rattlesnake, they say.
Alya'óots uu'ítsnyá,	The one they call Alya'óots,
'ashée a'íim 'íik 'et.	(that) means buzzard, they say.
Nyáava,	As for these,
shiimúly vatháts,	these clan names,
'atsaayúu,	well,
'iipáak ayémk athúum,	they follow the male line of descent,
siiwáak athúuk 'etəma.	and they continue, they say.
***[96]	***
Mashaxáyts na'áyvək avuuváak,	A girl has a father,
nyáanyəm shiimúly atháwk awityá.	and from him she gets her name.
Na'áyənya.	(From) her father.
Nyaathúum,	Then,
makyík sata'ótsəny nyiiáay lya'émk avuuváak;	she never does pass the name on to her children;
mashtxáats nyaathúum makyík shiimúly nyiiáaylya'émk.	if they are girls they do not pass on their clan names.
Maxáyənyts,	The boy,
uuxamíixaym,	when he fathers children,
maxáyənyts shiimúlyk 'ityá.	the boy carries the clan name, they say.

Nyáanyts xuutsamáar shiimúly
   nyiiáayk.⁹⁷
Sanyts'áakənyts
a'íim voonóonyək,

nyaapúyəm,
nyaanyamáam.
Namák 'et.
'Íis
aváts,
siiwáa lyaskyíik.

'Aavé kwatáyənyts,
nyáanyi,
aatspáatsəntik 'etəmá.
Atséwəm aatspáatsk;
'aavé taaxán a'ím,⁹⁸
'aavé síi a'ét,
kwaatsnyii'áalyk 'et,
xam'aavíir a'ím,
'aksár,
xan'aapúuk 'íikəm;⁹⁹
nyáany tsáaməly atséwk 'eta.
'Aavéts,
'aavéts avuuthúutsk athúm 'ítya.

Marxókavékts
avuuváak 'eta.
Piipáa nyiiwík —
Kukwiimáatt-ts uuváam,
nyáanyts nyiiwík.¹⁰¹
Avuuváaxaym,
'aavényts tsakyíwk 'etəma.

Nyáany avuuváaxaym,
tsakyíwətəm athúm,
apúyk 'eta.

He is the one who gives his children
   their clan name.
The women
go on being called (by their clan
   name all their lives),
and when they die,
that is the end of it.
They leave it behind, they say.
But
that (man),
(his clan name) still continues.

The big snakes,
at that point,
they appeared, they say.
He made them and they appeared;
they were called rattlesnakes,
they were called gopher snakes,
they were called red racers,
they were called water snakes,
and sidewinders,
and they were called king snakes;
he made all of those, they say.
Snakes,
that's what kind of snakes they were,
   they say.¹⁰⁰

Marxókavék
was there, they say.
He helped people —
Kukwiimáatt was there,
and he was the one who helped people.
(Marxókavék) was there, and suddenly,
a snake bit him, they say.

There he was, and suddenly,
and it bit him, and so,
he died, they say.

Apúyəm ayúuxayk,	When he saw that (Marxókavék) had died,
Kukwiimáatt-ts ookavék,	Kukwiimáatt brought him back,
ookavékəm 'iipáyk athúntik 'et.	he brought him back (so that) he was alive again, they say.
Aványa,	That one,
'atsaayúu,	well,
'aavé,	the snake,
'aavé kwatsakyíwəny,[102]	the snake that had bitten him,
nyáanyi,	at that point,
nyáany atháwk,	he took that (snake),
aaxwésxwéshk,	and he spun him,
'aayúu matxávily xwérər awétk atáp,[103]	he threw him and sent him spinning to the north,
aváts.[104]	this one (did).
Nyáanyi,	There,
nyáanyiiáapk 'etá.	he threw him there, they say.
Nyaanyiimánk,	Starting then,
mattooxaméeyk voonóoxaym,	(the snake) went about reproducing,
'atsaayúu,	and, well,
'axály oonóots,	they are in the water,
'amáy oonóok athum,	they are in the sky,
athúuk 'etá.	they are, they say.
'Aavéts uuthúutstəsáa,	They are snakes, but
xáam uuthútsk athúm.[105]	they are different kinds.
'Amáy 'Aavé a'ét.	He is called 'Amáy 'Aavé (Sky Snake).
Nyáanyts 'amáyəny uuváak;	He is the one who is up in the sky;
ayérək lyavíik uuváak 'ityá.	he seems to be flying, they say.
Nyáanyiimánk,[106]	Starting then,
pa'iipáats,	people,
pa'iipáanyənyts —	the people —
xuumáar nyiivasháwk uuváxaym,[107]	when they were taking care of children, then suddenly,
'aláayk avuuváxaym,	if (one of the kids) was bad, then suddenly,
'aayúu kanáavək 'etá.	they would tell him things, they say.

"Athúum,
nyamuuvám,
'atsaayúu 'aave kwa'atsláytsəny nyii'aqáasəm,[108]
apák
veemawémxá!"
a'íik 'eta.

Athúum,
viitháwnyək,
pa'iipáany iiwáatsənyts sàqasáq 'etəm;
makyík mattshoopóow 'ím athúulya'émk,
mattvaashqwék 'ím.

Kukwiimáattənyts
nyáany ayúuk awétsáa,
***[109]
"Viitháwnyək,
nyaa'aláaytanəm,[110]
'atsaayúu,
'atsaayúu,
aví 'a'áw aráa 'ím;
nyáanya,
'aayúu aráak mattapéem mayúutxá."
Nyáany a'ét.

'Amátt énən,
énənən 'í av'áarəm,
nyáany ashék 'ityá.
Nyáanyi aqásəm,
nyiiqáasəm,
pa'iipáa nyiitatpóoy 'ím.
A'étəsáa,
Kumastamxó
xuumáyənyts,
nyáany xuumáyənyts a'ím.[111]

"So,
as you are here,
I will summon the bad snakes and things,
and they will come here
and take you away!"
they said, they say.

So,
there they were,
and people were restless;
they never had gotten to know each other,
and they disliked each other, they say.

Kukwiimáatt
must have seen that, but
***
"Here they are,
and if they are bad,
well,
well,
a fire will blaze up there;
as for that,
you will see things blaze up in a terrible way."
That's what he said.

As for earthquakes,
(the earth) has always quaked,
and that's what he named them, they say.
He summoned them there,
he summoned them,
and they killed people, they say.
However,
Kumastamxó
was his son,
he was his son, they say.

Pa'iipáa 'atáyəm ashtúum —	He got many people together —
'atsaayúu,	well,
'amátt akúp mattapéets viivák 'etəma.	there was a great cave there, they say.
Vatáyk,	It was big,
nyáanya,	that (cave),
nyáanyily tsakxávək awim,	and he took them in there, and so,
'atsaayúu 'avíits mattapéek viitháwm athum,	there were big rocks and things, and so,
awíim,	he did it,
'asá kwanályts athúuk awím,	and there was snow that had fallen, and so,
'atsaayúu,	well,
xatsúurək nyiináamk viitháwm,[112]	it was terribly cold,
nyáanyi.	there.
Nyáany awíim	That's what he did,
ashtúum,	he gathered it,
nyáany,	that (snow),
'atsaayúu,	and, well,
'amátt akúp 'avuuyáany aatspíitt.[113]	he blocked the entrances to the cave.
'Atskwaráanyts athúum,	There was a fire,
'amátt énənyts athúum,	and there was an earthquake,
'atsaayúu 'axá sa'ílynya awíim,	and he did something to the ocean,
'aayúu,	well,
kaawémtəm athúm,	I don't know what he did, but
'amáytan axávək athúm,	it went right up into the sky, and so,
viiyáanyk viiyáanyk viiyáanyək,	it went on and on and on,
viiyáaxaym,	it went on, and suddenly
asáttəm.	it receded.
'Atsaayúu,	Well,
nyaanyiimánək,	from then on,
'atsaayúuts nyiitháwəm ooyóov av'áarək 'ityá.	things have been there that are still seen today, they say.[114]
'Avíits,	Rocks,
'avíi kwa'uutta'úuttányts athótk,	there are round rocks,
'avíi kwa'alméenyənyts athótk athúum 'ityá,	and there are tall mountains, they say,
nyáanyəm.	because of that.

'Axányənyts awíim 'ityá.
'Axá mattkwatsapéets.

Athúum,
viiyáaxaym,
viitháwnyək,
taarawíik viitháwk 'etá.
'Atsaayúu tsáaməly viiyáak,
'axóttk kayáamk viiyáat,
athót kwayuulyavíim ayúuk 'etəma.
Athúum,
oonóoxaym,
'anyáa 'ashéntək alyaváamk athúm,[115]
Kukumáatt vatsíinyənyts masharáyk 'etəmá.
Makyík uutar'úy lya'émk a'ím,
kaathómk a'ím.
Kaawíts awéey lya'émk 'et.
A'étk 'etəma.
Sanyts'áakts nyáany lyavée av'áarəm mayúuk.[117]
Ayúutk av'áartəm athúm,[118]
nyáanyiimánk,
'atsaayúu,
kaawém,
kaathóm,
'aláayapat aaly'íim uuváak uuváaxáym,[119]
kwas'iithíik awíi 'ím,
mattatháwk 'eta.
Nyáanyts mattatháwk awíim,

nyáanya,
apúyk a'ávtank waatsavátank,
apúyk viiyáak 'etəma.

Athúum,
viithíknyək,[121]

The water did it, they say.
A huge amount of water.

So,
(life) went on, and soon,
there they were,
they recovered, they say.
Everything went on,
it was going straight in a good (direction),
that's how it appeared to be, they say.
So,
there they were, and suddenly,
one day came, and so,[116]
Kukwiimáatt's daughter got angry, they say.
He didn't take care of her at all, she said,
that's how he was, she said.
He didn't do anything for her, she said.
She was just saying that, they say.
Women have always been like that, as you see.
He ignored her, and so,
starting then,
well,
she did something,
she behaved somehow,
she was thinking about being bad in turn, and suddenly,
she decided to use her powers,
and she bewitched him, they say.
That (daughter of his) bewitched him, and so,

as for him,
he felt himself slowly dying,[120]
he was going along dying, they say.

So,
he lay there,

Kumastamxó kanáavək a'ím.	and he talked to Kumastamxó.
"Máanyts,	"You,
'atsaayúu nyikamáanənya matséwxá,"	you will make the rest of the things,"
a'íim,	he said,
kanáavək 'eta.	and he told him (what to do), they say.
Nyaa'íim,	Then,
apúyk 'etəma.	he died, they say.
Nyaapúyəm,	When he died,
'atsaayúu,	well,
iimáattənya,	as for his body,
awíim,	they did it,
'atsaayúu mapís uuwítsnya lyavíik uutsáaw,	they did what they do nowadays,
nyáany uutsáawk awím,	that's what they did, and so,
ootanyéy a'ím avoonóonyək,	they went about getting ready to cremate him,
awíik 'etəma.	they did it, they say.
Nyaanyiimánk,	From then on,
tsuunyúuts av'áarək athútya.[122]	(people) have always followed that example.
Nyáavəm,	At this point,
athúu av'áarək.	they always do it.
Xatalwéts	Coyote
'atsaayúu nyáava avkwathútsəny ayúutank uuváanyək,	had been watching all these things that had happened,
mattáam nyakórtanəm ayúuk uuváak.	he had been watching for a very long time, for years.
Nyáany lyavíi xalyavíik 'eta.	Perhaps he wanted to be like that, they say.
Pa'iipáa nyiikwanáamts athúu a'ím,	He wanted to be a great person,
Kukwiimáatt 'atsuuthúutsnya lyavíi a'ím,[123]	he wanted to resemble Kukwiimáatt in character,
athótəsáa,	he did, but
makyík shoopóow aly'émk,	he didn't realize,

təsáa,
'atsaayúu nyáany uuthúutsənyts

aaíimk athúuly'émk athópka 'et.
Uuthútsənyts 'atsaayúu
  nyiikwanáamtan,
nyiikatsámtank viitháwm,
nyaanyiimánk,
athúum,
athúu av'áark athúuk 'etəma.

A'ávaly'émk,
avuuváak athúm.
'Atsaayúu,
Kukwiimáatt nyáany iimáatt
  atháwnyək kaathómxas awíi
  kaawémxayk,
nyaanyiimánk,[124]
nyiináam a'ím,
nyiikwanáamts athúu 'ím.
Athúum,
atséwk,
'atsaayúu atséwk avoonóot.
Ootanyék,
awíim,
nyáavi athíkxáym,
viithíkəm,
pa'iipáanyənyts a'ítsk voonóok
  'etá.[125]
Mattuutsuupáayk,
mattuutsuupáayk athúum a'íim,

viiwáak,
"Kaspérək![126]
Kakwanamíik!
Mattkuutar'úytsək!"[127]
a'íik a'ím.
Voonóoxáym,

however,
that those things that (Kukwiimáatt)
* had done*
were not done lightly, they say.
(The things) he did were great things,

they outdid (all other deeds),
and from then on,
(people) have done them,
they have always done them, they say.

He didn't listen,
and there he was.
Well,
he was planning to take a piece of
* Kukwiimáatt's body somehow,*

and from that point,
he intended to be great,
he intended to be a great (person).
So,
he made it,
he went about making it.
They cremated (Kukwiimáatt),
and so,
he lay here, and suddenly,
as he lay here,
the people went about saying things,
* they say.*
They comforted each other,
they said things in order to comfort
* each other,*
they went along (saying),
"Be strong!
Be brave!
Take care of each other!"
they said, they say.
There they were, and suddenly,

Xatalwényənyts avéshk axávək,	that Coyote ran in,
iiwáanya atháwk 'et.	and he took (Kukwiimáatt's) heart, they say.
Nyaatháwk athúm,	He took it, and so,
'anyáavik shathómpk veeyémk 'etá.[128]	he went off heading east, they say.
Avéshk viiyáanyək viiyáanyəm,	He ran on and on,
'atsaayúu,	and, well,
'avíits 'améek 'ashéntək nyáanyi av'óowk,	there was one tall mountain standing there,
av'óowm,	it was standing there,
ayúuk athúm,	and he saw it, and so,
nyáanyi nyaaváamk,	when he got there,
'atsaayúunya —	that thing —
iiwáanya —	the heart —
asóok 'et.[129]	he ate it, they say.
Nyáany 'atsaayúu 'axáyts,[130]	It was a wet thing,
iimáattk aatspáats,[131]	it came out of (Kukwiimáatt's) body,
iiwáa,	his chest,
iiwáanyək.	from his chest.
Avík aatspáatsk,	It came from there,
'amáttnyi atúsk 'et.	and it dripped on the ground, they say.
Nyaanyiimánk,	Starting then,
'atsaayúu a'íim ashét:	they named it something:
'Avíi 'Axás a'íim.	they called it Greasy Mountain.
Nyaanyiimánk a'ím 'itya.	Since then it has been called (that), they say.
Nyáany athúntim athúm,	That's what he did, and so,
Xatalwényənyts,[132]	that Coyote,
nyaamáam,	that's all,
pa'iipáa nyaakwévəts athótəsáa,	he's a good-for-nothing person, but
'atsaayúu,	well,
nyaakwév athúum,	he's good for nothing,
athóoyvək uuváanyək.	that's his character.
Nyáanyiimánk,	That's where it comes from,
'atsaayúu kamánk athúuk 'etá,[133]	things result from that, they say,
'atsuuwítsnyá.[134]	the things he does.

'Atsaayúu iiwáa aathóm,	He turns his heart towards it,
nyáanya aaxnók.	and he gets sick from it.
Athúum,	So,
nyáany lyavíik athúuk 'eta.¹³⁵	that's what he was like, they say.
Pa'iipáa nyaakwévəts.	He was a good-for-nothing person.
Pa'iipáa —	A person —
pa'iipáa tsakwshá nyaakwévəts athúum,	he was a person whose head was good for nothing,
athúum,	and so,
athúuk 'etəma.¹³⁶	it happened, they say.

Kumastamxóts nyáanyi tsaamánək,¹³⁷	Kumastamxó started there,
nyakóny uuwítsnya awíinypátk uuváak athúm,	he went about doing the things his father had done, and so,
uuváaxayk,	there he was, and suddenly,
'atsaayúu a'ávək 'et.	he heard something, they say.
Kaanáav viithíkəm:	There was a story:
'atsaayúuts —	something —
'aavé taaxan vatáytants avuuváak,	a big rattlesnake was around there,
'atsaayúu 'axótt lya'émk,	he was not a good thing,
'atsaayúu 'aláay athúm,	he was a bad thing,
awím,	and so,
pa'iipáanyts uuwár aly'ém.	the people did not want him.

Nyáanyi ayúu lyavíik piipáa,	At that point, it seemed that a person,
'iipáats,	a man,
nyiikwanáamts avuuváanypatk awim	a great one was there too, and so,
'atsaayúu,	well,
'atsaráav mattkwatspée athúuk 'etəmá.¹³⁸	he got a terrible sickness, they say.¹³⁹
Athúm,	So,
nyaayúuk athúm,	when he saw this,
piipáa,	the person,
piipáanyənyts avuuváam avathíkəm,	the (sick) person was around there, he was lying there,

nyaayúuk athúm,	and he saw him,
Kumastamxóts.	Kumastamxó (did).
'Aavé taaxán,	The rattlesnake,
'aavé nyáasily alykuuváatsnya,	the snake that was off in the distance,
aaxweshxweshk makyí áap athúum	(Kukwiimáatt) had thrown him spinning away somewhere
uuváany,	and there he was,
nyáanyi,	and at that point,
nyáany aqásk 'etá,	(Kumastamxó) summoned him, they say,
vathány.	this (snake).
Piipáa vathánya mattawík awim uumán a'ím.	He intended (the snake) to help this person and cure him.
'Aavé taaxán nyaaváam,[140]	The rattlesnake got there,
athúm,	and so,
tapúyk 'etəma.	he killed him, they say.
Kumastamxóts atháwk tapúyk 'et.[141]	Kumastamxó took (the snake) and killed him, they say.
'Atsaayúu,	Well,
nyeexwéttənyts	his blood
'óorts athúuk 'et.	became gold, they say.
Tsooyóqənyts	His spittle
'óor kwalyavíits kaxmáalyənyts athúuk 'et.	became something white that's similar to gold, they say.
'Atsaayúu,	Well,
tsakwshányənyts —	his head —
'avíi xóorəts viitháwm,	there is gravel here,
nyáany athúntik 'eta.[142]	his head turned into that (gravel), they say.
Iimáattənyts[143]	His body
'amátt kwa'ora'órnya shakwíinək,	encircled the earth,
'atsaayúu,	and, well,
nyáanyənyts 'apínyk athúuk 'éta.	that (area) became warm, they say.
Nyaanyiivák,	There it is,
aamél lyavíik,	it's like a belt,
'apínyk 'eta.	and it's warm there, they say.
Kumastamxó uu'íts nyáanyts,[144]	The one they call Kumastamxó,
'atsaayúu,	well,

'a'íi qweraqwér atháwk,
'amáttnyily ushák,[145]
a'ét.
Nyaanyiimánk,
'axányənyts avéshk viiyáak 'et.[146]
'Atsaayúu,
'uutáp nyáany atháwk,
nyaalyavíintits viithíkəm atháwk awím,[147]
'amáttnyi awíim,
aaqíirək,
aaqíishk viiwáanyək viiwáanyək,

nyáasily,
'axá sa'íly kamémək 'et.

he picked up a pointed stick,
and he stuck it in the ground,
they say.
From then on,
water has run there, they say.
Well,
he picked up that spear,
(something) like that was there and he picked it up, and so,
he did (something) to the earth,
he made a line in it,
he made a line and extended it and extended it,

and way over there,
he took it (all the way) to the salt water, they say.

Nyaanyiimánk,
nyáanyi amáarək,[148]
vatháts nyiithík 'ityá.
'Axá Kwaráw Kwaxwéttnya.[149]
Nyáanyts aviithík 'itya.
Kwatsáan nyamátt atóm viikwáama.[150]
Nyáany nyaawíim,
'atsíi atséwk 'eta.
'Atsíi 'atáyəm atséw,
xáam uuthútsnyəm,[151]
'atsayérəts,
'axányi xiipáan avkwathíkəny,[152]
nyáany awíntik,
'axály avkwathíkənya nyiitséwk voonóok 'ityá.[154]

From then on,
it has flowed there,
this (river) has been there, they say.
The Colorado River.
That (river) has been there, they say,
the one that goes through the middle of Quechan territory.
Having done that,
he made fish, they say.
He made many fish,
different kinds (of fish),
and birds,
the ones that live near the water,[153]
he did those too,
he went about making the water birds, they say.[155]

Nyamáam,
nyikapílym viithíixaym,
'atsíinyənyts vaathíik 'et.
Vaathíinyək vaathíinyək vaathíinyək,

Finally,
as soon as it got to be summer,
the fish would come, they say.
They would come and come and come,

makyéely apám.	and they would reach some distant place.
'Aayúu,	Well,
xatsúurək siitháwm,	it was cold there,
nyáanyily aváam,	and they got there,
apámk.	they all got there.
Nyaanyiimánk,	From that point,
'atsíinyənyts 'atáyk athúuk 'etəma.	there were a lot of fish, they say.
'Atsíi kwarts'áakənyts,[156]	The old fish,
nyáanya,	as for them,
nyáanyts oopóoyk 'etá.	they died, they say.
Nyakaváayk.	They were worn out.
Nyiikamáanənyts aakavék,	Their offspring went back,
'axá sa'íly kayáamk vaayáanyk,	they went straight to the salt water,
apámk.	and they got there.
Nyáasily athík athíknyək,[157]	There they were, over there, until
xaméera,	eventually,
aakavék,	they went back,
avathútsəntik athúu 'ím athúm,	they were going to do the same thing, and so,
nyaanyiimánk athúu av'áarək athópəka.	since that time they have always done it.
Viithíik,	They came,
viithíinyək,	they came, until
kaawíts kanyaathúum kanyaathúm,	somehow they managed to do it,
aakavék athót.	and they went back.
Nyaanyiimánk athúum 'ityá.	Since then they have done it, they say.
Kumastamxóts pa'iipáa nyiishtúum.	Kumastamxó got people together.
'Avíits,	A mountain,
'avíits viivám,[158]	a mountain was here,
nyáany nyiiuukayáamk 'etá.	and he brought them towards it, they say.
Nyáany a'íim:	That's what it was called:
'Avíi Kwa'amée 'et.	it was called 'Avíi Kwa'amée (High Mountain).
Nyáanyi,	At that point,
'atsaayúu atséwk athúum,[159]	he built something, and so,
nyaanyiivák athúuk 'etəma.	there it was, they say.

'Avá mattkyáaly uu'íts,
nyáany atséwk 'etəma.¹⁶⁰

'Atsaayúu,
***¹⁶¹
uuthúutsxanyá,
a'íim.
'Atsaayúu,
alyoovar'é lyavíik awíim,¹⁶²
nyáanyi athúu 'ítsk,¹⁶⁴
a'íim,
nyáany atséwk,
nyiioo'éeyk voonóok,
aavíirək 'eta.

Nyáanyi,
nyáanyts viitháwnyək,
viitháwnyək,
xaméera,
siiyáanyək,
nyáava,
uuwíts vatháts nyaanyamáam;
"Pa'iipáa avkoonóonyá,
aatsuuxáymək,
shatamatháavəxá,"
a'íim a'íikəta. ¹⁶⁵
Nyaawíim,
kaawíts nyiioo'éeyəntik avoonóok
   athúm,
'atsaayúu,
'atsaamáats nyáanya tsavóow a'ím,
nyiioo'éeyk athúm;
'atsaayúu xáam kuuthúutsnya
   uumáxats athúm,
viitháwm,
nyáany nyiioo'éeyəntik,
atháak kaawémk avoonóo 'ím.

It was called a ramada,
that's what he built, they say.

Well,
***
it was for them to use,
he said.
Well,
*he made something like a church,*¹⁶³
he intended them to use it,
and so,
that's what he made,
and he went about teaching them,
and he finished, they say.

At that point,
these (people) were here,
here they were,
and later,
they went along,
and as for this,
it is what he did, and that's all;
"The people who are around there,
they have no expertise,
they won't know,"
he said, they say.
Then,
he went about teaching them
   something, and so,
well,
he intended them to plant crops,
and he taught them;
there were other things that they
   could eat,
there they were,
and he taught them about those too,
he intended them to gather them and
   do whatever it was.

'Atsaayúu tsáaməly alynyiithúutsk viitháwk:
kaawíts tsavóowxaym,
xáak athótk athúm,
nyáanya,
vanyaa'íim:
merasíints athúuk 'etəma.
'Iipá uutsáawəntík 'eta.
Oo'éeyəm,
'iipá uutsáawk,
'uutáp awíim,
kaawíts xáam kuuthútsnya nyáanyəm awíim.[166]
'Axwáayk nyaathúum,
nyáanya uuwíits a'ím.
Nyáany nyiiaatsooyóoyk:
'atsaayúu oowéxanya,
'a'áw awíim ootséwxanya,[167]
nyioo'éeyəntík 'et.
Awim,
mattáam vikwayáanya,
uushíitənya nyiioo'éeyəntik 'et.
Nyáanyi,
xáam uuthútsəm 'ityá.
Nyaa'íim,
" 'Apínyək,"
" 'Apílyk,"
"Ayúushk,"
"Xatsúurək," awím,[168]
nyáany a'ím,
nyiioo'éey 'ím 'et.
'Atsaayúu,
shiimúlynya nyiiáayk athúm,
nyáavəm a'ím,
"Miiwáam mootséwnya,[169]
pa'iipáa nyiimashíitk awím a'étxá,"[170]
a'íim,

They were thinking about all these things:
as soon as they planted something,
it became different, and so,
as for that,
this is what happened:
it became medicine, they say.
They made arrows, they say.
He taught them how,
and they made arrows,
and they did spears,
and they did the (other) different things.
When there was war,
he intended them to use these things.
That's what he showed them:
how to make things,
how to make fire,
he taught them that too, they say.
So,
(in) the years that passed,
he taught them names too, they say.
At that point,
there were different (seasons), they say.
Then,
"It's warm,"
"It's hot,"
"It's cooling off,"
and "It's cold," and so,
that's what (the seasons) are called,
he tried to teach them that, they say.
Well,
he gave them clan names, and so,
at this point he said,
"Whatever you make of yourself,
that's what people will call you,"
he said,

shiimúly nyiiáayəntik 'et.[171]	and he gave them their clan names, they say.
Nyáanyiimánk, pa'iipáa xáak tsawémk 'eta.[172]	Starting there, he took the people in different (directions), they say.
Nyiikanáavək a'et:[173] nyáany makyí nyatsuuváay 'ím: 'anyaavi awétk, kavéevik awétk, 'anyaaxáapk awíim, matxávik awíim. Marxókavék, 'atsaayúu, Kwatsáan pa'iipáa nyiikwanáamts.[174] Uuváaxáyk, 'atsaráavək 'eta. 'Atsaráavək awim, nyamáam, kwara'ák athúm,[175] 'atsaráavək, apúyk athúm.	He told them (things), they say; he said where they would live: they (would) do it in the east, they (would) do it in the south, they (would) do it in the west, or they (would) do it in the north. As for Marxókavék, well, he was a great Quechan person. He was there, and all of a sudden he got sick, they say. He got sick, and so, finally, he got old, and so, he got sick, and he died.
Kwatsáanənyts, uu'ítsənyts, nyáanyts iimáatt atháwk, viiwáak, ootanyék aavíirk a'ím.	The Quechans, the ones called (by that name), they took his body, they took it here, and they cremated it and finished, they say.
'Atsaayúu tsáaməly, ookavék kanáavək athum.	All (these) things get told over and over again.
Nyáanyi viiwáak, 'Avíi Kwa'mée kwa'ítsəny alyawémk, nyáanyi, nyáanyi athík athutyá.	They took him there, they took him to what is called 'Avíi Kwa'amée, and there, that's where he lies.

Nyaanyiimánk,
'avíi nyáanyi alynyaayém.
Nyuuwítsk uuthúutsk a'ím,
nyáanya.
Pa'iipáa mattkamaawíinyts athúuk 'ím,
Kwatsáants athótk,
Xamakxáavəts athúum,
'Axá Xavashúupáayts athúum,
Xawáalyapáayts athúum,
Yáavapáay.
Amák athíintisáa,
'atsaayúu,
Xattpáa 'Anyáa a'étəma.
Iiwáa mattashék Pa'iipáa a'ét.

Vathány awíim voonóok nyaavíirək.
'Atsaayúu,
pa'iipáats 'uuxúutt nyaa'íim,
pa'iipáats 'uuxúuttk 'iipáyk voonóow 'ím,
Kumastamxó uu'ítsənyts.
'Amáttəny alyaxávək 'et.[176]
Nyaanyiimánk;
nyakónyənyts nyáanyi kamánk atspák awityá.[177]
Nyáanyəm,
mattwaaxáavək athúum,
makyík 'atsamáa lya'émk,
oovar'ék,
nyáasik awémk,
Pa'iipáa Nyiikwanáam nyáanyi,
awémk,
'atsaayúu tsáaməly kwatséwənya.[178]
Athúum,
viitháwnyək,
'anyáa tsuumpápəm,
nyaavíirək,
awim,

Since that time,
(people) have gone to that mountain.
They own it, they say,
that (place).
The people are his relatives, and so,
they are Quechans,
they are Mojaves,
they are Havasupais,
they are Hualapais,
and Yavapais.
(Some) might have come afterwards,
well,
they are called Maricopas.
They called themselves the People.

He went on doing this and finished.
Well,
he intended the people to be good,
he intended the people to be good and live (their lives),
the one called Kumastamxó (did).
He went into the earth, they say.
He came from there;
his father had come up from there.

At that point,
he fasted, and so,
he didn't eat anything,
and he prayed,
he sent (his prayer) over there,
to that Great Person,
he sent it,
to the one who had created everything.
So,
there he was,
for four days,[179]
and he finished,
and so,

viithíik,
'atsaayúu 'ashpáa tsuumpápk xáam kuuthúutsəny mattatséwk 'et.
Nyaanyiimánk,
pa'iipáany nyiiyúuk nyiiuutar'úyk avoonóow 'ím,[180]
a'íik 'et.

Nyáava 'uu'íts vathány,
kaanáav vathány,
Kwatsáananyts kanáavk 'ityá.
'Atsaayúu,
avoonóok,
'axótt a'ím,
Pa'iipáats Nyiikwanáam nyiiáaytan kwathútsəny.
Athúum athót.

he came,
and he turned himself into the four different kinds of eagles, they say.
Starting there,
he intended to watch over the people and take care of them,
they say.

This that I have said,
this story,
the Quechan people have told it, they say.
Well,
they are around,
and they intend to be good,
because the Great Person gave them (this intention).
That's how it is.

PART III:
A QUECHAN ACCOUNT OF ORIGINS

Retold in the Quechan Language
by George Bryant

Xiipúktánək,[181]	First of all,
'atsaayúu,	well,
'axáts aaíimk,	water was all there was,
tsáaməly aamáttk viivát.	and it covered everything.
'Amáttəny nyiiríish a'íim.[182]	There was no land.
Kukumáatt-ts athúum,	Kukwiimáatt was (there),
piipáa nyiiv'óowəntik,	and someone else was there too,
nyáanya,	and as for that person
makyík amúly —	whatever his name was —
amúly shoopóow aly'ém;	he didn't know his name;
áayts aly'émxáym.	he hadn't been given one yet.
Nyáanyts,	They were the ones,
'axá maxák amánk athót.[183]	they came from under the water.
***[184]	***
Avoonóoxaym,	There they were, and suddenly,
kaawíts kírən a'ím uu'áavək 'ét.	they felt something shake, they say.
Nyáanyəm,	With that,
Kukwiimáattányts atspák 'et.	Kukwiimáatt came out, they say.
'Axá 'amáy nyiiv'óowət.	He stood on top of the water.
'Ashéntits athúunypat 'étsáa,[185]	The other one wanted to do (the same thing) too, but
siiváxáyk,	he was still there,
Kukwiimáatt kwa'ítsnya nyáany,	and that one who was called Kukwiimáatt,
nyáany tsakakwék 'eta.	he asked him, they say.
"Kamathómk 'axám mathíik matspák mathúum?"	"How did you come out of the water?"
a'íim,	he said,
Kukumáatt-ts a'íim,	and Kukwiimáatt said,
" 'Eethóny 'uutstáaqəsh,"[186]	"I opened my eyes,"
a'íik 'et.	he said, they say.
Taaxánk,	(But what) really happened (was),
eethóny aaspáqs a'étk a'íik 'eta.	he must have had his eyes closed, they say.

Piipáa kwashéntəntínyənyts athúum:	That other person did it:
eethónya uutstáaq 'et.[187]	he opened his eyes, they say.
'Axáts alyaxávək,	Water went in,
eethó ta'aaláaym,	and it ruined his eyes,
eethó táarək 'et.	and he was blind, they say.
Atspák vanyaathíim,	As he was coming out,
Kukwiimáatt-ts a'ím,	Kukwiimáatt said,
"Kwara'ák Eethó Kwatáarée!" a'íim 'ityá.[188]	"Blind Old Man!" he said, they say.
'Atsaayúu tsáaməly tiinyáamk viitháwət.	Everything was dark.
'Anyáats nyiivá lya'émk,	There was no sun,
xaly'áts nyiivá lya'émk,	there was no moon,
xamashéts nyiitháw aly'émk,	there were no stars,
athúum,	and so,
viitháwk 'et.	here they were, they say.
Nyaany ayúukəm,	He saw that,
Kukwiimáattənyts,[189]	Kukwiimáatt (did),
'axóttəm ayúu lya'émk 'et.	and it didn't look good to him, they say.
Áar aly'ém.	He didn't like it.
Av'áak láak láak a'ím,	He walked, taking big steps,
aatsuumpápk,	he did it four times,
takavék,	and he came back,
nyáalyavíintík,	and it was like that again,
nyáalyavíi uutsáawəntík 'etá.	he did it like that again in the same way, they say.
Nyaaxáapk shathómpk,	He headed to the west,
xiipúk,	first,
takavék;	and he came back;
kavéely shathómpk,	he headed to the south,
takavék;	and he came back;
'anyáavi shathómpk,	he headed to the east,

takavék;	and he came back;
athúuk 'et.	he did, they say.
Nyaathúum,	Then,
'axányanyts asáttk a'et.	the water receded, they say.
Iisháalynya 'axály shathúunk,	He put his finger in the water,
aakwíin aakwíin awíik 'etá.	and he made it go around and around, they say.
" 'Anyaats 'ashaakwíink va'oonóok,	"I am stirring it around,
'anyaats 'ashaakwíink va'oonóok,	I am stirring it around,
kúur a'ím,	and soon,
'amáttənyts arúvəxa.	the ground will be dry.
Kúur a'ím,	Soon,
'amáttənyts arúvəxa,"	the ground will be dry,"
a'íim,	he said,
aashváarək.	he sang it.
Nyiiv'óowk,[190]	He stood there,
nyiivoo'óowənyá,[191]	and there where he stood,
'atsaayúuts atspák;[192]	something came out;
'axányi atóly avák 'et.[193]	it was in the middle of the water, they say.
'Amáttəts.	It was land.
" 'Aaqáa,"[194]	" 'Aaqáa,"
'et,	he said,
'atsaayúu Piipáa Eetho Kwatáaránynyts.	the Blind Person or whoever he was.
"Tsapéevt.	"It is small.
Tsapéevtəm,	It is small,
kaawémk,	so how is it
piipáats 'atáyk vanyoonóowúm?"	that a lot of people might be there?"
a'íik 'et.	he said, they say.
"Náq ka'íim,"	"Be silent,"

a'ét.	he said.
Kukumáatt-ts a'ím.	Kukwiimáatt said it.
Piipáa Eethó Kwatáarənyts 'amátt nyiinák,	The Blind Old Man sat down on the ground,
'aayúu mas'ée ashtúum,	and he gathered some mud or something,
xantap'óop atséwk 'et.	and he made a doll, they say.
Nyáanya,	As for that,
mapísá,	nowadays,
xuumáarts uutsáawk awityá,	children make them,
xantapa'óop nyáany.	those dolls.
Nyáany lyavíim atséwk 'et.	He made something like that, they say.
Aaíimtank,	He just did it,
iiwáam,	on his own,
iiwáam,[195]	on his own,
alynyiiuuthúutsənya awíim atséwk.[196]	he used his ideas to make them.
Nyáanya,	About those dolls,
Kukwiimáatt nyáany makyík " 'Anykawík!" a'íi lya'ém.	he never said to Kukwiimáatt, "Help me!"
Vaawíim:	He did it like this:
mas'éenya ashtúum,	he gathered the mud,
iiwáamtan alynyiiuuthúutsəny awíim	he used his very own ideas
atséwk avoonóok 'et.	and he went about making (the dolls), they say.
Nyáany makyík avány tsakakwíivək a'ávək awíi lya'ém.[197]	He never did ask him and listen (to what he had to say).
Nyáanya tatsháattk nyiixítsək awíik 'et.	He stood them up and lined them up in a row, they say.
Kukwiimáattənyts,	Kukwiimáatt,
nyáany,	as for that,
piipáanya,	that person,
Eethó Kwatáar nyáany shalyamák nyiiv'óowk av'óowk.	he stood there behind that Blind One.

"Kaawíts matséwk ma'ím
  avmuuváak mawíim?"
"Pa'iipáa,"
a'íik 'eta.
Eethó Kwatáaránys.
" 'Anyáats xiipúk 'awíim,
mayúuk,
mawéxa,"
a'íikəta.
Kukwiimáatt a'íim.

Piipáa Eethó Kwatáarány,
kaa'ém alya'émk 'etá.
Masharáyk viivák.
Kukwiimáatt-ts a'íim,
" 'Atsaayúu xaly'á xiipúk
  'atséwxa,"
nyaa'íim,
'anyáavik shathómpk,
iisháaly kapáar nyáanyi tsayóq,

'amáynyi tsasvék,
vaawée vaawée awíik 'eta.
Nyáanyəm,
tàkaták 'anyáayk uuvák 'et.

Eethó Kwatáarənyts a'íim,
"Kaawíts viithíik!
Kaawíts viithíisá."
" 'Atsaayúu xaly'á 'a'íim 'ashéxá,"
a'íik 'et,
Kukwiimáattányts.

Nyáany 'ashéntəm atséwk 'eta.
Kukwiimáatt-ts a'íim,
"Vatháts,
xaly'á vatháts,
mattkwashéntəny nyiivá lya'émxá.

"What are you trying to make?"
  (he said).
"People,"
he said, they say.
The Blind One (did).
"I will do it first,
and you may watch,
and you may do it,"
he said, they say.
He said it to Kukwiimáatt.

(To) the Blind Person,
(Kukwiimáatt) said nothing, they say.
He was angry, sitting here.
Kukwiimáatt said,
"First I will make the moon or
  something,"
and then,
he turned toward the east,
and he spat on the tip of his finger
  there,
and he rubbed it on the sky,
he went like this and like this, they say.
With that,
it was round and shiny, they say.

The Blind One said,
"Something is coming!
Something might be coming."
"I will name it the moon,"
he said, they say,
Kukwiimáatt (did).

He made that one (thing), they say.
Kukwiimáatt said,
"As for this,
this moon,
it will not stay in the same place.

Nyáavi amánk
viiyáanyk viiyáanyk,
'anyaaxáapk shathómpk
　viiyáanyk aváamxá."
Eethó Kwatáarənyts a'íim,
"Viiyáaxayk,
'axaly axávətxá.
Kaathómk atspámxa'ənká?"
a'íikəta.
***198
" 'Amáynya 'atawáamk,199
vaawée 'awíim,
nyáany,
xaly'ányts matxávik aváak
　nyaaváamk,200
viiyáanyək,
'anyáavik aváam;
takavék
nyáanyi aváamxa,"
a'íik 'et.
"Tsaváamk athúuwúm,"
nyáany a'íik 'etá.
Eethó Kwatáaránynts.

Nyáanyəm,
piipáa atséwk,
suuvák awíik 'etk,
uuvám,
ayúuk,
Kukwiimáattənyts anák,
awíinypat:
'atsaayúu mas'ée ashtúum.

'Atsaayúu,201
Piipáa Eethó Kwatáarənyts
　xiipúk awíim,
pa'iipáa nyiitséwxá,
aaly'íim.

It will come from here
and go on and go on,
it will go on heading toward the
　west and get there."
The Blind One said,
"It will go along, and all of sudden,
it will go into the water.
How will it get out?"
he said, they say.
***
"I will turn the sky,
I will make it go like this,
and as for that,
the moon will reach the north,

and go along until
it gets to the east;
it will go back
and get there,"
he said, they say.
"That would be impossible,"
that's what he said, they say.
The Blind One.

With that,
he made people,
he sat over there intending to do it,
there he was,
and seeing him,
Kukwiimáatt sat down,
and he did it too:
he gathered mud or something.

Well,
the Blind Person would do it first,

he would make people,
he thought.

Nyáany áar aly'ém.
Awéxáym,²⁰²
piipáanyts xáak athúum,
'aláayíi kaa'émxa,
makyík uutar'úyk atséw aly'ém.

Xiipúk,
Kwatsáan 'iipáa atséwk 'et.
Nyaamák,
Kamayáa atséwk,
nyaawíim,
mashaxáy Kwatsáan awíim,
Kamayáa mashaxay awíim 'et.
Nyaamák,
Kwa'aapá 'iipáa atséwk,
Xattpáa 'Anyáa 'iipáa atséwk,²⁰⁴
Kwa'aapá sanya'ák atséwk,
Xattpaa 'Anyáa sanya'ák
  atséwəntík 'et.
Nyaawíim,
'amátt nyiitháwk,
viitháwk 'eta.
Nyiitsáam athum,
nyáanyi atháwk avatháwk.

Piipáa Eethó Kwatáarənyts
  Kukumáatt aatsooyóoyk 'etá,
piipáa ootséwənyá.
Eeméts athótəsáa,
eemé kapáarəny nyiirísh a'íim.
Iisháaly kapáarəny nyiirísh a'íim.
A'étəm athúm,
'axótt alya'ém.
Iisháalyəny takyévək
  shanàpanápk 'et.²⁰⁵
"Kaawémk

(Kukwiimáatt) didn't want that.
If (the Blind One) did it,
the people would be different,
they might be bad,
for he was not making them
  carefully at all.

First,
he made a Quechan man, they say.
After that,
he made a Kamia,²⁰³
and then,
he did a Quechan woman,
and he did a Kamia woman, they say.
After that,
he made a Cocopa man,
he made a Maricopa man,
he made a Cocopa woman,
and he made a Maricopa woman
  too, they say.
Then,
they lay there on the ground,
they lay there, they say.
He placed them there, and so,
that's where they lay.

The Blind Person showed them to
  Kukwiimáatt, they say,
the people that he had made.
There were legs, but
there weren't any toes.
There weren't any fingers.
Therefore,
they were no good.
The fingers were joined together
  and webbed, they say.
"How is it

pa'iipáanyts uuxáyk uuváaxanká?	that a person will know how (to use them)?
Makyík 'axóttəm atséw aly'ém.	He didn't make them well at all.
'Anyáats nya'awíim,	When I do it,
'aayúu iisháaly kapáarnya 'atséwk.	I make fingers and things.
Iisháaly kapáara kwaqóolnya 'atséwəntík" a'ím,	I make long fingers too," he said,
"Iisháaly kwaly'ooxóo 'atséwəntík,	"I make fingernails too,
eemé 'atséwk,	I make feet,
eemé kapáarnya.	and the toes.
Eemé kwaly'ooxóony 'atséwəntík," a'ét.[206]	I make the toenails too," he said.
Piipáa Eethó Kwatáarəny iiwáanyts 'axótt aly'ém viiv'óowt.	The Blind Person felt bad, standing there.[207]
"Vathány,	"As for this one,
vatháts 'axóttk athútyá,	this one is good,
'anyép 'ootséwənyts.	the one that I made.
'Atsaayúu 'amáttnyi atháwəm,	If there are things on the ground,
ashtúu a'éxayk awíim,	if he wants to pick them up he can do it,[208]
'axóttxá."	and that will be good."
"Kaváarək," 'étk,	"No," he said,
awíim,	he did,
Kukwiimáatt-ts.	Kukwiimáatt (did).
"Máany piipáa mootséwənyts 'axótt alya'ém.	"The person you made is not good at all.
Iisháaly kapáarnya,	As for the fingers,
iisháaly kapáarənyts shaaxúukəm 'atséwətk awityá.	I made mine with ten fingers.
Piipáats —	A person —
xalyavímtəm	it is possible
kaa'íts nyáanya	that some of those (fingers)
kaathómk aráavxáyəm,	might get hurt somehow,
'axótt alyaskyíitxa,	but it would still be all right,
oov'ótstəntík kwathútsəny.	because other (fingers) would be there.

Awíi lyaskyíik,	He could still use them,
iisháalyəm kaawémǝm,	he could do something with his hands,
'axóttəxá.	and it would be all right.
Nyaathúum,	Then,
máany mootséwənyts 'aláayexa.	the ones that you made would be in bad shape.
Iisháalynya taaráavxáym,[209]	If (one of them) hurt his hand,
'atsaayúu tsáaməly aráavək 'et.	the whole thing would be hurt.
Aráavəxa."	It would be hurt."
Nyaa'íim,	Having said that,
táqsh a'ím,	he jumped up,
'atsaayúu,	and, well,
Piipáa Eethó Kwatáarənyts siiv'óowm,[210]	the Blind Person stood there,
'atsaayúu ootséwənya,	and as for the things that he had made,
ka'ák ka'ák awíim,	(Kukwiimáatt) went kick! kick!,
'axály aatspáxk 'et.	and he cast them into the water, they say.
Pa'iipáa Eethó Kwatáarəny,	As for the Blind Person,
mashuuráyəny mattapéem;[211]	his anger was terrible;
'axály axávək,	he went into the water,
siiyáak 'et.	and he went along, they say.
Awéxáym,[212]	When he did so,
'axá shaakwíints mattapéek, nyaanyi;	there was a terrible whirlpool, there;
nyáanyi avák 'eta.	there it was, they say.
Nyáanyts athúum:[213]	That's what happened:
'atsaayúu 'atsiiráavts mattapéem,	there were a lot of sicknesses and things,
mattapéek siitháwənyk,	there were a lot of them over there,
aatspáatsk 'ét.	and they came out, they say.
Avathúum,	That happened,
'atsuuráavək athúuk 'et.	and (people now) get sick, they say.
Nyáany ayúuk oov'óowxayk,	As soon as he saw that,
Kukumáattənyts,	Kukwiimáatt

eeménya awíim shapéttk 'et.

'Atsaayúu kwa'anyóyməts,
kaa'íts aatspáatsk 'et.
Athúu lya'émk 'ís,
piipáats 'atsuuráav aly'émtəxá,
nyáava kwathíkəny.

Piipáa Eethó Kwatáarənyts
'axá maxák alyavák,
siivák 'eta.
'Atsaayúunyts aatspáatsk avoonóo:
'atsiiráavəts.
Kukwiimáatt,
nyáanyi 'amátt nyiiv'óowk ayúuk,[215]
siiv'óowk 'eta.
Vasháwək.

Kukumáatt-ts takavék,
piipáanya kayáam,
ootséwənya.
Piipáa Kwatsáanənya atháwk 'et.

Atháwk awim,
tskalypónyi,
nyáany nyiiwíim,
matxávik aashathómp,
ookavék ookavék awím,

takavék,
awím,
nyiiv'óowəntík 'eta.

Nyaamák,
'anyaaxáapk awémk,
wiishaawíish nyaawíntík,

used his foot and covered (the whirlpool), they say.

The ugly things,
some of them had come out, they say.
If it hadn't happened,
people would not get sick,
as is now the situation.[214]

The Blind Person
stayed underwater,
there he was, over there, they say.
Things kept coming out:
sicknesses.
As for Kukwiimáatt,
he stood there on the ground there and watched,
he stood over there, they say.
He guarded it.

Kukwiimáatt returned,
and he went straight toward the people,
the ones he had made.
He picked up the Quechan person, they say.

He picked him up
by his armpits,
that's what he used,
he sent him (swinging) to the north,
he made him go (swinging) back and forth,

and he came back,
and so,
he stood there again, they say.

After that,
he sent him to the west,
he made him swing back and forth again,

nyáavik awíntík,
awíik 'et.

Xiipúkətánk,
piipáa vatháts,
piipáa nyáavi kwathíkənya,[216]
isháály lyavíik 'aqóolk 'et.
Aawinyawínyk

nyiimánxaym,
'aqóolk alóq a'ím,
athúuk 'et.

'Atsaayúu tsáaməly shoopóowk
   viiv'óowətəs a'ét —
'íis a'étk[217] —
makyík tsaqwér aly'émk 'et.
Kukwiimáatt-ts a'íim,
"Eethóny kashatpíittk
   kav'óowk!" 'eta.

Nyaathúum,
Kukwiimáatt-ts piipáanya
   nyiikamáanənya awíntik 'eta.
Nyiiwíntik:
Kwa'aapánya awíim,
Xattpáa 'Anyáa awíim,[218]
a'étəsáa
makyík Xattpáa 'Anyáany
   kavéely ooshathómp aly'émk
'eta.[219]
Athúum,
nyáanyts viiyáak,
nyáasi nyaváy a'íim.

Kukwiimáatt-ts,
nyaamák,
tsooqwérəny piipáa nyiiáayk 'et.

he did it again towards here,
he did it, they say.

At first,
this person,
the person that was here,
he was as long as one's hand, they say.
(Kukwiimáatt) swung him back
   and forth,
and from then on,
he was very long,
he was, they say.

He stood there, aware of
   everything, but —
but —
he couldn't talk at all, they say.
Kukwiimáatt said,
"Close your eyes and stand there!"
   he said.

Then,
Kukwiimáatt did the rest of the
   people in turn, they say.
He did them in turn:
he did the Cocopa,
and he did the Maricopa,
but
he never did turn the Maricopa to
   the south,
they say.
So,
that (Maricopa) went along,
intending to live over there in the east.

As for Kukwiimáatt,
after that,
he gave the people language, they say.

Kwatsáan,	The Quechan,
piipáa Kwatsáannya nyaatháwək,	as the Quechan people were standing there,
xáak tsavóowk,	he put them on one side,
a'íim,	and he said,
"Katsaqwérək!"	"Speak!"
a'íik 'eta.	he said it, they say.
A'ávk viiv'óowsáa,	(The Quechan man) understood him, but
makyík tsaqwér aly'émk 'eta.	he could not speak at all, they say.
Uu'íts nyaatsuumpápəm,	The fourth time he said it,[220]
nyáanyəm,	at that point,
'anóqəm tsaqwérək 'et.	(the Quechan man) spoke a little, they say.
Piipáa nyáanya amúly áayk 'et.[221]	(Kukwiimáatt) gave that person a name, they say.
Kwatsáan a'íim.	He called him Kwatsáan (Quechan).
Nyáanyi uutsáawəntík,	Doing it in the same way,
Kukwiimáatt kwa'ashíinəntínya a'íim,	Kukwiimáatt said (something) to each of them,
tsatsuuqwáarək 'eta.	and they spoke, they say.
Makyíny uu'ítsəny:[222]	What he said was who they were:
Kamayáa,	Kamia,
***[223]	***
Kwa'aapá,	Cocopa,
Maricopa,	Maricopa,
Xattpáa 'Anyáa a'íikəta.[224]	he said Xattpáa 'Anyáa (Maricopa), they say.
Kukwiimáattənyts sanyts'áak nyiiáay lya'émk 'et,[225]	Kukwiimáatt did not give it to the women, they say,
tsooqwér nyiiáay lya'ém.	he did not give them the power of speech.
Nyáanyts ookavék,	He sent it back

'iipátsənya,	(with) the men,
a'íim nyiioo'éeyk 'et.	and so he intended (the men) to teach (the women).
'Iipáa Kwatsáanənyts,	The Quechan man,
'aayúu,	well,
Kamayáany eethónya asháamk 'et.	he looked into the face of the Kamia, they say.
Ayúuk ava'óow.	He stood there looking.
Mattkiiyíik 'et.	They became friends, they say.
Kwa'aapá,	As for the Cocopa,
Kwa'aapányənyts Xattpáa 'Anyáany taxkwéevk viiv'óow,	the Cocopa stood next to the Maricopa,
nyáanyts mattkiiyíintík 'et.	and they likewise became friends, they say.
Kwatsáan 'aakóoyənyts alynyiithúutsk viiv'óowk 'et.	The Quechan woman stood there thinking, they say.
Alynyiithúutsk a'ím:	She thought about it and said:
"Kaathúntək a'ím,	"Why is it
Kukwiimáatt-ts 'anyétsa awíim,[226]	(that) Kukwiimáatt, in doing us,
xáak awíim atséwk awím?"[227]	did things differently?"[228]
a'éta.	she said.
"Kaathómk	"How is it
xuumáarts aatspáatsxanká?" 'et.	that children shall be born?" she said.
Piipáats siiv'óownyək,	A person stood there in the distance,
a'ávək siiv'óowəny,	he stood there in the distance listening,
a'íikəta.	they say.
" 'Ayáak	"I shall go
Kukwiimáatt 'atskakwékm a'ávəka."[229]	and ask Kukwiimáatt and hear (what he has to say)," he said.
Kukwiimáatt-ts ava'óownyək a'ím, 'aakóoyəny a'íikəta.	Kukwiimáatt stood there, and so, he said something to the woman, they say.
'Anyáats 'anykóor 'ashoopóowk 'athutyá	"I already know

alynyiimuuthúutsnya.	about your thoughts.
Nyáanya,	Those (thoughts),
miiwáaly matsathúly viimav'óowəs athót,	you are hiding them in your heart, but
'ashoopóowk.	I know about them.
Kaathúntək a'ím	Why is it
aaíimk ma'íilyma'ém?	that you don't just say them?
Mashtxáats iiwáam makyík xuumáar ayúu aly'émk.[230]	Girls cannot have children on their own.
Mayáak,[231]	You (must) go,
Kwatsáan 'iipáanya makayáamxá,"	you must go to that Quechan man,"
a'ét.	he said.
Nyaa'ávk awim,	When she heard him, then
'aakóoy —	the old woman —
sanya'ákíi —	the woman, perhaps —
mashaxáyts,	the girl,
'a'étxa,	I will say,
nyáanyts,	that (girl),
iiwáanyts 'axóttk 'et.	she felt better, they say.
Avathótəs a'ét,	Even so, she said,
" 'Anyáats,	"As for me,
'iipáa 'iixán 'áartəka'e.	I want a good-looking man.
Makyík avány Kwatsáanənya 'áar aly'émtəka'e.	I don't want that Quechan at all.
Kwa'aapányənyts 'iixántəmash.	The Cocopa is good-looking.
Kwatsáannya 'áar aly'émtəka'e,"	I don't want the Quechan,"
a'íim,	she said,
viiv'óowk 'ityá.	and she stood there, they say.
Kwa'aapánya atsúyxa lyavíik.	She felt like marrying the Cocopa.
Ayúuk,	She looked at him,
a'íitstank viiv'óow.	and she stood there flirting with him.
Kukwiimáatt-ts a'íim,	Kukwimáatt said,
"Kwa'aapánya makyík matsúy alyma'émxa.[232]	"You will not marry the Cocopa.
Máanyts mathúum,[233]	You are you,
nyáanyts athúum,	and he is he,

makyík mattkwa'ashéntəly nyamoonóo lya'émxa," a'íiket.	and (the two of) you will never be in the same place," he said, they say.
Mashaxáyənyts makyík a'áv aly'émk 'et. Viiyáak, avata'ár avuuváak, avuuváak 'et.	The girl didn't listen to him, they say. She went along, she was sulking, there she was, over there, they say.
Piipáa Eethó Kwatáarənyts xáak athíik atspák.[234] Siivám ayúuk 'et. Nyaayúuk a'íim, "Kukumáatt-ts uu'ítsnya, makyík ka'áv alyaka'émk. Kaawémk 'atsmawéeyúm?	The Blind Person came out from one side. He saw her there, they say. Seeing her, he said, "Whatever Kukwiimáatt says, don't listen to him. What could he do for you?
'Ís 'anyép nyaama'ávəm, 'atsaayúu 'atáytanəm manyuuwítsxa. 'Atsmuumátsənyts 'atáy athóxa, xuumxúukəm 'anyáa kwashíintənyám." Kukumáatt shoopóowk 'eta. Aváts, Eethó Kwatáaránłyts, nyiiuuváam, nyáanyts, a'ávtəsáa,[236] makyík ayúulya'émk 'et.	If only you were to listen to me, you would own many things. You would have many meals,[235] six of them each day." Kukwiimáatt knew about it, they say. This one, the Blind One, he was there, and that (Kukwiimáatt), he sensed it, but he couldn't see him.
Viiyáak, viiyáak, sany'ákənyts — mashxáyənyts siiv'óowxáym, viiyáamk awítya.	He went, and he went, and as the woman — (or rather) the girl stood there, he went past her.

Piipáa Eethó Kwatáaránnyts
maxák alyaxávək 'et.
Maxák alyaxávək 'anyéw,

awim,
Kukwiimáatt-ts mashxáyəny a'íim,[237]
"Makyík 'atsaayúu 'uu'ítsəny
　ma'áv alyma'émk.[238]
Nyuukanáavxaym,
makyík ma'áv alyma'émk.
Nyáavi amánk,
nyiinytatpóoyxá!
Máanyts athúum,
piipáa nyiikamáanənyts!"

Kukwiimáatt-ts matxávi
　shathómp,[239]
tsaqwérk uuráwtan aatsuumpáp.
Nyaanyi amán,
oov'óowk viitháwnyək,
nyaatsuumpáp.
'Axányənyts 'amáttnya aamáarək 'et.
Piipáanyənyts 'axám áamk
　avoonóoxayk 'et.
Oonóoxaym,
oov'óowənyts akwévək a'ét.

Kukumáatt-ts 'a'íi ashtúum,
a'íim,
" 'Atsaayúu mashtaráts
　nyiinyatséwxá,"
a'íik 'et.

Piipáa Kwa'aapánya atháwk
'atsaayúu shakw'iiláa atséwk
　'et.[240]
Kamayáany awíim,[241]
'aqwáaq nyiitséwəntík,

The Blind Person
went under the water, they say.
He went under the water and
　disappeared,
and so,
Kukwiimáatt said to the girl,
"You did not listen to what I said.

I told you,
and you never listened.
Starting here,
I will kill you!
It is you (whom I will kill),
and the rest of the people!"

Kukwiimáatt faced north,

and he spoke very rapidly four times.
From that point,
it went on raining,
four times.
The water covered the land, they say.
The people were swimming around,
　they say.
There they were, and suddenly,
the rain stopped, they say.

Kukwiimáatt gathered wood,
and he said,
"I will make you into wild things,"

he said, they say.

He took the Cocopa person
and made him into a mockingbird
　or something, they say.
He did the Kamia,
he made them into deer,

Xattpáa 'Anyáanya 'ashée nyiitséwk,	and he made the Maricopa into buzzards,
'ís	but
Kwatsáan,	as for the Quechan,
nyáanyts 'ashéntək,	he was the only one,
pa'iipáa lyavíik oov'óowk 'et.	he remained in human form, they say.
Nyáanyi,	At that point,
ashék 'ím,	he named him,
Marxókavék a'íim ashék 'ét.	he named him Marxókavék, they say.
" 'Atsaváamk 'atsáam 'oowéxanya 'awíiyúm,[242]	"I can't do everything that I should do.
'Aayúuts 'atáyəm 'oowéxats viitháwk 'itya,"	There are so many things for me to do,"
a'íik 'eta.	he said, they say.
Marxókavékts a'íim.	Marxókavék said it.
Kukwiimáatt-ts a'íim,	Kukwiimáatt said,
" 'Anyáats nyoo'éeyəxá.[243]	"I will teach you.
'Anyáats nyoo'éeyəm,	I will teach you,
piipáa matséwxá.	and you will make people.
Nyáany mawíim 'anymawíikəm,[244]	You will do that to help me,
'amátt vatháts 'axóttxá.	and this world will be better off.
'Anyáats 'amáttəny 'atséwk 'awim,	I made the earth,
'amáyəny 'atséwk 'awim,	I made the sky,
xaly'á 'atséwk,	I made the moon,
xamshé 'atséwk,	I made the stars,
tiinyáaməny 'atséwk,	I made the darkness,
'awétk 'awím,	I did, and so,
aaíim,	anyway,
'aayúu kwanyméts viitháwm 'atséwəntixá,"	I will make other things (that will) be here,"
a'íikət.	he said, they say.
Kukumáattányts	Kukwiimáatt
'axá 'amáynyi av'óowk av'óowk 'eta.	was standing on top of the water, they say.
Nyiiv'óowxáyk aashváarək 'et:	He stood there and suddenly he sang, they say:

" 'Axá vatháts 'àra'ár alya'ém;²⁴⁵
'anyáats avány 'asíim tsáaməly
  'atsáavxa.
'Axányanyts 'axóttk;
'ooséxats athúum."

Nyaa'íiva.
Marxókavék a'íim,
"Meethó kashatpíittk," a'ím,²⁴⁶
awéxaym,
'axányənyts takavék atsénk,²⁴⁷
a'íim,
atsénək siiyáaxáym,
'amáttəny 'amáyənyi ava'óowk
  a'ím,
soov'óowk 'et.²⁴⁸

"Piipáa siipxúuk 'atséwk,
makyík nyuu'áav aly'émk.²⁴⁹
Nyáava 'awíntik,
shaaxúuk aaxavík 'amáyk
  tsuumpápm 'atséwxa.
'Atséwm,
nyáanyts 'axóttxá."

Nyaa'íim,
av'áak viithíik viiyáak 'eta.

Xiipúk 'anyaaxáap kayáamk,
takavék 'anyáavi kayáamk.

"Nyáavi 'amátt-ts atóvi athúum
  athutyá.
'Amátt atónyi nyáavi avák.
Nyáavi avák.
'Avá kwatiinyáamənya 'atséwxa."²⁵¹

"This water is not deep;
I will drink all of this up.

The water is good;
it is fit for me to drink."

That's what he said.
He said to Marxókavék,
"Close your eyes," he said,
and as soon as he did so,
the water went back down,
and so,
as soon as it went down,
they were standing on the surface
  of the land, and so,
they were standing over there, they say.

"I made eight people,
and they never listen to me.
When I do this again,
I will make twenty-four.

I will make them,
and they will be good."

Having said that,
he walked back and forth, they
  say.²⁵⁰
First he headed west,
and then he turned back and
  headed east.

"This is the center of the earth.

The center of the earth is here.
Here it is.
I will build my dark house."

A Quechan Account of Origins

Nyaawíim,	Then,
nyii'íly tsuumpáp ashtúuk 'eta.	he gathered up four lice, they say.
Iimáattk uuthíik.[252]	He got them from his body.
Nyaawíim —	Then —
nyaawíim,	then,
mas'éenyi,	into the mud,
nyáanyi,	there,
nyáanyi aapáxk 'eta.	that's where he threw them, they say.
Awéxáym,	He did, and right away,
nyaayúuts athúuk 'eta.	they turned into something, they say.
***[253]	***
Xanapúuk.[254]	Piss ants.
Nyáany a'íim 'ityá.	That's what they are called.
'Ís	But
vatátsk 'axwéttxay,	if they are big and red,
tsamathúly a'íim.	they are called ants.
Nyíilyk vatáyk uuvá,	(Some) are big and black,
avkoonóonya,	the ones that are around here,
tsamathúly 'avíi a'íikəta.	and they are called rock ants, they say.
Nyáanyts 'amátt uutskúpk avoonóok	Those (ants) went about making holes in the earth,
'ityá.	they say.
Nyáany nyaawíim,	That's what they did,
'amátt mas'éenya awíim oonóom,	they went about doing something to that muddy place,
arúvək.	and it dried up.
"Kamawémk,	"How will you do it,
manyavá matséwxa'ənká?"	how will you build your house?"
a'ét.	he said.
Marxókavékts a'íim.	Marxókavék said it.
'Atsaayúu,	Well,
'a'íi kaayúm,	he had no wood,
'ax'áa kaayúmtan,	he had no cottonwood,
'éxáyk,[255]	and immediately,
alynyiithúutsxáyk atséwk 'eta,	by thinking about them, he created them, they say,
nyáanya,	those (things),
'uu'íts avány.	these (things) that I mentioned.

'A'íi tuutsháattəny tsuumpápəm atséwk 'et,
kwatiinyáaməly.
Kaawíts avatháwəntim ashtúum,

'atsaayúu,
'avá kwanyíilyá atséwk 'et.

"Nyáava,
viikaváts vathány,
'Axá 'Avoolypó 'a'íim 'ashéxa,"

a'íikət.

Marxókavék pa'iipáa atséwk mas'éem.
Pa'iipáa atséw.
Makyík kwakyáav aly'émk 'etá,
kaawémk ootséwxanyá.

Nyáany piipáanyənyts[257] —
aaíim — alymata'órxats athót.

Ayúuxáyk,
atáqshk,
shalyamákəny alytaxrámpk 'et.[258]
Kukumáatt-ts a'íim,
"Nyáanyamáam,
alymata'órtəm athúm,
makyík av'áak,
makyík eemé shalyamák kwatháwnya av'áa lya'émxa.[259]
'Alaavúur 'a'ím 'ashéxa,"
a'íik 'et.

***[260]

He created four wooden posts, they say,
in the darkness.
He gathered whatever else was there,

and, well,
he made the black house, they say.

"As for this,
this (thing) that is sitting here,
I will name it 'Axá 'Avoolypó (Water Housepost),"

he said, they say.

Marxókavék made a person out of mud.
He made a person.
He didn't ask for any help, they say,[256]
with what he was somehow going to make.

It was a person —
anyway — it was something you could ride on.

As soon as he saw it,
he jumped,
and he clung to its back, they say.

Kukwiimáatt said,
"Now,
you have ridden on him,
and he will never walk,
he will never walk on his hind legs.

I will name him Burro,"
he said, they say.

***

Kukwiimáatt-ts,
Kukwiimáatt-ts
mashaxáy atséwk,
'iipáa atséwk awet.
***261

Maxáyənyts mashaxáyəny a'íim,
"Kukumáatt-ts kaawíts
  kwa'anyáawənya
  muukanáavám?"262
a'íik 'et.
"Kaváarək,"
mashxáyənyts a'íim.
"Kaváartəsáa,
'ayáak 'atskakwék 'a'ávəxá,"

a'íikəta.
Mashxáyənyts viiyáak,
'avá kwatiinyáaməny ayémk 'eta.

Marxókavékts Kukwiimáatt
  aqásəm,
viithíik.
"Máanyts piipáa Kwatsáanənya
  matsúyly 'aaly'éta,263
'ootséwxáyənya,"264
Kukwiimáatt-ts a'íim.
" 'Atsaayúu,
xuumáar 'ayúuxa lyavíita'a,"
a'ét.
Mashxáyənyts a'íim.
" 'Ayúuxa lyavíitəsáa,
uuxáyəmk athúuk 'eta."

Kukumáatt-ts a'íim,
" 'Anyáats nyaatsooyóoyxá.
Athótəs
makyík pa'iipáa kuukanáav
  alyka'émk,"265

Kukwiimáatt,
Kukwiimáatt
made a girl,
and he made a man.
***

The childless man said to the girl,
"Has Kukwiimáatt told you any
  secrets?"

he said, they say.
"No,"
said the girl.
"No, but
I will go and ask him and hear
  (what he has to say),"
she said, they say.
The girl went along,
she went to the dark house, they say.

Marxókavék summoned
  Kukwiimáatt,
and he came.
"I think you should marry the
  Quechan man,
the one I have just made,"
Kukwiimáatt said (to the girl).
"Well,
I would like to have children,"
she said.
The girl said it.
"I would like to have them, but
he says he does not know (what to
  do)."
Kukwiimáatt said,
"I will show you.
But
don't tell anyone,"

a'íik 'et.
Mashxáyəny iiwáanyts apúyəm
 oov'óowk 'eta.

***266

Kukwiimáatt-ts mashxáyəny
 a'íim.
Amúly ashék a'ím,²⁶⁷
Xavashúum Kulyíi a'íik 'et.

Maxáyənya,
Xavashúum Kuwáa 'íik 'et.

'Anyáa tsuumpápəm
mashxáyənyts 'atsarávək 'eta.
Kwas'eethée ayúuxa lyavíik
 a'íim kanáav,
athótəsáa,
makyí uuváak athúu lya'emk,
athúuk 'et.

Athótəsáa,
xuumáar eetóly kavátsənyts
 'anykóor shoopóowk 'et.
Kwas'eethée athóoyəny
 shoopóowk 'et.
Uukanáavək 'ím:
"Kapáam!"
a'íik 'eta.
Nyaanyi amánək awím,
'anóqtan mattatséwk 'et.
'Anóqtan mattatséwk athúm,
mashxáyənyts aráavəxa lyavíim.

'Akór aly'émxáym,
av'áak

he said, they say.
The girl was surprised, standing
 there, they say.

***

Kukwiimáatt said (something) to
 the girl.
He called her by name,
he called her Xavashúum Kulyíi,
 they say.
As for the young man,
he called him Xavashúum
 Kuuwáa, they say.
It was four days
that the girl was in pain, they say.
She told him she would like to see
 a doctor,
but
there were none,
that was the situation, they say.

But
the child in her belly already knew
 things, they say.
He knew what doctors did, they
 say.
He explained it to her:
"Lie down!"
he said, they say.
Starting from there, he did it,
he made himself very small, they say.
He made himself very small,
(because) the girl was likely to feel
 pain.

It wasn't long, and right away
he walked

tsaqwérək,	and he talked,
athót.	he did.

Kukumáatt-ts a'íim:	Kukwiimáatt said something:
amúly ashék,	he called him by name,
Kumastamxó a'íikət.	he called him Kumastamxó, they say.
Nyáanya a'íim,	That's what he said,
xuumáyts athúuk 'et.[268]	and (Kumastamxó) was his son, they say.

Awík,	He would help him,
'atsaayúu atséw a'íim	he would fix things
'amáttnyá.	(in) the world.

"Tiinyáamk aav'áarək viitháwxanká?"	"Will it always be dark?"
a'ét.	he said,
Kumastamxóts a'íim.	Kumastamxó said it.
"Xaly'ányanyts	"The moon
xamshényənyts	and the stars
makyík 'anyáaytan alya'émt."	are not very bright at all."

Kumastamxóts[269]	Kumastamxó
iisháalynyi tsayóq.	spat into his hand.
'Amáynyi tsáaməly 'amáyk tsayóq,	He spat all over the sky,
nyáanyəm,	and with that,
xamshéts athúuk 'et.	there were stars, they say.
Nyaawíim,	Having done that,
iisháalynyəm tsasvéq avoonóok,	he went about wiping them with his hand,
aaíim 'anyáaytanək,	and they became bright in varying degrees,
nyaawíim,	and then,
'amáynya uushtúuk iiwáam kayáamk 'et.	he pulled the sky toward himself, they say.
Nyaawíim,	Then,
eethó atséwk 'et.	he made a face, they say.
Tsasvék avoonóoxaym,	He went on rubbing, and right away,
'anyáaytank 'et.	it was very bright, they say.

"Kama'émk mashéxanká,
avány?"
a'íik 'eta.
Kukwiimáatt-ts a'íim.
"Vathány 'anyáats.
Xaly'ávats viiyáak,
nyaaxáapk kayáamk,
takavék athum.
Apúyk,
'anyáa xavíkəm atspákəntík.
Athúuk," a'ét.

"Xáak 'awíim,
xáak athúum;
'anyáany 'atséwətk 'awityá.
Athúm,
nyamooyémənyts xáak athóxá,"
a'ím.
Kumastamxó aaíimk a'íim,
Marxókavékts 'aayúu 'anyáanya
  'anyáay atséwk,²⁷⁰
tiinyáam atséwt.
'Ís
"Xuuvíkəly,
tiinyáamtank viitháwk,
'anyáaytank viitháwk,
makyík eethóny ta'aaxótt
  aly'émxá.²⁷²
Avathótəm athum,
aalyoovéevk,
tiinyáaməxá.
Aalyoovéev 'anyáam'əntixá.

Pa'iipáanyənyts kwatiinyáam
  aashmátsk,
'anyáamkəm 'iipáy
  avuuthúutsxá."

"What do you call it,
that one?"
he said, they say.
Kukwiimáatt said it.
"This is the sun.
The moon goes along,
it heads to the west,
and it returns.
It dies,
and in two days it is born again.
(That's what) happens," he said.

"I did it differently,
and it is different;
I made the sun in a different way.
So,
its path will be different,"
he said.
Kumastamxó said something,
and Marxókavék made the sun
  give off light,²⁷¹
and he made darkness.
But
"Both of them,
if it were really dark,
or if it were really light,
that would not be good at all for
  the eyes.
That's how it is, and so,
half (of the time),
it will be dark.
And half (of the time) it will be
  daytime.
People will sleep in the darkness,

and creatures will do so (when) it
  is daytime."

Kukumáatt-ts Kwatsáan 'iipáa
    atséwəntík,
Kamayáa 'iipáa atséwəntik,
nyáanya,
'avá atóly,
'avá tiinyáam atóly tsakxávək,
kaawíts nyiioo'éeyk.
Kwa'aapá atséwəntik,
Xattpáa 'Anyáa atséwəntik.
***273

Xawáalyapáay atséwk,
'Axá Xavashuupáay awíim,
Tsamoowéev awíim,
Kawíiya uu'ítsnya awíim.[274]
Nyaatsavéts awéeyk atséwk,
nyiiwéeyk.
Marxókavékts a'íim,
"Vatháts nyaanyamáam 'axótt-
    tək athutyá.
'Ís,
awíntik avoonóok,[275]
piipáats 'atáyəm,
'amáttənyts 'anóqtəm athum,[277]
'aláayxá."
Kukwiimáatt-ts uukanáavək
    a'íim,
" 'Atsaayúu
'amátt kwa'ora'ór vatháts
vatáyk thúutt a'ím viitháwk,
athópəke,"
a'íikət.

Kumastamxóts
'amátt ka'ák ka'ák awíim,
'atsaayúu tsáaməly —
athót,

*Kukwiimáatt made another
    Quechan man,
and he made another Kamia man,
and as for that,
in the house,
he put them in the dark house,
and he taught them things.
He made another Cocopa,
and he made another Maricopa.
****

*He made a Hualapai,
he did a Havasupai,
he did a Chemehuevi,
and he did the one called Cahuilla.
He made wives for them,
he did it for them.
Marxókavék said,
"This is fine now.

But,
if he keeps on doing it,[276]
there will be many people,
and there will be too little land,
and that will be bad."
    Kukwiimáatt explained it to him,
        saying
"Well,
this round earth
is getting bigger,
it is,"
he said, they say.

Kumastamxó
went stamp! stamp! on the ground,
and everything —
he did it,*

'aayúu tsáaməly masheethéevət.²⁷⁸
Kukumáatt-ts 'avá kwatiinyáamənya
  alyavák siivát.²⁷⁹
Shoopóowk 'et,
Kumastamxó 'aayúu 'amáttəny
  uuqáq,
uuqáqəm,
'aayúu kaawíts aatspáatsk
  oov'óts 'ím.²⁸⁰
'Atsaayúu xavashúunyányts.
'Atsaayúu 'iisáv 'et.

'Iisáv xiipúk atspák athutyá
'atsaayúu 'amátt kwaqáaqənyá.

Kumastamxóts tsaqwérək
  aatsuumpápk:
" 'Amáy tathíts asílyxá,"
a'íik 'et.
A'étəsáa,
'atsaayúu,
'aayúu kwasílyəny,
nyáanyts,
'amáy tathíts athúu lya'émk 'et.
Taaxán tathíts athúuk 'et.²⁸¹
Piipáanyts uumáavək avoonóok
  'et.
"Tsáaməly kuumáav alyka'émk!"
a'íik 'et.
Kumastamxóts a'íim.
"Kaa'its katsavóowk."
"Ee'é.
Ka'wémk 'atstsoovóowxanká?
'Iisháalyəm?"
a'íikəta.
Pa'iipáany matxávik tsawém,
'a'íi aayáak 'et.

and everything was frightening.
Kukwiimáatt was sitting in the
  dark house.
He knew, they say,
that Kumastamxó was making
  cracks in the earth,
he was making cracks,
so that things would sprout and
  stand there.
Green things.
Arrowweed or something, they say.

Arrowweed was the first to sprout
  (through) the cracked earth or
  something.

Kumastamxó spoke four times:

"Hail will fall,"
he said, they say.
He said it, but
well,
whatever fell,
as for that,
it wasn't hail, they say.
Really it was corn, they say.
The people went about eating it,
  they say.
"Don't eat it all!"
he said, they say.
Kumastamxó said it.
"Plant some of it."
"Okay.
How shall we plant it?
With our hands?"
he said, they say.
He sent the people north,
and they got sticks, they say.

Piipáa kwashíintənyts 'a'íi 'ashéntəm shtuutúutk 'etəma,²⁸² 'atsaayúu 'a'íi qweraqwéra.	*Each person got one stick, they say, a sharp-pointed stick or something.*
"Vathány tathíts," a'íikət.	*"This is corn," he said, they say.*
Kumastamxóts a'íim.²⁸³	*Kumastamxó said it.*
"Kashtúum! Katsavóowk!"	*"Gather it! Plant it!"*

***²⁸⁴   ***

'Axmá athíts athúum, tsam'eetó, awíim, atséwk a'ét.	*There were tepary seeds, and melons; he did it, he made them, they say.*
'Atsaayúu tsooyóqəny nyáanyk uuthíik, Kwa'aapá nyiiáayk 'et.	*He brought them out of his spittle or something, and he gave them to the Cocopa, they say.*
'Atsaayúu athíts, 'a'á athíts,²⁸⁵ nyáanya Xattpáa 'Anyáa nyiiáayk 'et.²⁸⁶	*Seeds of something, seeds of the prickly pear, he gave those to the Maricopa, they say.*
Piipáanyənyts athítsnya tsatsoovóowk, awíik 'et, 'atsaayúu 'amátt kwa'axáyənya.	*Those people planted the seeds, they did, they say, in the wet earth or something.*
Piipáats makyí uuváak, oov'óowəny atséwk shoopóowk athúu ly'émk 'et.	*People were everywhere, (but) they did not know how to make rain, they say.*
"Xattpáa 'Anyáa 'ashéntiny nyáany 'áayk," 'eta.²⁸⁸	*"To the Maricopa alone²⁸⁷ I give that (power)," he said.*
"Nyáaym oov'óowk akwévk athóxá," a'ét.	*"And I give you (another power) so that it will stop raining," he said.*
Kumastamxóts a'íim.	*Kumastamxó said it.*
"Piipáats matxá nyoopóoyk,	*"When people are thirsty,*

nyáanyəm,	at that point,
'anyép alynyiithúutsiyú.	let them think of me.
'Anyáats 'awíim,²⁸⁹	I can do it,
'atsaayúu 'atáy 'ashoopóowk,	I know many things,
'aayúu 'anyáa avány 'ashapéttxa, kwa'anyáaya.	I can cover the sun, the bright thing.
Nyaayúu 'atséwk,²⁹⁰	I make things,
nyaayúu 'awíim.	I do things.
***²⁹¹	***
Oov'óow matxá 'awíntik.	I too make rain and wind.
Pa'iipáats athíts 'amátt arúv nyaawíim,²⁹²	When someone is going to use seeds in the dry earth,
nyáanyts 'anyép alynyiithúutsəxá.	he should think of me.
'Anyép 'amúly nyaashém,	If he calls my name,
nyaanyayúum,	if he sees me,
nyáanyəm oov'óowk,	at that point, it will rain,
'anyáa tsuumpápk,	for four days,
'anyáa saarápíi kaa'ém,	or maybe for five days,
athúum,	and so,
nyáanyəm,	at that point,
athíts tsavóowəxa."	he may plant his seeds."

***²⁹³   ***

Kukwiimáatt-ts a'íim,	Kukwiimáatt said,
" 'Anyáa matt'atsaxóxtank,	"I am really exhausted,
'apúytantəka'é.	I am dead tired.
'Anák kúur a'éxa,"	I will sit for a while,"
a'íim.	he said.

"Nyáanyamáam,	"That's all,
'atsaayúu kwatiinyáam uuwárək athutyá,"	they want darkness or something,"
Kumastamxóts a'íim.	said Kumastamxó.
Nyaa'íim,²⁹⁴	Having said that,
" 'Atsaayúu tsáaməly —	"Everything —
'atsaayúu tsáaməly 'anyáay lya'émxá.	everything will not be light.

'Anyáay makyí avá lya'émxa."²⁹⁵
Nyaawíim,
'amáynya kaawémk,
uuváaxaym,
'atsaayúu,
'anyáanyts atspák aly'ém a'ím;

awíim atséwk 'et.

Kukwiimáatt-ts 'amátt ka'ák
  aatsuumpápk 'et.²⁹⁷
Awéxáym,
'amáy avats
'axóttk,
takavék 'axótt alyaskyíik,

a'ím,
'anyáanyts takavék atspák
  uuváak 'et.
Kumastamxóts 'avá
  kwatiinyáamənya alyuuváak.²⁹⁸
" 'Anyáayk viithíim 'ayúush.
Makyíts awíim athúm?"
" 'Anyáats 'awésh,"
'étk 'et.
Kukwiimáatt-ts a'íim.

Marxókavékts²⁹⁹
piipáa atséw a'ím uuváak 'et.
Xiipúk,
xatalwé awíik 'et.
Xatalwényənyts atspámk ayúuk;
kaawíts xalykwáak uuváak 'et,
'atsamáxa lyavíim.
Matsáam apúyk 'et.
Makyík av'óow aly'émk.

There will be no daylight anywhere."
Then,
he did something to the sky,
there he was, and suddenly,
well,
the sun did not come up any more,
  they say;
he did something and made (that
  *happen), they say.*²⁹⁶

Kukwiimáatt stamped on the
  ground four times, they say.
He did, and suddenly,
the sky
was all right,
it went back to the way it was, and
  it was still all right,
and so,
the sun came back up and there it
  was, they say.
Kumastamxó was in the dark
  house.
"I see that it is getting light.
Who did that?"
"I did it,"
he said, they say.
Kukwiimáatt said it.

Marxókavék
was trying to make people, they say.
First,
he did Coyote, they say.
That Coyote went out and looked;
he was hunting for something, they say,
because he felt like eating.
He was starving, they say.
He couldn't stand still.

Marxókavékts 'atsaayúu
　kwanyamé 'atséwəntík 'eta.³⁰⁰
Namé atséwk 'et,
póosh kwalyavíinya.
Nyáanya,
lyavíintik uuvám,
Xatakúly uu'íts;
nyáany atséwk.
Kukwiimáatt-ts Xatalwény
　oosha'órək 'et.
Nyáanyts alytanák athúuk 'et.
Pa'iipáa alytanák a'íim,
vathány nyiivasháw 'ím.

Marxókavékts,
nyaamák,
mashxáy awíim,
maxáy awíim,
atséwk.
Amúly nyiiáay 'étənyk
　uuváaxaym,
Xatalwényənyts a'íim³⁰¹
" 'Anyáats 'awéxa lyavíita'a,"
　a'íikət.
Xatalwényənyts mashaxáyəny a'íim,
"Shakílykíly Nyamáa," a'íim'
maxáynya,
" 'Axály Mattnyakótt," a'íik 'et.

'Axály Mattnyakót.³⁰²

Kukwiimáatt-ts ayúuk
　uuváaxaym,
piipáa vatháts makyík 'uuxúutt
　'ím athúu lya'émk avathík 'eta.
Naményanyts,
avány ooshéxayənya,
Shakílykíly Nyamáa vaa'ét,³⁰³
nyáany tavérək uuváak 'et.

Marxókavek also made something
　else, they say.
He made Bobcat, they say,
the one that is like a housecat.
As for that one,
there was another one like it,
the one called Mountain Lion;
he made that one.
Kukwiimáatt pointed to Coyote,
　they say.
He said he was the leader.
He said he was the leader of the people,
and he was supposed to take care
　of them.

As for Marxókavék,
after that,
he did a girl,
and he did a boy,
he made them.
He was about to give them names,
　when suddenly,
Coyote said,
"I want to do that,"
he said, they say.
Coyote said to the girl,
"Shakílykíly Nyamáa," he said;
and to the boy,
he said " 'Axály Mattnyakótt,"
　they say.

Or 'Axály Mattnyakót.

Kukwiimáatt looked at them, and
　suddenly,
these people were not behaving
　well at all, they say.
As for that Bobcat,
the (girl) who had just been named,
the one called Shakílykíly Nyamáa,
he was chasing her around, they say.

Kukwiimáatt-ts a'íim,
"Nyáany kanamák!" a'íim,
a'éxaym,
apúy lya'émk 'eta.
Nyaamák,
viiyáak:
'atsvée Marxókavék,
Kumastamxó,
nyáany Kukwiimáatt,
nyáanya nyiishtúu 'íim awíik
  'étəntima.
" 'Anyáats piipáa vathány
  nyii'áar aly'émk!
'Ashaaíimxá!"
a'ét,
Kukumáatt-ts a'íim.
Nyaa'íim,
mattatsáaməly nyiiqáask,
piipáany 'avá kwatiinyáam
  alyaakxávək 'et.

Nyáanyi tsaqwértank,[304]
oov'óowk awim;
uuráwk a'íikət.
Nyáany 'amáyəny a'íim 'ityá,[305]
'avá kwaaxwíir nyáanyi.
Uukayáamk a'íikəta.

Oov'óow kwiixáaly kwakyáavək.
Xiipúktank,
'atsaayúu ampóttk 'aláay tánk
  'et.
Nyaamák,
oov'óowk shaaxúuk aaxamók
  kayáamk 'et.
'Axányənyts makyík 'avá
  kwatiinyáam alyaxáv aly'émk.

Kukwiimáatt said,
"Leave her alone!" he said,
(but) when he said it,
(Bobcat) wasn't tired, they say.
After that,
he went after them:
what's-his-name, Marxókavék,
and Kumastamxó,
and that one, Kukwiimáatt,
they were the ones he was trying to
  catch, they say.
"I don't want these people!

I will destroy them!"
he said,
Kukwiimáatt said it.
Then,
he summoned all of them,
he brought the people into the dark
  house, they say.

At that point he spoke,
and he made it rain;
he did it fast, they say.
He said it to the sky, they say,
from there in the corner of the house.
He brought (disasters) that way,
  they say.

He asked for rain and floods.
First of all,
there was a dust storm, and it was
  very bad, they say.
After that,
it went on raining for thirty days,
  they say.
The water did not get into the dark
  house.

Piipáa 'atsláytsəts mata'ár oov'ótsk,
nyáanyi,
Kukwiimáatt kwakyáavək:
" 'Aakxávapátəlyá!"
a'íik 'et.
"Kaváarək," a'íim,
avoonóok 'eta.

'Atáytanək,
'axály oopóoyk 'et.

'Alaavúurənyts,
nyáanyi amánk,
'atsaayúu,
xamáalyk toxatóx a'ím,
nyáanyi eetó nyiitháwm athúuk
  'et.

'Aqáaqts 'amáyk kayáamk
  viiyáak 'et.
Viiyáanyək,
nyáanyi,
'amáynyi sawénk 'etəma,
'atsaayúu,
iiyáanyi.
Uutaxalúk,
nyáanyi athúum,
nyáanyi,
nyáanyi athúuk 'et.
'Axányts aváamk,
'axányənyts akúulyk viiyáanyək
aa'árəny ta'aaxáyk 'et.
Mayúuxaym,
nyáanyts athúu kwa'átstəmash.
'Axányənyts nyaa'axáyk,
nyáanya naqám,
nyáanyts —

The bad people stood outside,
and at that point,
they asked Kukwiimáatt a favor:
"We want to come in too!"
they said, they say.
"No," he said,
and they were moving about there,
  they say.
There were a whole lot of them,
and they drowned, they say.

As for Burro,
from then on,
well,
he has been white, with spots,
he has had them there on his belly,
  they say.

Crow went straight into the sky,
  they say.
He went along,
and there,
he hung from the sky, they say,
(by means of) something,
by means of his mouth.
He hooked it,
and that's where he was,
there,
that's where he was, they say.
The water reached him,
the water went rising up until
it got his tail wet, they say.
When you see it,
it really is that way, just as they said.
The water was wet,
and it touched that (tail of his),
and as for that (Crow) —

nyáanyi amánk athúuk athúuk 'etəma,	he has been like that ever since, they say,
'atsaayúunya.	that thing.
'Aqáaqənyts.	Crow.

Nyaathúum,	Then,
Kumastamxóts awíim,	Kumastamxó did something,
'axányənyts asáttk viiyáak.	and the water went down.
Piipáa makyípats —	Whichever creature it was —
'atsayérts 'axály apúyxa lyavíim,	the bird was likely to drown,
nyáany áar aly'émk;	and he didn't want that to happen;
'iixánk uuváam,	(the bird) was handsome,
ayúuk 'et.	and he saw that, they say.
'Aqáaqts anyíilyk,	Crow was black,
xiipúk nyíilyk athúm,	at first he was black,
nyáanyi amánk,	and starting at that point,
ooshétsənyts 'Aqáaq a'ét.[306]	his name has been 'Aqáaq (Crow), they say.

Kumastamxóts	Kumastamxó
'atsaayúu malyxó ashtúum,	gathered his feathers or something,
xáam uuthúutstant.[307]	and they became very different.
Tashoonyótsənyts xáam uuthúutsək.	Their colors became different.
Nyáanyi,	At that point,
nyáanyi amánək uumúulyk 'ím:	starting at that point he named him:
Qwaqxó a'íik 'et.	he called him Qwaqxó (Woodpecker), they say.

Kumastamxóts 'avá atséwk awíim,[308]	Kumastamxó built him a house,
aví nyaváy a'íim awíik 'eta.	he did it intending him to live here, they say.

Nyáany,	As for that,
nyaawíim,	when he did it,
'axáts viiyáaxaym,[309]	the water was going along here, and suddenly,
'amáynyəm áamk athúuk 'etəma.[310]	(the house) floated on top, they say.
Waapóor lyavíik.	It was like a boat.
Kumastamxóts,	Kumastamxó,

'atsaayúu,	well,
'atsayér nyavány atséwk 'eta.	he had made the bird's house, they say.
Aaíimtank awíikəta.	He made it without any special design, they say.
Makyík kaawíts xalykwáak awíi lya'émk.	He didn't look for things to use.
Nyáany Qwaqxó uu'ítsnya,	The one called Woodpecker,
wanyamayáatank athúum,	(Kumastamxó) loved him,
nyáanyi,	and for that (reason),
nyáanyi amánk awíik 'et.	for that (reason) he did it, they say.
'Atsaayúu,	Well,
nyaványanyts,	that house of his,
'atsayér nyaványənyts,	the bird's house,
viiyáanyək,	it went along, until
'amátt nyiivák 'eta.	it rested on land, they say.
Nyiivátəm athúum,[311]	It rested there, and so,
Qwaqxó atóly avák athúum,	Woodpecker sat in the middle of it, and so,
nyáanyts veeyémək,	he (wanted to) leave,
atspámxa lyavíik 'et.	he felt like getting out, they say.
Nyaathúum,	Then,
atspám nyaa'íim,	wanting to get out,
takavék 'ím athúuk a'éta'a.[312]	he said that he intended to come back.
'Axótt-tank,	He would be very good,
nyiiwík uuváaxa.	he would be there to help them out.
'Atsvée Kumastamxó aatooqwérək.	He would be with what's-his-name, Kumastamxó.
Aatooqwérək viiyáa;	He would go along with him;
aaíimk makyí nyaayémǝm,	wherever (Kumastamxó) went,
ayáanypatk athúuk 'et.	he would go too, they say.
Ayérək viiyáak,	He would fly away,
'amáytan axávək 'ím,	he would go into the sky,
atsénək viithíik,	and come down,
'aayúu uuyúutsnya kanáavək 'et,	and tell (Kumastamxó) what he had seen, they say,
aaíim kaawíts nyaayúuk.	if he happened to see something.
'Atsaayúu,	Well,
piipáa 'axwáats viithíixaym,	if an enemy came,

nyáasily athótəsáa, a'ávək a'ét. Vuuthíi nyaa'ávək.³¹³	he might be way over there, but he would hear him, he said. He would hear him coming.
'Axáts nyaasáttk vanyaathíim, 'amáttənyts atspák, 'amáttənyts athúuk 'etəma.³¹⁴ Kukumáatt-ts piipáa nyii'íim aaíimk vaayáak, aatspáats a'ím. 'Amátt kwatiinyáam alyoonóok avoonóonyək.	As the water was receding, the land appeared. It was land, they say. Kukwiimáatt said to the people that they should just go, he said they should go out. They had been there inside the dark place.
Nyaaxáapk kayáamk, 'atsaayúu, matxá kwaspérənyts viiyáak; nyáasi kayáamk athúuk 'et.	Heading to the west, well, the strong wind went along; it was heading over there, they say.
'Axányts asáttk avoonóonyək, 'aayúu 'axá sa'ílyənyts³¹⁵ 'anóqtank alyatháwk áampk 'et.	The water went on receding, until the ocean or whatever it was was very small and had little (water) left in it, they say.
Piipáa Eethó Kwatáarənyts mashathék 'eta. 'Atsaayúu tsáaməly arúvək 'et,³¹⁶ 'aláayxa lyavíim. Tsaxtáattk atspák 'eta,³¹⁷ matxávik. Nyáanyəm atspák 'et.³¹⁸ Xavashúum Kulyíits siivám ayúuk; Xavashúum Kuuwáats alyatháwk 'etəs 'et, 'avá kwatiinyáamənya. Nyaa'íim, 'atsaayúuts 'atáyəm nyiiáayəxa a'íikət.	The Blind Person was afraid, they say. Everything was drying up, they say, and was likely to be bad. He crawled out, they say. in the north. That's where he came out, they say. He saw Xavashúum Kulyíi over there; (she and) Xavashúum Kuuwáa must have been there, they say, in the dark house. Then, he said he would give them many things, they say.

Aványa aatooqwérəts lya'ém
  'ím,[319]
Kukwiimáatt uu'ítsnyá.
Nyiiuukanáavək 'ím,
"Kukwiimáatt-ts mattapúy 'ím
  uuváak athópəká,[320]
kúur a'ím."
***[321]
Athótəsáa,
Xavashúum Kulyíits
  thomtaayúuk a'éta.[322]
"Kaváarək,
athúu lya'émxá,"
a'íim.
Nyáany nyaa'íim mashthék
  uuváak.
Piipáa Eethó Kwatáarənyts
  shatríiq 'ím uuváa,
avéshk veeyém.
Atháwk.
Shav'óowk 'ím,

" 'Atsaayúu,
'atsmuumátsá xuumxúuk 'anyáa
  kwashíintím 'anyáayxá,"
a'íik 'et.
"Kuuthíik,
nyaathúum!"
a'íikəta.
Mashaxáyənyts a'íim.
" 'Awéxa lyavíitəsáa,
Kukumáatt 'amashthétka'é."
Kukumáatt-ts viithíik 'et.
Viithíixaym,
Piipáa Eethó Kwatáarənyts
  'amátt alyaxáv 'im veeyémk
  'et.
"Aa'árvək,

He did not want them to associate
  with that (person),
(with) the one called Kukwiimáatt.
He told them,
"Kukwiimáatt is going to kill you,

pretty soon."
***
However,
Xavashúum Kulyíi made it clear,
  they say.
"No,
it won't happen,"
she said.
(But) when she said that, she was
  afraid.
The Blind Person tried with both
  hands to restrain her,
(but) she went running away.
He caught her.
Intending to keep her standing
  there, (he said,)
"Well,
I will give you six meals each
  day,"
he said, they say.
"Bring them,
then!"
she said, they say.
The girl said it.
"I would like to do it, but
I am afraid of Kukwiimáatt," he said.
Kukwiimáatt came along, they say.
He came, and suddenly
the Blind Person
  was about to sink into the earth,
  they say.
"He had a tail,

iisháaly kwaly'ooxóonyts 'aqóolk
   lóq 'et," a'ím,
a'íik 'eta.
Xavashúum Kulyíi uu'ítsənyts.[323]
Iiwáam a'íikəta.[324]
"Máany matháwk,[325]
'amátt maxákəly matakxáv a'ím,"
a'íikət.
Kukumáatt-ts a'íim.
"Kamawémk
nyaany maxáktan nyaamayémk?
'Atsmamáxanká
nyáasily?"
a'íikət.

Xavashúum Kulyíits av'áak
   viiyáanyək,
piipáats oov'ótsk soov'ótsəm,

aváamk.
Nyaaváamk a'ím,
a'íik 'etəma.
Nyiiuukanáavək a'ím:
"Vaamawíim,
vaamawíim,
moonóok,
xuumáar matséwtəxa,"[326]
a'íikəta.
A'éxaym,
makyík uu'áv aly'émk.
"Kaváarək,
athúu lya'émxa."
a'íikəta.[327]

***

Kukumáatt-ts athótəm athúum,
awíim vanyuuváak:

and his fingernails were very long,
   they say," she said,
she said it, they say.
That's what Xavashúum Kulyíi said.
She said it herself, they say.
"He intends to grab you
and take you down under the earth,"
he said, they say.
Kukwiimáatt said it.
"What would you do
if you were to go down below?
(How) would you eat
over there?"
he said, they say.

Xavashúum Kulyíi went walking
   along,
and there were people standing
   over there,
and she got there.
She got there, and so,
she said it, they say.
She explained it to them:
"This is what you do,
this is what you do,
you go on doing it,
and you will make children,"
she said, they say.
When she said it,
they didn't believe her at all.
"No,
it won't happen,"
they said, they say.

***[328]

Kukwiimáatt did things, and so,
he went on doing things:

kaawíts atséwk,	he made something,
kaawíts awíim,	he did something,
uuváany,	he went on, until
mattatsaxóxk 'et.	he became exhausted, they say.
Nyaawíim,	When this happened,
'amátt ka'ák,	he stamped on the ground,
awéxaym,	and as soon as he did,
'anyáanyənyts veeyémk 'eta.	the sun went away, they say.
Veeyémәntík 'et.	It went away again, they say.
Kumastamxóts masharáyk 'eta.	Kumastamxó got angry, they say.
Nyáany a'íim,	When that happened,
masharáyk,	he got angry,
a'íim,	and he said,
" 'Anyáats thúutt a'ím av'uuváak 'athutyá!	"I am the one who does more!
'Anyáap nyiikwanáamts!"	I am the important one!"
Kukumáatt-ts a'íim,	Kukwiimáatt said,
"Máany 'anyép maxuumáyts.[329]	"You are my son.
Nyaxuumáyk 'ityá.[330]	I call you son.
Mashoopóow alyma'émk.	You don't know anything.
Ka'awémk 'awínypátúm!"	I will do it somehow!"
a'íikəta.	he said, they say.
Kumastamxóts	Kumastamxó
'avá kwatiinyáam alyaxávək 'et.	went into the dark house, they say.
Nyaaxávək,	When he went in,
"Kukwiimáatt!" a'íim,	he said, "Kukwiimáatt!"
"Marxókavék!" a'íim,	he said, "Marxókavék!"
nyiishék,	he called them by name,
'atsuurávxá a'íim.	so that they would get sick.
Soonóok 'et.	There they were, they say.
Kukwiimáattənyts tsakwshály yaakapéttk 'eta.	Kukwiimáatt became crazy in the head, they say.
Nyaayúu,	Well,
'amáynya,	the sky,

A Quechan Account of Origins 99

'amáynya awíim tsakwíin,
tsakwíink,
matxánya 'anyaaxáapk awém 'ím,[331]
athúuk 'et.
Nyáanyiimánk,
av'áak,
'avá kwatiinyáaməny atspámk,
shaly'áyly kayáamk siiyáak.

Siiyáak athúm,
'anyáavik shathómpk aváamk.
Takavék,
'anyaaxáap kayáamk.
'Atsaayúu,
'amáyəny xáak awíim ashéeməntim athúum,
nyiivák 'et.
Makyík tsayém aly'émk.[332]
Xwérər a'íi lya'em.
"Nyawíkúum?"
a'íikət,
Kumastamxóts.

Kukumáatt-ts anák,
'avíi 'amáy anák 'im,

alynyiithúutsk,
a'ét.
"Nyáanya,
piipáa 'atséwənti 'a'ím,"

'atsaayúu 'a'íi tsapéev atháwk,

nyaayúu mas'ée ashtúum,
iisháalyəm shoo'órnya nyáany 'amáyk awíik 'eta,

he did something to the sky and made it rotate,
he made it rotate,
he tried to take it from the north to the west,
(that) was (the situation), they say.
Starting there,
he walked,
he went out of the dark house,
he headed for the desert and went along over there.

He went along over there, and so,
he went towards the east and got there.
He turned,
and he headed west.
Well,
he had moved the sky in a different direction, and so,
there it was, they say.
He couldn't loosen it at all.
It wouldn't rotate.
"Can I help you?"
he said, they say,
Kumastamxó (did).

Kukwiimáatt sat down,
he sat down on top of a mountain, and so,
he thought about it,
they say.
"As for that,
I intend to make more people," (he said,)
and he picked up a small stick or something,
and he gathered mud or something,
and he used the tip of his index finger, they say,

kwakapáarnyi atsáam.³³³	and he put mud on the end of (the stick).
Nyaawíim,	Then,
'a'íinya,	that stick,
aaxweshxwéshk áapk awet.	he threw it spinning away.
Awexáym,	Immediately,
masharáyk 'et.	(the stick) became angry, they say.
Nyáanyəm,	With that,
nyaanyiimánk,	starting at that point,
'aavéts athúuk 'et.	it became a snake, they say.
'Aavé taaxán a'íim 'ityá.	It's called 'aavé taaxán (rattlesnake), they say.
Mas'éenyənyts athúum,	It was that mud,
nyáany alyuusíirmənyts athúuk 'et.	that's what became the rattles, they say.
'Aavé,	As for the snake,
'aavé taaxánənyts,	the rattlesnake,
piipáa nyiimashthék 'et.	it was afraid of people, they say.
Ookavék mashthétsapátk,	They in turn were afraid of (the snake),
a'ím,	and so,
piipáanyts ooyóovək aakakyáavək 'et.	the people looked for it and surrounded it, they say.
Athoxáym,	Immediately,
sanya'ák — 'aakóoy tavérək,	it chased after a woman — an old woman,
awéxáym,	it did, and suddenly,
piipáa 'axwáa,	an enemy,
nyáanyts athúum,	that's what he was,
uuváanyək atháwk 'eta.	he was there and he grabbed (the snake), they say.
Sharéq.	He took hold of it.
Awíi nyaawíim,	He did, and then,
kaawémk aamélk 'et.	somehow he put it around his waist, they say.
Aamél lyavíim.	It was like a belt.
Kukumáatt-ts nyáany nyiiáaym 'ityá.	Kukwiimáatt had given him that (power), they say.
Athúum,	So,

'atsaayúu,	well,
kaawíts awíi nyaa'ím,	when he wanted them to do something,
nyáany nyiiáayəntík 'etá.	he gave them that (power), they say.
***334	***
'Aavé taaxánənyts piipáa nyiitsakyíwk 'et.	The rattlesnake bit people, they say.
'Ashéntits Marxókavékts athúuk 'et.	One (of the people he bit) was Marxókavék, they say.
Piipáa tsáaməly a'íim,	All the people said,
" 'Aavé avány katapúyk!"	"Kill that snake!"
uu'íitsk 'et.	they said it, they say.
A'étəsáa,	However,
Marxókavékts nyáany áar alya'émk,	Marxókavék did not want that,
a'íim,	he said,
nyaawéxaym,	(because) if he were to do it,
vathány,	this one,
piipáa 'axwáanya,	the enemy,
nyáanyts masharáyxa lyavíim.	he would be likely to get angry.
Marxókavéts a'íim,	Marxókavék said,
" 'Anyáats 'apúyxá 'aaly'étk.335	"I think that I will die.
Athúu 'íim avuuváak."	It is going to happen."
"Kaváarək,	"No,
tsaváamk mapúyúm,"	it is impossible that you should die,"
a'íik 'et.	he said, they say.
Kukumáatt-ts a'íim.	Kukwiimáatt said it.
Nyaamák,	After that,
uuváany,	there he was,
piipáanya nyii'íim:	and he said something to the people:
" 'Aavé taaxánnya katháwk!	"Get that rattlesnake!
Alyuusíirmənya koomóq!	Pull out his rattles!
Nyáanyi amánk,	From that point on,
piipáa nyiitsakyíwəntixa.	he will not bite people.
Makyík ta'aaláay lya'émxa.	He will not destroy anything.
Apúy lya'émxa."	No-one will die."336

Kukwiimáatt-ts 'aavé taaxánəny atháwk,	Kukwiimáatt got the rattlesnake,
aaxweshxwéshk,	and he flung it,
matxávik awémk.	he sent it to the north.
'Atsaayúu alyuusíirm aanáwtank a'íik 'et,	The snake made noise with its rattles or something, they say,[337]
takavék atspák.	and they grew back.[338]
Atspák a'íim.	He wanted them to grow back.
Piipáats siiv'óowk,	Someone was standing over there,
a'íim,	and he said,
"Iiyáanyily,	"In his mouth
atháw alyaskyíitəsh," 'et.	they are still there," he said.
Kukumáatt-ts nyaa'ávək awim,	Kukwiimáatt heard him, and so,
atháwəntík 'etá.	he caught the snake again, they say.
Atháwəntík athum,	He caught it again, and so,
iiyáany uutáq ayúu 'ím.	he opened its mouth in order to take a look.
Awexáym,	When he did,
makyík alyuusíirmənyənyts nyiiríish a'íik 'eta.	there were no rattles there at all, they say.
Eethóots nyiiríish a'ím,	There were no teeth,
'atsaayúu kwa'aláayənyts nyiiríish a'íntík 'et.	there was nothing bad either, they say.
Nyaatháwk awím,	He picked it up,
'aavé,	the snake,
'aavé taaxán,	the rattlesnake,
nyaawíntik 'eta.	and he did it again, they say.
Aaíimk aaxweshxwéshk,	He just flung it so that it spun uncontrollably,
kúurtan,[339]	really far,
matxávik awémk.	he sent it to the north.
Aaxweshxwéshnyək,	He flung it so that it spun uncontrollably,
'axá sa'ílyəny alyaxávək 'etá.	and it went into the salt water, they say.

Muuvílytank,	It went really fast,
'axám áamk veeyém,	it swam away,
veeyémxayk nyaakwévək 'et.	it went away and that was the end of it, they say.

'Ís	But
maxák kayáamk viiyáanyək,[340]	it went straight to the bottom,
nyáasi uuváak,	and it stayed there,
nyaváyk,	it lived there,
asháyk;	and it got fat;
vaanóok 'et.	it was huge, they say.

Pa'iipáanyts 'aványi Kumastamxónya tsakakwék a'im,	The people in the house asked Kumastamxó,
"Xalyavímtəm,	"Is it possible
'ats'uurávəxa?	that we will get sick?
'Ats'uurávxaym,	And if we get sick,
makyíts nyiitséevxa'ənká?"	who will cure us?"

"Pa'iipáats avoonóo,	"People are around,
nyáany uuwíts a'íts avoonóok,"	they can do that,"
a'ét.	he said.
Kumastamxóts a'íim.	Kumastamxó said it.

***[341]   ***

"Tsaváamk athúwúm,"	"It is not likely that that would happen,"
uu'íitsk 'eta,	they said, they say,
pa'iipáanyənyts.	the people (did).
"Máanyts miiwáam 'atsnyaamarávəm,[342]	"When you yourself get sick,
miiwáam mattmatséev alya'emk," a'ityá.	you can't even cure yourself," he said.

Kumastamxóts Kwatsáan 'iipátsənya nyiishtúum,	Kumastamxó gathered the Quechan men,
'avá kwatiinyáaməly alyaatsakxávək 'eta.[343]	and he brought them into the dark house, they say.

"Mátsa,
mátsa wanyuukaváarək,³⁴⁴
'atsaayúu tsáaməly nyiinyuukanáavəxá,
thomkwayúuv alykwa'éma."³⁴⁵

Nyaawíim,
'amátt ampótt mattkwatsapée awíim.
'Anyáavik amánk,
viithíit.
Nyáanyənyts 'anyáa aamáttk 'eta.
Tiinyáam lyavíik.
"Nyamáam,
kaashmátsk!"
a'íik 'et.
Kumastamxóts a'íim.

Avatíivək,
shatuumáatsk a'ét.
Pa'iipáa 'ashéntəts ayúuxaym,
Kumastamxó eethónyənyts aráavək 'et.
Eethó kwa'uur'úurənyts aráavək,
aráavəm ayúuk 'et.

Nyáanyəm,
tsooyóqəny awíim,³⁴⁶
awéxaym amánk 'et.

Pa'iipáa kwanyaméts Kumastamxó ayúuxaym,
'atsiiráav — ***
nyatsasháak tuutkyáavanyts arávək 'ét.
Apásk;
kwarávənyts nyiivák,³⁴⁷

"As for you,
I am fond of you,
and I will tell you everything,

even (things) that don't make sense."

Then,
he did a big dust storm.
It started in the east,
and it came this way.
That (dust) covered up the sun, they say.
It was like night.
"Now,
sleep!"
he said, they say.
Kumastamxó said it.

They lay there,
and they had dreams, they say.
One person looked, and suddenly,
Kumastamxó's eyes hurt, they say.
His eyeballs hurt,
and (the person) saw that they hurt, they say.

At that point,
he used his spit,
and as soon as he used it, it cured them, they say.

Another person looked at Kumastamxó, and suddenly,
a disease — ***
his joints hurt, they say.

He pressed on them;
the pain was there,

kwarávəny a'ávək.	and he felt the pain.
Atséevək,	He doctored it,
atséevəm atspák 'eta.	he doctored it and (the pain) came out, they say.
Pa'iipáa kwanymé uuyúunyá,	What another person saw
Kumastamxóts —	was that Kumastamxó —
eetóts 'aláayk a'eta.	his stomach had gone bad, they say.
Arávək 'aláayk 'éta.	He was sick and in bad shape, they say.
Kumastamxóts aashváarəm —	Kumastamxó sang —
Kumastamxóts aashváarək a'éta.	Kumastamxó sang, they say.
Aashváarəxáym,	And when he sang,
pa'iipáanyənyts aapúk aashváarənypátk 'etá.	that person sang too, accompanying him, they say.
Aashváarapátk 'etá.	He sang too, they say.
Awéxaym,	He did, and suddenly,
amánk 'ét.	(Kumastamxó) recovered, they say.
Pa'iipáats 'atsaayúu xáak nyaa'íim,	When someone said something in a different way,
Kumastamxóts tsanák 'et.	Kumastamxó stopped him, they say.
Tsanákəm,	He stopped him,
pa'iipáa kwanyaméts tsaqwérəntí 'et.	so that another person could speak, they say.
"Maapa'iipáaváts,	"You people,
'atsaayúu 'axóttm ma'étk,"	you say good things,"
nyaa'íim,	he said;
"Kwas'eethée nyamkwanáamts muuthúutsəxa.	"You will be respected doctors.
Pa'iipáats 'atsarávəxáym,	If someone gets sick,
Kwatsáan kwas'eethée aqásəxá."	he will call a Quechan doctor."
Marxókavék,	As for Marxókavék,
Marxókavék,	as for Marxókavék,
'aavé tsakyíwm apúyk.[348]	the snake bit him and he died.
Kukwiimáatt-ts a'íim,	Kukwiimáatt said,
"Kathíik,	"Come,

maakwas'eethéeva,[349]	you doctors,
vathány kuumánk!"	and cure this one!
Pa'iipáa vathány kuumánk!	Cure this person!
Nyáavəts matháavək," a'éta.	This one is difficult," he said.
"Nyakór apúyk viithík.	"He is already lying here dead.
'Anyáats nyaatsooyóoym mayúuxá."	I will show and you will see."
Nyaa'íim,	Then,
Marxókavék iisháalynya sharéqək 'et.	he grasped Marxókavék's hands, they say.
Aalynyiithúutsk 'ím.	He thought about it.
Marxókavékts ooyéey lyaskyíik a'ét.	Marxókavék was still breathing, they say.
"Pa'iipáa vatháts apúy lya'émk nyaathúuva.	"This person is not dead.
Ashmáam athótkitya.	He is sleeping.
'Ashamánəxá."	I will wake him up."
Nyaa'íim,	Then,
nyaa'íim,	then,
shoothómp kwatsuumpápəny,	in (each of) the four directions,
láak a'étk,	he took a step,
av'áa lyavíit.[350]	as if he were walking.
Takavék,	He went back,
láak a'ím,	and he took a step,
av'áa lyavíit.[351]	as if he were walking.
Uuthútsənyts tsuumpápk:	He did it four times:
matxávi kayáamk,	he went due north,
'anyaaxáap kayáamk,	he went due west,
kavée kayáamk,	he went due south,
'anyáa kayáam.	and he went due east.
'Axá sa'ílyəva nyaaváamk;	He reached the salt water;
nyáanyts 'amátt nyaakwíink athútya.	that (salt water) is what surrounds the land.
Xamsheekwérəts viithíik aváak;	A whirlwind came and got there;
Marxókavékts avathíkm,	Marxókavék was lying there,
'amáyk ooyéeyk.	and (the whirlwind) breathed on him.

Eethó shatpíittk lyaskyíik av'óowk a'ét.	While his eyes were still closed he stood up, they say.
Kukwiimáatt-ts uuqásəny aqásk a'éta. Nyaaxáapk amánk; aqásk avuuthíik. 'Amátt tsáaməly 'anyáayk 'eta.	Kukwiimáatt summoned the thunder, they say. It came from the west; he summoned it and brought it there. The whole world became bright, they say.
Marxókavék eethónyənyts atáaqək a'ét. Kukwiimáatt-ts 'ím, "Máanyts mashmáam 'akór mayémk. 'Akór mayéməm, athúm, nyashamánk 'athútya." " 'Aavényts nyatsakyíwm, nyaanyiimánk, 'ashmáxa lyavíim av'uuváat," a'ét. Marxókavékts a'íim.	Marxókavék's eyes opened, they say. Kukwiimáatt said, "You went on sleeping for a long time. You went on for a long time, and so, I woke you up." "A snake bit me, and from then on, I felt sleepy," he said. Marxókavék said it.
"Kaváarək, mapúypəva," a'eta. Kukwiimáatt-ts a'íim, "Mapúyəsh," a'ét. "Nyáanyəm, xamsheekwérənyts aváak, matséevk muumánk athútyá."[353] Pa'iipáanyts vathány uu'áavək avoonóoxay, "Kwas'eethéenyənyts ookavék nyiinytapóoytəntíxá," a'ítsk a'éta.	"No, you died," he said. Kukwiimáatt said, "You died," he said. "At that point, a whirlwind came,[352] and it cured you." When the people heard this, "Doctors might turn around and kill us," they said, they say.

" 'Amshtatháavək av'oonóok
    'athúuva,"³⁵⁴
uu'íitsk 'ét.
Uu'íitsk 'ét,
mashtatháavək vanyoonóok.

***³⁵⁵

Mashtxáanyanyts matta'íim,
"Kaawíts 'eetóly aváta'á!"
Xavashúum Kulyíi tsakuukwíitsk
    'éta.³⁵⁷
"Kaathóntim athúm?"
a'ítsk.
A'ítstəsáa,
makyík kanáav alya'émk 'ét.
Xuumáar tsáaməly,
xuumáar tsáaməly aatspáatsk 'éta,
'anyáa kwashéntənyá.
Sanyts'áakənyts,³⁵⁹
sanyts'áakənyts wanymooyéts
    alya'émk,³⁶⁰
a'éta.
"Kaathúntik 'anaqóorək athúum?"
uu'íitsk.
"Pa'iipáa vatáts 'uuwárək
    va'oonóoxaym 'athúum.
Vatháts ee'é kaayúumk athutyá
    tsakwshányi!
Av'óow a'ím,
nyeekwéevəntík!"
Shtamatháavək 'ityá,
nyáanya.
Xuumáarts nyaatspáatsk,³⁶¹
makyík 'uukúuts alya'émk,
'alméts alya'émk.
Kukwiimáatt-ts a'íim,

"We are afraid,"
they said, they say.
They said it, they say,
(because) they were afraid.

***

The girls said to each other,³⁵⁶
"There is something in my belly!"
They asked Xavashúum Kulyíi,
    they say.
"What is happening?"
they said.
They said it, but
she didn't tell them anything, they say.
All the children,
all the children were born, they say,
on the same day.³⁵⁸
The women,
the women didn't like them,

they say.
"Why are they so small?"
they said.
"We wanted big people.

These have no hair
    on their heads!
And when they try to walk,
they can't do that either!"
They didn't know, they say,
about that.
When children are born,
they're not grown up yet,
they're not tall yet.
Kukwiimáatt said,

"Xuumáar mooyóov
    alyma'əməntixá,³⁶²
makyík 'iipátsa mashtoopóow
    alynyaama'émək."³⁶³

Kukwiimáatt-ts pa'iipáa
    tsuumpápəm atséwtəntik,³⁶⁴
a'éta.
Xawáalyapáay awíim,
Xàmakxáv awíim,
Pa'iipáa Kwaxamáalyəny awíim,
Xeykó Taaxán awíim;
nyiitséwəntík 'étəma.
Kaa'íts makyík pa'iipáa
    alyaaxwélyts aly'émk athúuk 'eta.
Mattnyiiuunáamək.
Kukwiimáatt-ts 'amátt ka'ák,
aatsuumpápk 'et.
Masharáyk.
Nyaawíim,
'atskwaráats aaíim makyí atháw
    aaly'ét.
Makyí atspák aaly'ét.

Kumastamxóts pa'iipáa kaa'íts
    ashtúum,³⁶⁵
oopóoy lya'émk,
a'ét.
'Atsaayúu xanapáats 'amáyk
    nyiitsáam.
Xeykó Taaxánányts
Pa'iipáa Kwaxmáalyənyts
    satuukyáanyk 'eta.

"Vatháts 'axótt alya'əməsh,"
a'ét.
Kumstamxóts a'íim.

"You won't have any more
    children,
if you do not know men."

Kukwiimáatt made four more
    people,
they say.
He did Hualapai,
he did Mojave,
he did a White,
and he did a Mexican;
he made them in turn, they say.
Some of them did not mix with the
    (other) people, they say.
They were proud, they say.
Kukwiimáatt stamped on the ground,
he did it four times, they say.
He was angry.
When he did that,
there were fires everywhere.

They appeared everywhere.

Kumastamxó gathered some of the
    people
and they didn't die,
they say.
He put snow or something on top
    of them.
The Mexicans
and the Whites ran away, they
    say.

"This is no good,"
he said.
Kumastamxó said it.

"Pa'iipáa nyaamatséwk,
nyaamák,
nyiimashaaíimk,
mawét.
Mootséwənyts 'axótt alya'ém,[366]

nyaama'íim."
Kukwiimáatt iiwáanyts 'aláayk,
'aláayk 'eta.
Nyaawíim,
kwaráanya tamaspátsk a'ét.
Oov'óowk,
'amáyk nyioov'óowəm.

Kukwiimáatt-ts 'a'íi xamáaly xavíkəm ashtúum 'et.
'Ashénti,
'anyáavi aaxweshaxwéshk awémk a'ét.[369]
Nyáanyənyts takavék 'axatt-ts athót.
'Axátt masínyəkts athót.
'Ashénəntíny 'axály áapk 'et.

'Axály áapxáym,

waapóorəts athúuk a'ét.
Waapóorəny awíim,
'axátt masínyk awíim,
ashtúum,
Pa'iipáa Kwxamáaly nyiiáayk a'ét.
Kumastamxóts
Pa'iipáa Kwxamáalyəny
'avá kwatiinyáaməly nyaakxávəm,
kaawíts nyiioo'éeyəxa.
A'éxáym,

"You made people,
and after that,
you destroyed them,
you did.
The ones you made did not turn out right,
that's what you said."
Kukwiimáatt felt bad,
(he felt) bad, they say.[367]
So,
he put out the fires, they say.
It rained,
it rained on (the fires).[368]

Kukwiimáatt got two white sticks, they say.
One of them,
he sent it spinning toward the east, they say.
That one came back and became a domestic animal.
It became a horse.
The other one he threw into the water, they say.
As soon as he threw it in the water,
it became a boat, they say.
He did a boat,
and he did a horse,
and he gathered them up,
and he gave them to the White people, they say.
Kumastamxó
(told) the White people
that if they went into the dark house,
he would teach them something.
But when he said this,

makyík nyiiuu'áav aly'émk 'eta,	(the Whites) didn't listen to him, they say,
uutsaváarək.	and he didn't get it done.
'Ompées,	(They had) money,
'atsnyiiuuwíitsənya 'atáym awíim,	they had many possessions,[370]
awítstəsáa	they had them, but
xalytuu'íishk 'et.	they were stingy, they say.
Kumastamxóts shiitamúulynyá nyii'íim;	Kumastamxó said the names of the clans;
"Nyiikakatspáatsk!"	"Drive them out!"
a'íikət.	he said, they say.
A'éxaym,	When he said this,
"Kaváarək."	"No," they said.
Iiwáanyts kaa'émam,	They were uncertain,
awíts aly'émk 'et.	and they didn't do it, they say.
Kumastamxóts,	As for Kumastamxó,
matxá aspér —[371]	a strong wind —
matxá aspér 'apíly aqásk.[372]	he summoned a strong hot wind.
Nyaawíim,	Then,
Pa'iipáa Kwxamáalyənyts satuukyáanyk,	the White people fled,
'anyaaxáapk kayáamk 'eta.	they went west, they say.
Waapóor alyatíivək.	They were sitting in a boat.
Pa'iipáanyənyts 'atsaayúu anáwatan uu'ávək 'etá,	The people heard something loud, they say,
'axányik amánəm.[373]	it was coming from the water.
Nyáanyəm,	At that point,
'atsaayúu Eethó Kwatáarany ootséwəny,[374]	the things that the Blind One had made,
Kukwumáatt-ts kats'ák;	Kukwiimáatt had kicked them;
'axály aatsuupáxányts,[375]	they were the (things) he had thrown into the water,
takavék 'iipáayk a'ét.	and they came back to life, they say.
Nyáanya,	These (things),
Xanamóots athúum,	they were Duck,
'Apénts athúum,	and Beaver,
Kapétt-ts athúum,	and Tortoise,

Yaaláqts athúum,
uuthúutsk a'éta.
Iisháalytsənyts eemétsənyts
  shuunàpanáapk a'ét.[376]

" 'Anyáats 'amshathéevətka'e.
Ookavék nyiinytatpóoyəxa lyavíim,"
a'ét.
Kukwiimáatt-ts a'íim.

Kumastamxó
Kumastamxóts 'uutíish atséwk,
'iipá atséwk,
awíik 'eta.
Nyaawíim,
pa'iipáa nyiisháattk 'ét.
Nyaawíim,
mas'ée ashtúum,
atápm.
Atápxaym,
matxávi uukayáamt.[377]
Matxávi uukayáam,
'éxaym,
'atsayérəts athúuk 'éta.
"Kakyáam!"
a'íik 'etá.
Pa'iipáa Kwa'aapányənyts akyáam.
Akyáam awétəsáa,
'iipányənyts alyéshk 'et,
'atsayérənyts 'avíi lyavíitəm
  kwathútsəny.
Pa'iipáa nyiiwáanyts 'aláayk 'éta.
'Iipáts,
'iipáts aavíirəm.
'Iipá aavíir awim,

nyaamáam nyiirísh a'ím.
Kumastamxóts 'iisáv uuxwíip
  awím,[378]

and Goose,
that's who they were, they say.
Their fingers and toes were
  webbed, they say.

"I'm afraid.
They might turn around and kill us,"
he said.
Kukwiimáatt said it.

As for Kumastamxó,
Kumastamxó made a bow,
and he made arrows,
he did, they say.
Then,
he distributed them among the people.
Then,
he picked up some mud,
and he threw it, they say.
When he threw it,
he sent it to the north.
He sent it to the north,
and when he did,
it became a bird, they say.
"Shoot it!"
he said, they say.
The Cocopa person shot at it.
He shot at it, but
the arrow broke, they say,
because the bird was like a rock.

The person felt bad, they say.
As for arrows,
the arrows were finished.
They had finished off the arrows,
  and so,
that was all, there weren't any more.
Kumastamxó pulled up an
  arrowweed, and so

'iisávəny tsatspátsk 'éta.[379]	he took out an arrowweed, they say.
Awíim awím,	He did, and so,
pa'iipáa nyiiaatsooyóoyk 'eta,[380]	he showed the person, they say,
'iipáa ootséwənya.	(how) to make an arrow.
Nyaawíim,	Then,
nyaaxáap kayáamk,	he headed west,
nyaayáak,	and as he went along,
'aqwáaq mattatséwk 'et.	he turned himself into a deer, they say.
Kwatsáan 'iipáanya a'ím,	He said to the Quechan man
'aqwáaqnya akyáaw 'ím,	that he should shoot the deer,
a'íik 'et.	he said it, they say.
A'éxaym,	As soon as he said it,
"Kaváarək," a'ét.	"No," he said.
Shoopóowk 'éta,	He knew, they say,
Kumastamxóts athúum.	that (the deer) was Kumastamxó.
Yaavapáay 'Axwáanyənyts shamathíitk athúm,	The Apache didn't know about it, and so,
shamathíitk athúm,	he didn't know about it, and so,
shalyamáknyi akyáam 'eta.	he shot it in the hindquarters, they say.
Awéxáyəm	He did, and right away
'amáttnyi apámk 'et.	it fell to the ground, they say.
Nyatsaqwély,	As for its hide,
awíim,	he did it,
aashkwáalyk atháw 'íinyək,	he tried to peel it off and take it,
Kumastamxóts a'íim,	and Kumastamxó said,
"Pa'iipáa nyaamakwévəts!	"You are a good-for-nothing person!
'Aqwáaq avány 'avíits athópəke!"	That deer is made of stone!"
a'íik 'et.	he said it, they say.
Vathány,	As for this,
kuunáav avány,	what it explains,
a'íim,	they say,
Yaavapáay 'Axwáanyənyts 'aqwáaq uukyáats av'áarək athúuk 'eta.	is why the Apaches always shoot deer, they say.
Kumastamxóts masharáyk 'et,	Kumastamxó was angry, they say,
Yaavapáay 'Axwáanyənyts uukayáamk akyémtan kwathútsəny.	because the Apache had aimed at him and shot at him.
Nyaanyiimánk,	From then on,

'iipány awíim,
'uutíish awím,
Kwatsáan nyiiáayk awíik 'et.

Nyaanyamáam;
awíik 'et.
Nyiikamáan,
nyiis'íilyk.

'Avíi vatáyts 'amáttk athíik viithíik 'et.[381]
Nyáava 'uutíishts athúuk a'íim.

Kukwiimáatt-ts kwiixáaly atséwəntík 'etá.
Kwanymé atséwəntík 'et.

Nyáany,
'axányənyts awíim,
'axányənyts 'amáttnya atsúuttxaym,[382]
'avíi 'almétsnya atséwtk awitya.[383]
Avathúum,
nyaanyiimánk,
nyáany lyavíik;
'avíinyənyts 'almétsk,[384]
'amáy kayáamk atháwk,[385]

vanyaatháwk.
Nyáany,
athúu aly'émxaym,
'amáttənyts làpalápk viithík.
Nyaanyamáamk 'et.

Kumastamxóts —
'iipáa 'ashéntim,
sanya'ák 'ashéntim,
nyiishtúum 'eta,

he did arrows,
and he did bows,
and he gave them to the Quechan, they say.

That was the end of it;
he did it, they say.
As for the others,
he forbade it to them.

A big rock was coming out of the ground, they say.
This was the bow, they say.

Kukwiimáatt made another flood, they say.
He made another one, they say.

As for that,
that water did it,
that water pushed the ground up, and right away,
it made tall mountains.
That's what happened,
and from then on,
that's what it was like;
those mountains were tall,
they went straight up into the sky and there they were,

there they were.
As for that,
before he had done it,[386]
the land had been flat.
That's all, they say.

As for Kumastamxó —
there was one man,
and there was one woman,
and he picked them up, they say,

pa'iipáa avkoonóonya,	the people that were there,
xáam kuuthúutsnya.	the different ones.
Nyáanya,	These (people),
miivíi nyiitsáam 'et.³⁸⁷	he put them on his shoulder, they say.
Nyikamáanənyts vaayáak,	The others went along,
'Avíi 'Xa'atásh 'amáyk oov'ótsk.³⁸⁸	and they stood on top of 'Avíi Xa'atásh.
Nyáavəts Kumastamxó a'íim,	These (people) said to Kumastamxó,
"Nyiinykawík!"	"Help us!"
a'éxaym,	they said, and suddenly,
ookavék	he turned around
'avíi nyiitséwət.	and he turned them into stone.

Oov'óowk,	It rained,
'anyáa shaaxúuk aatsuumpáp kayáam,³⁸⁹	it went on for forty days,
akwévət.³⁹⁰	and it stopped.
Kumastamxóts iisháalyəny uutstáaq aatsuumpápk a'et.³⁹¹	Kumastamxó opened up his arms four times, they say.
Nyaawíim,	Then,
'axányts asáttk 'et.	the water receded, they say.
Atsénk asáttk a'ét.	It went down and receded, they say.
'Amáttənyts nyaarúvəntím,	When the ground was dry again,
Kukwiimáatt-ts pa'iipáa 'ashéntənti atséwət:³⁹²	Kukwiimáatt made one more person:
'Aakóoy Kwatsáan.	Old Lady Quechan.
Xavatsáats uu'ítsnya kamánk athúuk 'et.³⁹³	She came from (the clan) called Xavatsáats, they say.

Kukwiimáatt-ts nyaavée kaayúumk,³⁹⁴	Kukwiimáatt didn't have a wife,
təsáa,	but
vatsíits uuváak 'eta.³⁹⁵	his daughter was there, they say.
Vatsíik uuváak 'et.	He called her his daughter, they say.
Eemé Kwalàpaláp Kwaxavshúu.³⁹⁶	Eemé Kwalàpaláp Kwaxavshúu (Green Sole-of-the-Foot).³⁹⁷
Nyáavəm,	These (days),
nyaanyiimánk,	ever since then,
Xaanyénya	Frog

Xavatsáats a'íim 'ityá.	has been called Xavatsáats, they say.
'Axály atspáam,	She was born in the water,
'axály atspáam 'ét,	she was born in the water, they say,
Kukwiimáatt lyavíik.	like Kukwiimáatt.[398]
'Avá Kwatiinyáaməly nyatsuuváayk 'et.	They lived in the dark house, they say.
Kukwiimáatt-ts atóly matxávik nyiithík a'ét.[399]	Kukwiimáatt lay inside on the north (side), they say.
Xavatsáats tsala'íshk,	Frog was naked,
'avuuyáanyi athík 'et.	and she lay by the door, they say.
Kukwiimáatt,	As for Kukwiimáatt,
Kukwiimáatt 'atsarávək a'ét.	Kukwiimáatt felt sick, they say.
'Aka'ák 'íim atspámk,	He staggered out,
atsérəq ayáaw 'ím.	intending to go and defecate.
Viiyáaxayk,	As he went,
Xavatsáats avathíkəm,	Frog lay there,
apáask 'éta.	and he touched her, they say.
Iisháalyəm apáask.	He touched her with his hand.
Kavéely ayémk,	He went south,
atsérəq.	and he defecated.
Xavatsáats nyaanyiimánk,	Frog started from there,
aakavéek,	she turned over,
'amatt alyaxwélyk,	and she dug in the earth,
'amátt axávək.[400]	she went into the earth.
Viiyáak,	She went along,
Kukumáatt nyuuthík alynyuuvátsnyi aváamk.	and she got to (the place) where Kukwiimáatt was.
Iiyáa uutáqək,	She opened her mouth,
awéxáym,	she did, and suddenly,
atsérəq tsuumpápk alyanáalyk 'eta.[401]	four pieces of shit fell into it, they say.
Nyaawíim,	Then,
takavék,	she went back,

'avényi kayáamk,	she headed for the house,
axávək,	she went inside,
apáam avathík 'et.	she lay down and there she was, they say.
Uuthútsnya lyavíik,	She was just as she had been,
xiipúk uuthútsnya lyavíik.[402]	she was just as she had been before.
Kukwiimáatt-ts atspák:	Kukwimáatt reappeared:
viithíik,	he came along,
'avényi alyaxávək.[403]	and he entered the house.
Tsakwshányənyts xwéshəsh 'ím.	His head was spinning.
" 'Áax! 'Aax!" a'étk viithiik 'etá.[404]	He came along saying "Aah! Aah!" they say.[405]
Iiwáam soopérənyts namák a'ét.	His own strength had left him, they say.
Xavatsáatsənyts a'íim,	Frog said,
" 'Ana'áyá!	"Father!
Kaawíts 'aláayám?'"[406]	What is wrong?"
" 'Ats'aráavək,	"I am sick,
'ats'aráavək,	I am sick,
kaathúuntik a'ím 'ats'aráavk?[407]	why am I sick?
Kaawíts awíim 'atsarávək?	What made me sick?
'Akwé oov'óowənyts awíim 'ats'arávám?	Did a raincloud do something so that I am sick?
Matxá kwa'aláayənyts awíim 'arávám?	Did a bad wind do something so that I hurt?
'Atsakwsháts aráavək,	My head hurts,
'eetóts aráavək,	my belly hurts,
'iimáatt atóly aráavək,[408]	my body is sick on the inside,
'iiwáanyts aráavək,"	my heart is sick," (he sang).
Kukumáatt-ts apáam,	Kukwiimáatt lay down,
tsakwshány tsawáamk,	and he turned his head
'amátt nyamuushíitənya,	to each place that he had named,
kwatsuumpápənya,	the four of them,
athót.	he did.
Pa'iipáanyənyts nyaanyiitíivək aakakyáavək,	The people were all around him,

kwas'eethée tsáaməly makyík uumán alya'émxats athót.	but, of all the doctors, none could cure him.
Maxwáanyənyts shaly'áy ayúush kamémk,	Badger brought cool sand,
iiwáanyi atsáam.	and he placed it on his heart.
Maxwáa kwas'eethéets 'atsathúu lya'émtəsáa,	Badger was not a doctor,
uuxáymtəsáa,	he didn't know (what he was doing), but
iiwáam uuwítsənya awét.⁴⁰⁹	it was something he did on his own.
Kukwiimáatt-ts a'íim,	Kukwiimáatt said,
" 'A'axóttk vi'athíit kwayúulyavíita'a,"	"It seems that I am getting better,"
'éxáyk,	he said, and suddenly,
'atsarávək thúutt 'íikəta.⁴¹⁰	he was sick and it got worse, they say.
A'íim,	He said,
" 'Atsaváamək 'a'iipáyk 'uuváantiyúm.	"It is impossible that I should keep living.
'Anyáats 'apúyxa.	I shall die.
Athótəsáa,	It is happening, but
xaméera 'a'axóttk,	later on I will be all right,
takavék 'a'axóttxa."	I will be all right again."
***411	***
Pa'iipáanyts shtamatháavək 'eta.	The people did not understand, they say.
" 'Apúyəxa,"	"I am going to die,"
uu'ítsənya.	that's what he said.
Nyaanyiimánk.	It started there.
Oopóoyəny xiipúk tsaamánk athútyá.	His death was the first one and started it.
***412	***
" 'Apúyk," uu'ítsənya, shtamatháavək 'et.	"I die" is what he said, and they did not understand it, they say.
Pa'iipáanyts⁴¹³ shtamatháavək 'et.	People did not understand it, they say.

Kaawíts 'íim,
" 'Apúyk," 'íim 'ítya.
Die,
then;
nyáanyi,
xiipúkts athúuk 'eta.
Oopóoyənya.

Kukwiimáatt-ts xalyashútsk.
Xalyashútsənyts tashoonyóts
  xamáalyk.[414]

***[415]

'Apénts nyuu'áaly ashtúum,[416]
'amáyk atsáatsk a'et,
xatsúurtəm kwathútsəny.
Avathúum,
pa'iipáanyənyts nya'áalytst
  athutyá.

Kukwiimáatt-ts Kumastamxó
  aqásk a'ét.[417]
"Xuumáréey![418]
Kathíik!"
Uu'íts nyaatsuumpápəm,
a'ávək.
Kukwiimáatt-ts kanáavək,
" 'Anyáats vi'ayémúm.[419]
'Akórəly 'ayémúm.[420]
'Atsaayúu tsáaməly máany
  nyáayxa.
Mavasháwxa.
'Uuwítsxanya kaavíirək!
Nyoo'éeypa mayúumək."
"Nyaayúu tsáaməly 'uutar'úyk
  'awíim."
Xaanyéts a'ím,

He said something,
he said "I die," they say.
Die,
then;
at that point,
it was the first one, they say.
His death (was).

Kukwiimáatt sweated.
His sweat was white paint.

***

Beaver got some clothes,
and he put them over him, they say,
because it was cold.
He did this,
and people have worn clothes
* (ever since).*

Kukwiimáatt called to
* Kumastamxó, they say.*
"Child!
Come here!"
When he said it the fourth time,
he heard him.
Kukwiimáatt told him,
"I am going to go away.
I am going to go far away.
I will give everything to you.

You will take care of it.
Finish what we were doing!
I have taught you and you've seen it."
"I will take care of everything
* properly."*
Frog said,

"Nyamáam apúy atsémk,
nyaaviimánk 'asakyínyək vi'ayémúm,"
nyaa'íim,
'amátt axwélyk,
maxák axávək,
a'et.

'Anyáats atspák vanyaathíim,
Kukwiimáatt-ts apúyk.

'Avá Kwatiinyáamənya,
'Avá Kwatiinyáam alyathík.
Tsakwshányənyts 'anyaaxáap shathómp.
Pa'iipáa tsáaməly nyiishnyítsk uu'íitsk.
Athótk,
ashmáam viithík aaly'ítsk.
Xanavtsíipts a'íik 'et:[421]
"Apúyk viithík,
nyaanyamáam;
mattkwiisháyts,
matxáts,
nyaaviimánk tsaváamk mashoopóowəntiyum."

Kukwiimáatt-ts apúy 'ím vanyaathík,
Xatalwény a'íim,[422]
"Nyaanyamáam.
Máany alynyuutanák.
***[423]
Muutara'úyk avmuuváaxa.
Muutara'úyk muuváam,
pa'iipáanyts mooyóovəxa.
'Atsaayúu 'axótt mathúuk," a'ím.

"Now he is almost dead,
and at this point I will run away,"
and saying that,
she dug in the ground,
and she went underneath,
they say.

As the sun was coming up,
Kukwiimáatt died.

The dark house,
he lay in the dark house.
His head was turned to the west.
All the people were silent.
So,
they thought he was sleeping.
Wren said it:
"He is lying here dead,
and that's the end of it;
he is a shadow,
he is a wind,
and from now on it is impossible for you to know him."

As Kukwiimáatt was lying there about to die,
he said to Coyote,
"That's all.
I make you leader.
***
You will do it properly.
You (will) do it properly,
and the people will be watching you.
You must do good things somehow," he said.

A Quechan Account of Origins   121

Kukwiimáatt shoopóowk 'etá,	Kukwiimáatt knew it, they say,
Xatalwényənyts iiwáany kwatsíts a'íim shoopóowk.[424]	he knew that Coyote was going to steal his heart.
Nyiikamáants nyáany lyavéek 'eta.	The others were like that too, they say.
Shatoopóowk avoonóok.	They knew it.
Xanavtsíipts a'íim,[425]	Wren said,[426]
Xanavtsíip Xatalwény a'íim,	Wren said to Coyote,
" 'Iiwáany matháwətxa,	"You will take my heart,
mashaqámk.	and you (will) be changed.
'Anyép 'iiwáa matháwk matsanyóxa."	You will take (after) my heart and follow (its example)."
Pa'iipáanyts shatoopóowk 'étəma.	The people knew it, they say.
Xatalwényənyts Xanavtsíip iiwáanya atháwk,	They knew that Coyote took Wren's heart,
taaxánk atháwk,	that's what he really took,
makyík Kukwiimáattəny iiwáany a'íilya'émk.	he never did take Kukwiimáatt's heart.
Xanavtsíipts alynyiithúutsk 'et.[427]	Wren thought about it, they say.
Náq a'íim av'óowk alynyiithúutsk.	He stood there in silence, and he thought about it.
"Kaawématank,	"Whatever he does,
Xatalwénya,	Coyote,
Xatalwény,	Coyote,
Xatalwé oowéxanya awíilya'éməxá,"	Coyote won't be able to do what he is planning to do,"
nyaa'íim,	and then,
iiwáam mattatskakwék a'ím,[428]	he asked himself,
"Iimáattəny 'atathúulytsiyúum?	"Shall we hide the body?
'Atháwk 'axály 'atápuum?[429]	Shall we take it and throw it in the water?
'Atapómk 'aavíirúm?"[430]	Shall we burn it up?"
" 'Ataráak 'atapómtəxa."[431]	"We shall make a fire and burn it."
Xanavtsíipts nyaamák 'Apénəny a'íim,	Wren then said to Beaver,

" 'Ax'áa,
'ax'áa,
'a'íi 'ax'áa matxá kamán makaméxa.
Nyáasi oov'ótsəm mayúuxa.⁴³²
Oov'ótsk,
arúuvək oov'ótsk,
ootanyéxats athúum."

'Apénts tatkyíttk,⁴³³
'Apénts eethóonyəm tatkyíttk 'et.⁴³⁴
Iiyáanyəm awíim,
eethóom awíim⁴³⁵
atsík a'ét.⁴³⁶

Xanavtsíipts Maníish Aa'ár a'íim,
"Nyáavi kaxwélyk,
kamuuvíly kaxwélyk,
'aqóolək,
avlyéwk,
'àra'árək,
pa'iipáa lyavíik.
'Iipáa lyavíik."

'Aayúu,
'amatt uukúpk,⁴³⁷
'amatt uukúpk nyaatséwəm,

nyaavíirəm,
Xanavtsíipts a'íim
'Apén,
'Apén a'íim
tamáark aavíir 'ím,
'iisávəm awíim,
nyaamák,
a'íits xamókəm,
akúpəny aapétt a'ím;

"Cottonwood,
cottonwood,
you must bring cottonwood logs that come from the north.
You will see them standing over there.
They are standing upright,
they are dry and standing upright,
and ready to burn."

Beaver chopped them down,
Beaver chopped them down with his teeth, they say.
He used his mouth,
he used his teeth
to gather them up, they say.

Wren said to Ant-lion,
"Dig here,
and dig quickly,
(so that) it's long,
and wide,
and deep,
(so that) it's like a person.
(So that) it's like a man."

Well,
he made a hole in the ground,
he made a hole in the ground and when he had made it,
when he was finished,
Wren said
to Beaver,
he said to Beaver
that he should fill it up,
using arrowweed,
and then,
with three logs,
he should cover the hole;

'a'íi xavíkəm awíim,[438]	he should use two (more) logs,
aapár a'ím,	they would be at the end,
aapárəntixa.	and (two more) would be at the other end.

'Apénts tsuumpáptan kamémk,[439]	Beaver brought only four logs,
'étá.	they say.
Awíi nya'ím,	He did, and then,
xamók áampk.	there were three remaining (to be brought).

'A'íi vathány,	As for these logs,
'Apénts nyikamáanənya awíim:[440]	Beaver used the rest of them:
'amáyk atsáatsk.	he piled them on top.
'Iisáv awíntik.	He also used arrowweed.
'Avá tiinyáam 'avuuyáats nyiiríish a'íim.[441]	The dark house had no door.
"Makyík 'uutaqək[442]	"Where shall we open it up
iimáattəny 'atháwú?"	in order to take out the body?"
a'ét,	he said,
Kumastamxóts.	Kumastamxó (did).
Kumastamxóts Marxókavék tsakakwék.[443]	Kumastamxó asked Marxókavék.

A'íim,	So,
kavéevily awém 'ím.	they decided to take (the body) out on the south side.

Xanavtsíipts nyaa'íim,	Wren said,
" 'Anykaa'íts matxávik 'amáantəm 'athúm,	"Some of us come from the north, and so,
nyáanyik mawémtəxá."[444]	you should take it that way."

Xanavtsíipts a'íim,	Wren said,
"Kuukamnáawk katháwk!"[445]	"Lift him up!"
a'ét.	he said.
Nyaauutháawk,[446]	When they picked him up,
iisháalyəm uutháawk,	they picked him up with their hands,
iimáattənya iisháalyəm uutháawk.	they picked up his body with their hands.

Vuu'áats aa'ashéntim,
vuu'áats aa'ashéntim láak a'ím,
matxávik ayém,
ookavék tsamíim.
'Avá atóly oonóo lyaskyíik.

Kumastamxó,
Kumastamxóts matxávi
 kwatháwənya uutáqək awét,
makyík naqám aly'émək.
Nyaanyiimánk,
láak 'ím,
matxávik shathómp,
ookavék tatsénk,
awím.
Nyáanyəm,
uukayáamk láak uu'ítsək,

aatsuumpápk,
nyaathúum,
nyaawíim,
tsakwshánya kavéely
 ooshathomk,[449]
aa'ámpk,
'a'íi ootséwənya,
nyaawíim,
'a'íi ashtúum,
awím,
'a'íi ashtúum,
'iisáv ashtúum,
nyaawíim,
'amáyk atsáatsk.[450]

'Atsaayúu tsáaməly uulyavíim
 viitháwət.[451]
Təsáa,
'a'áaw kaayúumək.

One step,
they took one step,
they took him towards the north,
and they put him back down.
They were still in the middle of the
 house.

As for Kumastamxó,
Kumastamxó opened the (side)
 that was on the north,[447]
without touching it at all.[448]
Starting there,
they took a step,
they headed north,
and they put him back down,
they did.
At that point,
they took him one step in that
 direction,
they did it four times,
and then,
when they had done that,
they turned the head to the south,

and they laid him face down,
on the pyre,
and then,
they gathered wood,
and so,
they gathered wood,
they gathered arrowweed,
and then,
they put it on top.

They got everything ready and
 there it was.
However,
they had no fire.

A Quechan Account of Origins

Xanavtsíipts Xatalwénya 'anyáavik ooshathómp,	Wren sent Coyote to the east,
ooshathómpəm,	he sent him,
'a'áw aráa ayáaw a'ím.	so that he could get fire.
Kanáavək 'ím,	He told him,
"Kamuuvíly kavéshk!"	"Run fast!"
nyáasik ayémk.	and he went over there.
'Amátt nyáanyənyts nyiivák athútya,[452]	That place was there,
Kumastamxó iisháalyi tsayóq nyamtsasvém,	where Kumastamxó had spat in his hand and rubbed it,
'atsaayúunya,	that thing,
'amáy,	the sky,
'amáynyi tsasvém.	he had rubbed it against the sky.
Xatalwény,	As for Coyote,
Xatalwényts nyiiuuváam áar aly'émk avuuváak.[453]	he didn't want Coyote to be there.
Xatalwéts viiyáanyək —	Coyote went along —
'anyáa atspák siivám,	the sun was coming up over there,
nyaanyiimánk[454] —	it was rising from there —
'anyáa tsuupáknyi aváam.	and he reached the place where the sun was rising.
Táqshatáqsh a'im,	He jumped,
aatsuumpápk,	he did it four times,
aatsuumpápənyəm atáqshək aváamk.[455]	and on the fourth time he jumped and got there.
Aa'árəny,	As for his tail,
'aayúu xamáalyts apómk viivám,	something white was burning there,
nyáanyily aanákt.	and he rubbed his tail in it.
Voonóoxaym,	There they were, and suddenly,
Xanavtsíipts sanyts'áak xavíkəm a'íim	Wren said to two women
'a'áw aráa atséwk.	that they should make a fire.
Nya'ashénti Xalyasmóts,	One of them was Fly,

'ashént Xalyasmó Kav'ashóo
  a'íim amúlyk,[456]
nyikuuváantinyənyts.
***[457]

'Atsaayúu,
'iisáv 'a'íinya atháwk,[458]
'eethóo awíntik,
nyáany awíim,
shaaxwérək avoonóot.

'Ashéntəts awéxaym,
nyaanamákəm,
kwanyaméts,
nyiikuuváantinyənyts awínypatk
  'et.
Máam,
aráaw 'ím viiváxaym,[459]

'atsaayúu,
'eethóo[460] —
'a'áwənya,
'eethóony atháwk nyiitsáatsk
  a'ét.[461]
Ashtúum nyiitsáatsk a'íim.

Kumastamxóts a'íim,
nyáany uutsáawk,
'a'áw aráa atséwəxa.
A'íim,
nyiiuukanáavək.[462]

Kwaatúuly,
nyáanyi 'eethóony atháwk,[463]
awíim,
taráat,[464]
'a'áw aatapályək.[465]
'A'áw aatapályəm aráak.

and (the other) one was named
  Blue Fly,
the one who was around there too.
***

Well,
they took arrowweed and wood,
they used willow again,
that's what they used,
and they went on drilling them
  together (to make sparks).

One of them did it, and right away,
when she quit,
the other one,
the other one who was there did it
  in turn, they say.
Finally,
when it was about to burst into
  flame,

well,
willow —
as for the fire,
they took the willow and put it on
  (the sparks), they say.
They gathered it and put it on (the
  sparks), they say.

Kumastamxó said it,
(he said) they would do that,
they would make a fire that way.
So,
he explained it to them.

As for Chuckwalla,
at that point he got the willow,
and so,
he set it on fire,
he lit a fire.
He lit a fire and it blazed up.

Ayáak,	He went along,
nyaayáak,	and as he went along,
kavéely,	in the south,
kavéely athúum,	it was in the south,
nyáavik athúum,	it was over here,
kwaaxwíirnyi,	in the corner,
nyáanyi xiipúk aatapályk.	he lit it there first.
Viiwáamk,	He went along,
viiwáamk,	he went along,
aakwíink,	and he turned,
kwaaxwíirnyi aakwíink,	he turned the corner there,
viiwáanyək,	and he went along,
kavéely,	and in the south,
kavéely 'anyaaxáap kamémt.	he brought it into the southwest.
Awíntik,	He did it again as he had done before,
taráantik,	he set it on fire again as he had done before,
Xatalwéts atáqshatáqsh a'ím takavék,	and Coyote came bounding back,
athóxaym,	he did, and right away,
aa'árənyts apómk,	his tail was burning,
apómam,	it was burning,
atáqshək sanyaayáak,[466]	and he went bounding along,
'a'áw atséwənya aváamk.	and he reached the fire they had made.
Nyaaváamk,	When he reached it,
masharáyk,	he was angry,
aa'ár kapómənyts maspát.	and his burning tail went out.
Avathúum,	For that reason,
aa'ár kapáarənyts nyíily av'áarək athópəka.	the tip of his tail is always black.
"Koov'ótsk kaakakyáavək!"	"Stand surrounding the fire!"
uu'íitsk 'etá.	they said, they say.
Pa'iipáanyts uu'íitsk.	The people said it.
"Atáqsh a'ím avuuváak athútya!"	"He is about to jump!"
nyaa'ítsəm,	they said,
aakakyáavək,	and they surrounded it,

'a'áw aráanya aakakyáavək oov'ótsk 'eta.

Axáv xalyavíim,
Maxwáats
Xuumírts
'ona'óntanək avoonóot.
Xatalwényənyts 'amáy atáqshək,⁴⁶⁷
'amáym áamk amákəly av'óow.

Kukwiimáatt iiwáany atháwk,
iiyáanya,
iiyáanya,
iiyáanyəm atháwk.
Nyaathúum,
nyaatáqshəntik takavék athúuk 'ét.
Avéshtank,
kavéely 'anyaaxáapk alyayémt.⁴⁶⁸

'Ats'óorts,
'Ats'óor uu'ítsnyənyts pa'iipáa avésh nyiikwanáamts.⁴⁶⁹
Nyáanyi,
a'íim,
Xatalwény tavéerək,
a'ét.
Nyaawéxaym,
Xatalwényənyts
'Ats'óornya nyiikáamk awim,
namák 'et.
Namák,
alynamák 'eta.

Athúum,
siiyáak,
makyík av'óow aly'émk,
'ét.

they stood surrounding the burning fire, they say.

It was possible for him to get in,
(because) Badger
and Squirrel
were very short.
Coyote jumped over them,
he went right over them and landed behind them.

He picked up Kukwiimáatt's heart,
in his mouth,
in his mouth,
he picked it up in his mouth.
Then,
he jumped back over them, they say.
He really ran,
he went away to the southwest.

Hawk,
the one called Hawk was the best runner.
At that point,
they say,
he chased after Coyote,
they say.
When he did,
that Coyote
outran Hawk, and so,
he left him behind, they say.
He left him behind,
he left him behind there, they say.

So,
he went along,
and he didn't stop anywhere,
they say.

Xattpáa 'Anyáa nyamatt aváamtank,	He reached Maricopa territory,
nyaaváamk,	and when he got there,
nyaaváamk,	when he got there,
iiwáanya,	as for the heart,
'amáttnyi tsavóowk.[470]	he put it on the ground.
Sáa	But
nyamáam,	that's all,
asóok avoonóok 'et.	he went about eating it, they say.

Iiwáa,	As for the heart,
iiwáanyənyts,	that heart,
kwiiwáanyənyts 'avíi 'améets athót.[471]	that heart of his became a high mountain.
Nyaanyiimánk,	Starting then,
'Avíi Kwa'axás 'ím ooshéeyk a'et.[472]	they named it Greasy Mountain, they say.
Nyáanya,	That (mountain),
kwa'axásənyts iiwáanyik athíik athúuk 'et.	its greasiness comes from his heart, they say.

***[473]   ***

Xatalwényənyts kwiiwáanya asóok,[474]	Coyote ate his heart,
nyaasóom,	and when he ate it,
iiyáanyənyts anyíilyk,	his mouth turned black,
a'ét.	they say.
Iipályənyts 'axwéttk,	His tongue turned red,
nyaaxwétt lyavíik 'ét.	it was as red as his blood, they say.
Nyáavəts aráak apómk,	These (parts of him) blazed up and burned,
a'ét.	they say.
Kumastamxóts a'ím,	Kumastamxó said,
"Xatalwé,	"Coyote,
Xatalwény pa'iipáa nyaakwévəts athúum.[475]	Coyote is a good-for-nothing person.

Makyík 'iipáa lyavíi lya'émk," a'ét.	He is not at all like a man," he said.
"Nyaanyiimán, yaakapéttk avuuváaxa. Makyík 'atskiiyíi lya'émk, nyavá kaayúuməntík," a'ét.	"From now on, he will be wild. He will call no-one his friend, and he will have no house," he said.
Nyaanyi uuváak, aashuuthúlyk, 'avíinyi uuváak. 'Aayúu 'Ak'úly uu'íts avoonóom, nyáanyəm takyéevək aashmátsk 'et. Uuksaráaviyú amúly 'et.	There he was, sneaking about, there he was in the mountains. Something called Jackrabbit was there, and that's who he slept with, they say. He named him Uuksaráaviyú, they say.
Xatalwényts tsakwshály yaakapéttk. Vatsíits avuuváam, nyáany atháw 'etk avuuváak, mattshakyév a'ím.	Coyote was crazy in the head. His daughter was there, and he was going to take her, he was going to marry her.
'Anyáats viithíkəm, mashaxáyts uuváam, ayúuk 'et. Kapétt alyuuváam.	One day, a young woman was there, and he saw her, they say. She was in the dense brush.

***476   ***

Makyík namák a'éxaym, nyeekwévək a'ét. Mashaxáyənyts atháwk viiwáak,	He couldn't leave her, and that was the end of him, they say. The young woman took him and went along,
'amáy alytakxávək 'et. Xatalwény mayúu lyaskyíitəxa. Nyáanyi Xaly'ányəm uuvám mayúutəxa.477	she took him up into the sky, they say. You can still see Coyote. You can see him there with the Moon.

Pa'iipáa tsáaməly aviitíivək 'eta,

'atsaayúu apómk uuváxáym.
Kwa'uukúutstanənyts iiwáanyts 'atsláytstank a'ét.⁴⁷⁸
Nyáava aalyuuthúutsk;⁴⁷⁹
ooyóovxayk 'ím,
"Nyáany 'alyavéexá,
'anyáavi kwiiyáanya."⁴⁸⁰

Athótəsáa,
makyípəts uumítsnya shoopóow alya'émk 'etá.
Kwatsáan 'iipáanyənyts xiipúk amíim 'etá.⁴⁸¹
Xan'aaváa a'íim amúlyk 'et.⁴⁸³
Amíim,
tshíi tshíi a'íik 'et.
'Aanáalyts viiv'óowm,
nyáany alyavák uuvák 'etá.

'Amattnya ayúuk.
Nyaayúuk,
malyqé taanáwk a'ét.⁴⁸⁴
Taanáwk thúutt a'ét,⁴⁸⁵
anáw alya'émk 'et.
Nyaa'íntik,
xwórər xwórər a'ím,
avuuvák 'et.⁴⁸⁶

'Atsaayúu,
'eethóots oov'óowm,
nyáanyily avák a'íik 'et.

Nyáanyənyts,
mapísa,

All the people were sitting around it, they say,
while the thing was burning.
The oldest ones felt very bad, they say.
They thought about (the funeral);
as soon as they saw it, they said,
"We will be like that,
one of these days."

However,
none of them knew about crying.

That Quechan man was the first to cry, they say.⁴⁸²
He was named Xan'áaváa (Cicada).
He cried,
he went "Tshíi tshíi," they say.
A mesquite tree was standing there,
and that's what he was sitting on, they say.

He was looking at the ground.
As he looked,
he raised his voice, they say.
He raised it a little more,
but it wasn't loud, they say.
He did it again,
he went "Xwórər xwórər,"
there he was, they say.

Well,
a willow tree was standing there,
and that's what he was sitting on, they say.
As for that one,
nowadays,

nyáavatánəm,	at this (time),
xavashúuk athúuk 'et.[487]	he is green, they say.
Pa'iipáa tsáaməly tsaamánk matsats'íim.	All the people began to cry.
'Atsaayúu tsáaməly matsats'íim:	Everything cried:
matxányənyts amíim,[488]	the wind cried,
'amáyənyts amíim.	and the sky cried.
Kumastamxóts taanáwk tsaqwérək 'ím:[489]	Kumastamxó spoke louder:
"Nyáavi nyaamánk,[490]	"Because of this,
'anyakó 'ana'áy 'atstsuunáalyk 'athúm.	we (must) lose our fathers.
Pa'iipáa tsáaməly xaméra nyáany lyavíinypatxa.[491]	All people in the future will be like that too.
'Amaawíi,	Our relatives,
'amaawíi kuumánəny,	and the descendants of our relatives,
nyáany a'ítsapátxá."[492]	they will do that too."
Nyáany alynyuuthúutsk avoonóok athúuk 'étəma.	That is what they were thinking about, they say.
"Nya'uumáanənyts oopóoyk,[493]	"Our descendents will die,
oopóoyəm,[494]	they will die,
pa'iipáa tsáaməly oopóoyxa.	all people will die.
Pa'iipáats aatspáatstəm,	People will be born,
voonóonyək,	they will be here for a while,
oopóoy,	and they (will) die,
oopóoyəxa.	they will die.
Athúulynyaa'ém,	If it didn't happen,
pa'iipáats 'atáyk mattapéexa.	there would be too many people.
Athóxaym,	And then,
pa'iipáanyts ashmáaw nyaa'ím,	if people wanted to sleep,
pa'iipáa kwanyamé 'amáyk athík ashmáxa.	they would have to sleep on top of other people.
Xalyavímtəm,	And perhaps
pa'iipáa makyípəts 'amáyk matsérəqtəxá."[495]	some person would shit on you."

| | A Quechan Account of Origins |

Nyuu'áavək oov'ótsk,	They stood there listening,
pa'iipáa tsáaməly ee'ény aatskyítt.[496]	and all the people cut their hair.
'Atsaayúu,	Well,
malyxónya —	their feathers —
malyxúyk nyaathúum,	if they were feathered,
nyáany aakyíttk,	they cut those (feathers),
nyaawítsək,	and when they had done so,
ashtúum,	they gathered them up
'a'áwəly aapáxk 'et.	and threw them into the fire, they say.

'Aqwáaqts	Deer
'Ak'úlyts,	and Jackrabbit,
Xaly'áwts,	and Cottontail,
Maxwét,[497]	and Bear,
aa'ártsənya aatskyíttk	they cut their tails off
ashtúum	and gathered them up
'a'áwəly aatspáxk 'et.	and threw them into the fire, they say.
Nyaanyiimánk,	After that,
aa'árəny —	their tails —
aa'árənyts aatspáats 'éxáym,	when they wanted their tails to grow out again,
nyaakwéevək 'et.	they couldn't, they say.
Talypó,	As for Roadrunner,
Talypó,	Roadrunner,
nyáanyts 'ashént-tank,[498]	he was the only one,
aa'árəny 'aqóoləm namák athutyá,	he left his tail long,
aa'ár áartsəm kwathútsəny.	because he needed his tail.

Xamsheekwérts viithíik,	A whirlwind came up,
nyáanyi uuváak athúuk 'eta.	and it stayed around there, they say.
Pa'iipáatsənyts alyapáam alyuuthúutsk,	All the different kinds of people mistakenly thought
Kukumáattənyts atspák 'ím,	that Kukwiimáatt was about to appear,
uuváak athúuk kwayúu lyavíik.	for it seemed to them that he had stayed around.
"Kaváarək,"	"No,"
a'íik 'ét.	he said, they say.

Kumastamxóts.
Vathány,
'atsaayúuts,
xamsheekwér kwas'eethéets,"
nyaa'íim.
"Makayáamk,
xiipán uuváaxa.
Athótəsáa,
pa'iipáa mayúu alyma'émxá.
Ampóttk viitháwm mayúutxa."

Nyaa'íim,
aashváarək 'et:

"Matxányənyts av'áak uuváak,
av'áak uuváak,
matxányts av'áak uuváak,
av'áak uuváak."⁴⁹⁹

Nyaa'éxáym,
pa'iipáanyts tsáaməly,
pa'iipáanyts tsaamánk matsats'íim,⁵⁰⁰
a'ét.⁵⁰¹

Kumastamxóts a'íim,⁵⁰²
"Xanavtsíipts makyík vasháw 'axótt aly'éməsh.
Nyáaviimánk,
'iiwáam 'atsaavéshxa.
Tsáaməly 'atsaavéshxa.⁵⁰³
'Anyáats iiwáam 'a'áshéntk 'atsaavéshxa."⁵⁰⁴

Xaanyéts 'amátt maxák axwélyk uuváaxayk,
a'ét.

Kumastamxó (did).
"As for this,
this thing,
it is a spirit wind,"
he said.
"It will head straight for you,
and stay very close.
However,
you won't see anyone.
You will only see that there is a cloud of dust."

Then,
he sang, they say:

"The wind is traveling around,
it is traveling around,
the wind is traveling around,
it is traveling around."

When he said it, right away,
all the people,
the people started to cry,

they say.

Kumastamxó said,
"Wren did not take care of (things) well at all.
From now on,
I will run things myself.
I will run everything.
I will run things by myself."

Frog was digging underground,

they say.

Iiwáanyts apúym mashathéevək.⁵⁰⁵	She was surprised and afraid.
Nyaa'ávəm,	When she felt it,
nyaa'ávəm,	when she felt it,
nyaa'ávək a'íim,	when she felt it, they say,
atspák.	she came out.
Atspák,	She came out,
iiyáa uutáq,	and opened her mouth,
tsalyéq;	she let it gape open;
taayúush a'íim,⁵⁰⁶	she wanted to let it cool,
apómk uuvátəm kwathútsəny.	because it was burning.
'Aayúu atséerqənyts 'apílyk uuváxáyk,⁵⁰⁷	The shit had been hot,
nyáanya amáam.⁵⁰⁸	and that's what she had eaten.
Nyáany amáam athútya.	That's what she had eaten.
Amáam athútya.⁵⁰⁹	She had eaten it.

Athótəsáa,	However,
'atsaayúu,	well,
matsats'íim,	they were crying,
nyiixúu kwa'ítsənya nyaa'ávək.	and she heard the ruckus that they made.

Takavék,	She went back,
'amátt axwélyk atséntəntík 'etəma,	she dug her way down into the ground again, they say,
pa'iipáanyənyts ooyóovək	(because) those people (might) see her
tatoopóoy xalyavím.	and they might kill her.
Tsuupákənyts aatsuumpápk 'et.⁵¹⁰	There were four places where she came up, they say.

Siiyáanyək,⁵¹¹	She went along,
'amáttəm athíik atspákəta,	and she came up out of the ground, they say,
atspák aatsuumpápk.	she came up four times.
Xiipúkənyts 'Amátt Kaxwíts a'íim,	The first (place) was called 'Amátt Kwaxwíts,
'ashéntəts Shamkót Kavée a'íntik,	one was called Shamkót Kavée,
'ashéntits 'Avíi 'Ax'áa a'íim,	one was called 'Avíi 'Ax'áa (Cottonwood Mountain),

'ashéntits 'Avíi Xaanyé a'íntik.

Nyáanyəm athíik atspák aatsuumpápk.

'Avíi Xaanyé,
nyáanya,[512]
Xaanyényənyts,
nyaánya Xaanyénya 'avíi atséwk athutyá.
'Avíi mattatséwk.[514]

'Aavé Taaxánts
'axá sa'íly alyuuváa alyaskyíik,
a'ét.
Mashathéevək,
pa'iipáanyts avaathíik atháwk kaawémts xalyavíim,

oowéeyts xalyavíim,
Marxókavék tsakyíwəm.

Vuutáyənyts thúutt a'étank,
avanyaathúum,
'amátt —
'amátt kwa'ora'óra nyáany —
aakwíin aa'ashéntək athóxats athót.[515]

Pa'iipáanyənyts mashtatháavək 'et xalyavímtəm
'Amáy 'Aavétanyts aaíimk atspáam,[516]
thúutt 'ím viithíixáy,
'amáttnyi athíik[517]
nyiitatpóoy xalyavíim.[518]
Mashtatháavək a'éta.

and one was called 'Avíi Xaanyé (Frog Mountain).
Thus she came up four times.

Frog Mountain,
as for that,
that Frog,
that Frog got turned into a mountain.[513]
She turned into a mountain.

Rattlesnake
was still staying in the ocean,
they say.
He was afraid,
(because) people were likely to come and take him and do something to him,

they were likely to do something to him,
(because) he had bitten Marxókavék.

His size was really increasing,
and because of that,
the earth —
that whole round earth —
he could wrap (his body) around it once.

The people were afraid, they say,
(because) it was possible
that Sky Snake (might) somehow appear,
and get bigger and bigger,
and come onto the land
and kill them.
They were afraid of him, they say.

Kumastamxóts a'íim,[519]
"Xalyavímtəm
atsénk
'atsiiráav kamétəxá.[520]
Athúu,
pa'iipáa kwanyamé atsérəq amáam,
Xaanyé uuwítsəny uutsáawk." [521]
Vanyaathúum,
Kumastamxóts 'Amáy 'Aavéta tapúy a'ím.[522]
" 'Uuqáasəm,
nyáavi 'Axaavoolypó aváatxa,"

a'ét.
Kumastamxóts a'íim.
Nyaanyiimánk,
'anyáats nyiikamánəny 'awéxa,"
a'ét.

Kumastamxóts Xalytótt a'íim
ayáak
'Amáy 'Aavéta a'íim
'Axaavoolypó aváaxa.[524]

Pa'iipáa,
pa'iipáats 'atsaráavək avathíkm,[525]
nyáany uumán a'íim.
Nyáanyi,
Xalytótt-ts maxák axávət,
takavék.[526]
" 'Amáy 'Aavétats a'íim,
avathíixa lya'émk a'íim,"[527]
a'ét.

Ayáak,
'Amáy 'Aavétanya uukanáavəm[528]

Kumastamxó said,
"Perhaps
he will come down
and bring diseases.
Or,
he (might) eat another person's shit,
he (might) do what Frog did."
For that reason,
Kumastamxó decided to kill Sky Snake.
"We will summon him,
and he will come here to Water Housepost,"[523]
he said.
Kumastamxó said it.
"From now on,
I will do the rest,"
he said.

Kumastamxó said to Spider
that he should go
and say to Sky Snake
that he should come to Water Housepost.

Someone,
someone was lying there sick,
and (Sky Snake) could cure him.
At that point,
Spider went into the area below,
and he came back.
"Sky Snake says,
that he won't come,"
he said.

He went,
and he told Sky Snake

pa'iipáanyənyts apúytəxa	that the person would die
muuvílyk viithíi alynyaa'ém.	if he did not come in a hurry.[529]
Kumastamxóts a'íim,	Kumastamxo said it,
Xalytóttəny a'íim.	he said it to Spider.
Xalytóttənyts viiyáak,	Spider went along,
nyáanya kanáavəm,	and told him,
'Amáy 'Aavétats a'íim,	and Sky Snake said,
"Kwas'eethéets 'athótəm;	"I am a doctor;
'oowéxats athútyá,"	it is my duty,"
a'íik 'et.	he said, they say.
" 'Aaíimk 'ayáatxá,	"I will go anyway,
'ashoopóowəs 'athótk.	even though I know about it.
Muuwíitsxany 'ashoopóowk," a'ítya.[530]	I know what you will do," he said.
"Athótəsáa,	"However,
'atsaayúu 'ashéntəm 'akwakyáavəxa:	I will ask for one thing:
'Atathíts katawáak!	Grind corn!
Nyaakawíim,	Do that,
'anóqəm kashtúum,	and take a little,
nyiiuuváts aatsuumpápəm katsáam nyam'ooyémxanya.	and put it down in four places along my path.
Xalyavímtəm	Perhaps
matsáam 'apúy xalyavíim,"	I might get hungry,"
a'etá,	he said,
" 'akór alyavátəm kwathútsəny."	"because it is far away."

'Amáy 'Aavétats xiipúk alyuuváamənya aváamxayk,[531]	When Sky Snake reached the first stopping place,
'atathíts 'atáyk thúutt 'etá,	there was a lot of corn, and more and more,
tsáaməly uumáxats athúu lya'émt.	and he could not eat all of it.
"Alynyi'athúutsxay,	"I thought about it, and immediately
'ashoopóowəsh.	I knew.
Nyaanyamáam.	That's all.
Nyatatoopóoy a'íim awétk awítya.	They did it intending to kill me.
'Aayúu 'uumáxa nyáavi atsáatstəm kwathútsəny.[532]	They put things here for me to eat.[533]
Athótəsáa,	However,

'aaíim 'ayáatxa,	I will go ahead anyway,
'oowéxats athótəm kwathútsəny."	because it is my duty."
Xalytótt-ts a'íim,	Spider said,
"Mamuuvílyəxa.	"You must hurry.
Pa'iipáanyənyts apúytəxa	The person will die
mathúulynyaama'émǝm."	if you don't."
A'éxaym,	When he said this,
'Amáy 'Aavétats masharáyk 'et.	Sky Snake got angry, they say.
Aa'árəny sélǝl awíik 'et.	He made his tail rattle, they say.
Kwanáwǝnyts uuqás lyavíik 'ét.	The noise was like thunder, they say.
'Amátt ampóttk athúum,	The land was dusty,
uuráv mattapéek athótǝsáa,	and there was a lot of lightning, but
'Axaavoolypó aváamk a'ét.	he reached Water Housepost, they say.
Pa'iipáa,	As for the people,
pa'iipáa tsáamǝly,	all the people,
'avá kwatiinyáamǝly kwatíivánts —	the ones that were in the dark house —
'Amáy 'Aavétanyts tsakwshá tsuumpápk athúuk 'ét.	Sky Snake had four heads, they say.
Kumastamxóts 'ashéntǝk nyiivák uuvák,	Kumastamxó was the only one who stayed there,
aatooqwérǝk,	he was with (Sky Snake),
'aványi alyavák uuvák 'et.	he stayed in the house, they say.
'Amáy 'Aavéts 'avány axwíitsǝk 'ét.[534]	Sky Snake smelled that house, they say.
"Pa'iipáats nyiirísh 'ím viitháwk.	"There is no-one there.
Pa'iipáats nyiirísh a'íim nyaathúuva,"	There is no-one,"
uu'íits,	they said,
pa'iipáanyǝnyts.	the people did.
"Pa'iipáa 'atsarávǝts alyathík,"	"There is a sick person in there,"
a'ét,	he said,
'Amáy 'Aavétats.	Sky Snake (did).
"Ma'émpak,"	"You are right,"
uu'íitst,	they said,
pa'iipáanyǝnyts.	the people (did).
"Athúum,	"It is so,
athótǝsáa	but

aly'uuthútsk	we thought
máanyts ma'ashéntik avmuuváaxa,[535]	that you would want to be alone,
'ayétsəts aly'oonóoxa[536]	and (we wondered) whether we should be here
nyamathíik matséev nyaam'íim.	when you came to doctor him.
Nyaany athúum,	That is (the reason why)
'aatspáatstək 'athútya."	we came outside."
Kumastamxóts 'avá atóly av'óowk,	Kumastamxó stood in the middle of the house,
'anyaaxáapk —	and to the west —
'anyaaxáap axkyéek	he crossed to the west side
'avá shoopéttəny nyikavátsnya.[537]	of the winter house that was there.
Awétk,	He did it,
'amáttəny ashtúum,	he picked up some dirt,
'avá atónyi atsáatsk 'et.	and he put it in the middle of the house, they say.
Nyáava awíim	He did this
pa'iipáats nyiithík lyavíim.[538]	to make it seem like a person was lying there.
'Amáy 'Aavétats	As for Sky Snake,
tsakwshánya —	his heads —
tsakwshánya 'avuuyáaly takxáav a'íim,	he tried to put his heads through the door,
nyaakwévək.	but he couldn't.
Tapéttk.	It was blocked.
Kumastamxó awíim	Kumastamxó did something
'avuuyáanyənyts avalyéwk thúutt 'ét.	and the doorway got wider.
'Amáy 'Aavétanyts kaawíts axwíivəm a'ávək 'et.	Sky Snake could smell something, they say.
Nyáanya,	As for that,
Kumastamxó axwíivəm a'ávək 'ét.	he could smell Kumastamxó, they say.
Tsakwshá kwatsuumpápnya 'avály alytakxávək 'et.	He pushed his four heads into the house, they say.
Uuwíts aa'ashénti awíim,	With one act,[539]
Kumastamxóts tsakwshá kwatsuumpápənya aakyíttk,[540]	Kumastamxó cut off the four heads,
malyaqé kamán,	he started at the throat,

nyaatskyíttk 'et.⁵⁴¹	and he cut them off, they say.
Nyaawíim,	Then,
atáqshək	he jumped up
mat'ár aváam.	and went outside.
Tsakwshány,	As for the heads,
tsakwshá kwatsuumpápnya,	as for the four heads,
atóly atháw alyaskyíim,	they were still inside,
'aványily.	in the house.
'Asháak nyuuwítsəny atháwk,	He took his knife,
pa'iipáany nyiiaatsooyóoyk 'et.	and he showed it to the people, they say.
"Pa'iipáa 'atapúy," nyaa'íim.	"I have killed someone," he said,
"Vathány kawíim!	"Use this!
Kawím!"	Use it!"
Avathúm.	That's how it was.
Nyaanyiimánk,	From then on,
pa'iipáanyənyts 'asháak tsatsuu'úly av'áark athópka.	people have always carried knives, they say.
Atápk,	He threw it,
'amáyəly awémk,	he sent it up high,
atsénk viithíixaym,	and when it came back down,
qatt awíim atháwk 'et.	he caught it neatly in his hand, they say.
Kumastamxóts a'íim,	Kumastamxó said,
"Nyamáam.	"That's all.
'Amáy 'Aavétats apúyəm,⁵⁴²	Sky Snake is dead,
kwanyaméts oopóoyəntixa."	and others will die too."
Nyeexwétt-ts viitháwk,	His blood is there,
tsooyóqts,⁵⁴³	and his saliva,
'avíi nyiitháwk 'etá,⁵⁴⁴	they are there in the mountains, they say,
'Amáy 'Aavéta iimáattənyts nyiuuthíka.⁵⁴⁵	in the place where Sky Snake's body is lying.
Pa'iipáa kaxamáalyənyts,	The white people,
'óor uu'ítənyts 'axwéttk alyatháwk.⁵⁴⁶	what they call gold is (the) red (part) in there.
'Atsaayúu kwaxmáalynya,⁵⁴⁷	The white substance (i.e., silver),

'atsaayúu xamáaly nyiikwanáamts athúuk 'et.[548]	the white substance is something valuable (too), they say.
Kumastamxóts tsakwshá kwatsuumpápəny ashtúum,[549] aatskyíttəm — aatskyíttk ashtúum, kwa'ashíintənya. 'Axaavoolypó uu'ítsənya nyaaxáapk awétsa. Nyáany 'avíi 'axály kwatháwənyts athúum.	Kumastamxó gathered up the four heads, and he cut them up — he cut them up and gathered the pieces, each one. They might be west of what is called Water Housepost. They are the rocks that are in the water there.
Kumastamxóts a'íim,[550] " 'Ashoopóowəsh mátsəts mamashtatháavək ammoonóotk," 'ét. "Kwiixáalyts viithíi xalyavíim.[551] Nyáany kwiixáalyts aatsuumpápk athótk athútyá. Nyaaviimánk, athúunti lya'émxa. 'Anyáats pa'iipáa iimáatt kavatáy vathány atháwk xá kwa'úurnyi, 'amátt tsáaməly nyiikaváatsnya. Nyi'atsáam, 'axányənyts makyík akúuly alya'émxa. Athótəsáa, 'atsayér 'anyuuwíts, Qwaqxó, mawéxaym, 'axány a'íim,[552] akúulyk, 'axály nyammatatpóoyxá."	Kumastamxó said, "I know that you are afraid," he said. "A flood might come. There have been four floods. From now on, there will never be another one. I (will) take this big body of a person to the edge of the water, where all the land is. I will place it there, and the water will never rise above it. However, as for my bird, Woodpecker, if you do (anything) to him, I will say (something) to the water, and it will rise, and you will drown."

'Amáy 'Aavétats nyaapúyk,	When Sky Snake died,
avasútsk,	he urinated,
aaíimk avasúts aaly'ét.	he urinated as he pleased, all over the place.
Nyáanya	That
'axá kwasa'ílynya.	is the ocean.
Nyáanyts.	That's it.
'Axá kwasa'íləny avsúts athúuk 'et.	The ocean is his urine, they say.
Avathúum,	For that reason,
'asa'ílyk,	it is salty,
xamóolk,	it is foamy,
athúm,	and so,
mooséxats athúulya'ém;	you can't drink it;
'aláayt.[553]	it's bad.
Kumastamxóts a'íim,	Kumastamxó said,
"Nyáavi 'axótt aly'émək athutyá.	"It is not good here.
'Aványa 'atapómxa.	I will burn the house.
'Ootanyéxá."	I will cremate it."
Marxókavékts a'íim,	Marxókavék said,
"Kaváartək.	"No.
Kayúutəm oov'óowú.	Let it stand.
'Atsaayúu,	Well,
'atsayérnya nyi'aqáasəm,	I will summon the birds,
'atsaayúu mashtarátsnya nyii'aqáasəntim,	I will summon the wild things too,
nyáavi oonóok oonóoxa,	and they will be here, on and on,
matxávik 'ashathómpk vi'anayéməm."	(when) we go north."
" 'Aványənyts apóməxa.	"The house will burn.
Apóməxa.	It will burn.
'Aványənyts anáwəxa.	The house will make noise.
Anáwəxa.	It will make noise.
Aráaxa.	It will blaze up.
'Anyétsəts 'atsiimátsxa.	We will dance.
Ta'aanyáayəxa.	They will set fire to it.

Ta'aanyáayəxa.	They will set fire to it.
Aráaxa.	It will blaze up.
'Anyétsəts aatsiimátsxa.	We will dance.
Kaawíts,	Something,
kaawíts 'atsayér lyavíik,	there is something like a bird,
viithíik,	and it is coming,
'atsayér eemétsənyts 'amátt nyiitháwxa.	and there will be birds' tracks on the ground.
'Avá kwa'aláay vathány 'ata'aanyáaytsəxa.⁵⁵⁴	We will light up this bad house.
Nyáanyəm aráaxa.	With that, it will blaze up.
Aráaxa."	It will blaze up," (he sang).

Kumastamxóts av'áa,	Kumastamxó walked,
láak a'íim,⁵⁵⁵	he took a step,
aatsuumpápk athúuk a'ét.	he did it four times, they say.
'Aványa,	The house,
kwaaxwíirənya ta'aanyáayk,	he lit it at the corners,
kwaaxwíir kwatsuumpápənya.	the four corners.
Nyaa'íim,⁵⁵⁶	Then,
mattatsáaməly aatsiimátsk 'éta.	they all danced, they say.

Nyaatsavérək athúm,	When they were finished,
Kumastamxóts	Kumastamxó
'Uurúu aqásk a'éta.⁵⁵⁷	summoned Nighthawk, they say.
Nyáanyi,	At that point,
'Uurúuny oo'éeyəm aashváar uuxáyk,	he taught Nighthawk to sing,
a'éta.	they say.
'Atsaayúu,	Well,
nyamáam,	now,
nyaaqwalayéwk,	at dawn,
'anyáayk vanyaathíim,	when it's getting light,
pa'iipáa nyiishatamáan a'íim.	he tries to wake people up.

Kumastamxóts a'íim,	Kumastamxó said,
" 'Atsaayúu 'atáyəm mashoopóowxa.	"You will know many things

'uu'íts vathány mawíim avmoonóok maav'áarxáym."558	if you always do what I say."
" 'Anykayúutəm	"Leave me alone
'ashmáam,	(so that) I can sleep,
'anóqəm 'ashmáam vi'athíkəntiyúxa,"	(so that) I can sleep a little (longer),"
a'ét.	he said.
'Uurúuts a'íim.	Nighthawk said it.
Kúur nyaa'ím,	After a while,
'Uurúuts nyaa'ím,	Nighthawk said,
xərər xərər xərər 'et.	"Xərər xərər xərər," he said.
Vathánya,	As for this,
uu'ítsnya,	what he said,
pa'iipáanyts shatoopóowk a'éta.	people know (what it means), they say.
Uumáan 'ím a'íim.	It means that they are going to get up.
Kumastamxóts a'íim,	Kumastamxó said,
"Nyáavi 'antuumáak 'apúuttu."	"Let's leave him here and scatter."
Av'áak,	He walked,
láak 'étk,	he took a step,
aatsuumpápk,	he did it four times,
viiyáak,	and he went along,
matxávi kayáamk.	heading north.
Pa'iipáats aayáak aatuuqwíirk 'et.559	People followed him, they say.
'Uutátt 'a'íi nyuuwítsk 'ét.	He had a wooden spear, they say.
Kaawíts nyiirísh uu'íts viitháwm, nyáanyik uuthíik,560	There had been nothing there, and that (nothing) is what he brought it out of,
atséwk 'ét.	he made it, they say.
Nyaawíim,	Then,
'amáttəny uushák 'et.	he stabbed the ground, they say.
Ooqweraqwérnya,	As for the sharp point,
'amáttəny axávək,	it went into the ground,
qíir awím,	and he dragged it, making a line,
siiwáak siiwáak 'ét.	he took it along and took it along, they say.
Nyiioov'óow nyáanya,	(In) the place where he was standing,

qíir awíim,
aatsuumpápk 'ét.
Nyaawíim,
oomóqək,
matxávik awémk.[561]
'Axáts atspák mattapéek,

matxávi kayáamk 'et.

Nyaathúum,
sharéq 'ét,
naqám aly'émxáyk.
Awíntik 'ét:
'uutáttəny oomóqək,
'anyaaxáap ooshathómpək 'et.

Nyaawíim,
'axánya sharéq,
nyaawíntik awíim,
'anyáavi ooshathómpək,
'axánya shapéttəntik,
nyaatháwəntik,[563]
'anyáavik awémk 'et.
'Axánya sharéq 'et.
Nyaawíim,
oomóq,
qíir nyaawíntik,

kavéek,
kavéely uukayáamk,
ayúutəm,
'axányts avéshk siiyáak 'et.

Av'áa aatsuumpápk,
kavéely shathómpək,
láak uu'ítsnya aa'ashéntim,
awíim:

he dragged it, making a line,
he did it four times, they say.
Then,
he pulled it out,
and he took it toward the north.
Water came out, and there was a
   lot of it,
and it flowed north, they say.

Then,
he stopped it,
without touching it.[562]
He did it again, they say:
he pulled the spear out,
and he turned it towards the west,
   they say.

Then,
he stopped the water,
he did it again, and so,
he turned it towards the south,
and he shut off the water again,
and when he took it again,
he sent it to the east, they say.
He stopped the water, they say.
Then,
he pulled out (the spear),
and when he dragged it again,
   making a line,
to the south,
he brought it to the south,
and he let it be,
and the water went running along
   over there, they say.

He walked four times,
heading south,
and with one step,
he did it:

uuqárək a'étəm,	he broke through the rock,
'uutátt nyamawíim.	he did it with his spear.
Nyáany awíim,	That's what he did,
'axányənyts viiyáak,[564]	and the water went along,
'axá 'asa'ílyəny alyaxávək 'et.	and went into the ocean, they say.
'Atsaayúu 'uutátt,	The spear or whatever,
kwalàpalápənya,[565]	the flat (part),
nyáanya awíim,	(at the place where) he used that,
avlyéwk athúuk a'ét.	(the river) is wide, they say.
Xáak awíim,	Where he used the other side (of the spear),
qíir awéxaym,	he dragged it, making a line, and as a result,
'era'érək a'ét.	(the river) is narrow, they say.
Nyaawíim,	Then,
'axáts athúutt 'ím,	there was more and more water,
xáak ayémk aráwk 'et.[566]	and it flowed swiftly on one side, they say.
Yuma uu'ítsnya,	What they call Yuma,
'avíits oov'ótsəm,	there were mountains standing there,
nyáany,	and as for those (mountains),
uuqárk,	he broke them open,
uuqárəm,	he broke them open,
'axányənyts nyamaxáv a'ím.	so that the water could go through.[567]
Vuu'áats aatsuumpáp nyaathúntik,	When he had taken four steps,
nyaathúum,	then,
takavék,	he went back,
nyiuumáni aváamk 'et.	and he reached the source, they say.
"Vathány 'anyaxáts,	"This is my water,
'anyaxáts,	it is my water,
vathány 'anyaxáts,	this is my water,
'anyaxáts.	it is my water.
'Axánya wanym'ooyétsk,	We love the water,
'a'íi aaooxnéenya wanym'ooyétsk.[568]	we love the driftwood.

Avéshk voonóonyək voonóoxa.	It will go on running, on and on.
'Axányənyts avéshk avoonóok avoonóoxa.	The water will go on running, on and on.
Nyik'apílyk vanyaatháwm, atspák,	When it is summer, it will come out,
'amátt aamáarək,	and flood the land,
nyaathúum	and then
avéshk oonóok aav'áarxa."	it will go on running always," (he sang).

Kumastamxóts waapóor atséwk.⁵⁶⁹
Kaawíts makyí atháw alya'ém,
nyaanyiimánk atséwk 'et.⁵⁷⁰

Kumastamxó made a boat.
There had been nothing there,
and that's what he made it out of, they say.

Nyaawíim,
pa'iipáats tsuumpápəm
 nyiitsáam 'et:
Xattpáa 'Anyáats,
Kwatsáants,
Kamayáats,
Kwa'aapáts,
uuthúutsk.
Waapóorənti atséwk,⁵⁷¹
pa'iipáa kwas'eethéets
 tsuumpápəm alyatsáam:⁵⁷²
'ashénti Xamakxávəts athúuk 'et.
Pa'iipáa nyiikamáanənyts,⁵⁷³
vuu'átsk aatsénk,
a'et.

Then,
he put four people there, they say:

Maricopa,
Quechan,
Kamyaa,
and Cocopa,
those were (the people).
He made another boat,
and he put four medicine men in
 it:
one was a Mojave, they say.
The rest of the people,
they walked down,
they say.

Vaayáak;
'axámshuukwíints siivám,⁵⁷⁴
apámk a'ét.
'Aavé xiikwíirts kavéely
 shathómpək siiyáak 'eta,
'axá maxákəm.⁵⁷⁵
Pa'iipáa tsakyíw 'ím áarək
 uuváak athúm.⁵⁷⁶

They went on;
there was a whirlpool over there,
and they reached it, they say.
A Mojave rattler was going along
 heading south, they say,
under the water.
It wanted to bite someone.

Kumastamxóts atháwək a'ét.	*Kumastamxó caught it, they say.*
Kumastamxóts atháwk.	*Kumastamxó caught it.*
Pa'iipáa lyavíi lya'ém 'ím,	*Not wanting it to resemble a person,*
Kumastamxóts 'aavénya eethóo ootsmóq a'ét.	*Kumastamxó pulled out the snake's teeth, they say.*
Ootsmóqək a'ét.	*He pulled them out, they say.*

***577 ***

'Avíi Kwalyaatátt a'íim siivám,578	*(The place) called 'Avíi Kwalyaatátt was over there,*
nyáasi,	*over there,*
nyáasi apám nyiitíivəntik a'ét.	*and they got there and there they were, they say.*
Kumastamxóts Yaavapáay nyiikanáavək,579	*Kumastamxó said to the Yavapais*
Yaavapáay nyatsuuváy a'ím.580	*that the Yavapais would live there.*
'Axánya aatsxuukyíts a'íinyək,581	*They were going to cross the river,*
nyiis'ílyk 'et.	*but he forbade them, they say.*
'Axám áam 'ím aatsuuxáyəmək.582	*They did not know how to swim.*
Avoonóonyək,	*There they were,*
aatsxuukyítsk 'et.	*and they went across, they say.*
'Atsaayúu,	*Well,*
kwalyiináaw kwalxó alyatíivək,583	*they were in a boat made of tules,*
'axá aatsxuukyítsk a'et.584	*and they went across the water, they say.*

Kumastamxóts awíim.	*Kumastamxó did it.*
Kumastamxóts ta'aanyáayəm;	*Kumastamxó made a light;*
'avíi 'amáy amánk athúuk 'et.	*it came from a high mountain, they say.*
'Avíi Kwalyaatátt.585	*'Avíi Kwalyaatátt.*
Aaxkyéenyənyts tiinyáamk 'et.586	*The other side was dark, they say.*

Kumastamxóts pa'iipáa nyii'íim,	*Kumastamxó said to the people,*
"Pa'iipáa máanyts ma'uuxúuttəm,	*"You are good people,*
ma'uuxúuttəm athúm,	*you are good, and so,*
'amátt 'axótt makyí avám,	*there is a good place somewhere,*
nyáanyi moonóoxá.587	*and that is where you will be.*

Vi'aayáak,
av'uu'átsk vi'aayáak,
'avíi 'alméets suuvám,
nyáany 'aatsuukúlyxa.
Nyáasəm,
'atsaayúu tsáaməly
  nyiinyuukanáavək,
nyiinyoo'éeyk,
'awéxá.
Nyáanyi,
'amáysi,
'atsmayúuxa.
Mattatsáaməly thomayúuvəxá,"⁵⁸⁸
a'ét.

Vuu'átsəny aatsuumpápk,
athúntik,
pa'iipáanyts aatuuqwíirək a'ét.
"Vathány 'anyaváts.
Vathány 'anyamátt-ts.⁵⁸⁹
Nyáava 'Avíi Kwa'amée a'íim
  ashéts.
Nyáavi,
'avá kwatiinyáam nyiivák
  'axóttəxa,"⁵⁹⁰
a'ét.

'Apénəny a'íim,
"Kayáak
'ax'áa 'avoolypó kakamíim!"
Maníish Aa'ár uu'ítsənyts,⁵⁹¹
mattaxwélyk aatsuumpápk,
akúpk nyiitháaw.
Kwaatúuly,
Kwaatúulyts 'eethóonya kamíim
  'et.⁵⁹²
Tsamathúly 'Axwétt shaly'áy
  kamíim,

We will go,
we will go walking,
there is a high mountain over there,
and we will climb it.
Over there,
I will tell you everything,

I will teach you,
I will do it.
At that time,
over there in the high place,
you will see things.
Everything will be clear,"
he said.

He took four steps,
he did it again,
and the people followed him, they say.
"This is my house.
This is my land.
This is what they named 'Avíi
  Kwa'amée (High Mountain).
Right here,
it will be good for the dark house
  to be here,"
he said.

He said to Beaver,
"Go
and bring cottonwood houseposts!"
The one called Ant-lion,
he dug in the ground in four places,
and there were four holes.
As for Chuckwalla,
Chuckwalla brought willow, they
  say.
Red Ant brought sand,

'amáy nyiitsáatsk 'et.	*and he put it on top, they say.*
'Amáy nyiitsáatsk.	*He put it on top.*

Kumastamxó nyiioo'éeyətsnya matxá 'anyáa kwaaxwíir nyiitsáam,[593]	*Kumastamxó positioned the learners at the northeast corner,*
kwas'eethée kwa'uuxúuttənya kavéely 'anyáaxáap kwaaxwíirəny nyiitsáantik,[594]	*he positioned the good doctors at the southwest corner,*
pa'iipáa koopóoyəny[595] kavéely 'anyáavi kwaaxwíirnyi awíntik,	*and he did it again with the dead people in the southeast corner,*
nyáasi aayémk athutyá nyaaoopóoyk.	*(because) they go that way when they die.*

'Avuuyáanyənyts matxávik avát,	*There was a door on the north (side),*
Kumastamxóts pa'iipáa tsooqwér 'atsláytsənya nyiitsanáak,[596]	*and Kumastamxó made the people whose speeches were bad sit there,*
makyík mattatháw aly'ém 'ím,[597]	*so that they would not witch anyone,*
matt-ta'aaláay aly'ém 'ím.[598]	*and so that they would not ruin each other.*
Kumastamxóts iiwáamtan awíim 'ítya.	*Kumastamxó himself did that, they say.*

'Atsaayúu,	*The things,*
'atsiiráav pa'iipáa ootséevənya,	*the sicknesses that people could cure,*
'axótt 'ím,	*so that they were all right,*
nyaayúu,	*well,*
nyaanyiiáayk 'et.	*he gave them these, they say.*
Kumastamxóts a'íim,[599]	*Kumastamxó said,*
" 'Anyáats nyiinyavasháwk.	*"I (would like to) take care of you.*
Nyiinyavasháwk.	*I (would like to) take care of you.*
Nyáavi nyiinyaatsoonóoy xalyavíita.	*I might abandon you here.*
Athótsáa,	*However,*
pa'iipáats 'atáyk athúm,	*there are many people, and so,*
tsaváamk	*it is unlikely*
'atsmuuxáyúm.	*that you would learn things.*
Muuxáyəm matháavəxa.	*It would be difficult for you to learn.*
Vaathótəm athúm,	*This is how it is, and so,*

nyiinya'íim
matta'áar maatspáatsxá."
Nyaa'íim,
mattáar nyiitsatspáatsk 'éta.⁶⁰⁰

I say to you
that you should go outside."
Then,
he sent them outside, they say.

***601

Kumastamxóts
xamashé vatáy atséwk,
nyiiaatsooyóoyk a'ét,⁶⁰²
kwatiinyáamənyəm.⁶⁰³
"Vathám 'oonyénya kayúuk,
vathám manyavá kayúuk
kwatiinyáamtánəm.
Xamshé vatáyts.
Vathány xamashé vatáyts.
Katháwk,
katháwk vikawáak
'atsaayúu muuyúuxanyts
  nyaanyaakwéevəm."

***

Kumastamxó
made a big star,
and he showed it to them, they say,
in the dark.
"With this, see the road,
with this, see your house
in the dark.
It's a big star.
This is a big star.
Take it,
take it along with you
when you are unable to see things."

Piipáa —
Kumstamxóts
pa'iipáa kwas'itthítsnya
  'ashíintəm nyiiqáast.⁶⁰⁴

People —
Kumastamxó
summoned each of the doctor
  people.

***605

Nyiioo'éeyəm
piipáa tapúyxa
shamáts tsuumpápəm.

***

He taught them
how to kill a person
in four nights.

***606

Kumastamxóts piipáa tsáaməly
  nyiiqáask,
'avá kwatiinyáam
  alyaakxávəm'áshk 'et.⁶⁰⁷
Nyaawíim,
'atsaayúu tsáaməly aamáttk 'et.

***

Kumastamxó summoned all the
  people,
and he took them into the dark
  house once again, they say.
Then,
he covered everything, they say.

Tiinyáam.	It was dark.
Tsáaməly aashmátsk 'et.	Everyone went to sleep, they say.
Nyaawíim,	Then,
'amáyəly axávək ayérk veeyémk,	he went flying up into the sky,
piipáanyts makyí uuváam ooyóov aly'émək 'et.⁶⁰⁸	and the people could not see where he was, they say.
'Avá kwatiinyáaməly alyaxávəntík 'et.	He went back into the dark house, they say.

***⁶⁰⁹   ***

Nyáanyily uuvám ooyóovək 'et.⁶¹⁰	They saw him in there, they say.
Nyaamák,	After that,
'anyáanyányts,	the sun,
xaly'ányányts,	the moon,
xamashényányts,	and the stars
nyuupáyts.	were gone.
Kwashtuumátsənyts kathóly aaly'étk avoonóot.	The (people) who were sleeping did not know what to do.
Marxókavék⁶¹¹	Marxókavék
shoopóow aly'émtək 'ét,⁶¹²	did not know, they say,
kaawíts 'anyáay ootséwxanya,	how to make light or whatever,
ta'aanyáayxanya.	how to light things up.
Nyáany shamathíik.	He didn't know these (things).
Awéxaym,	So, right away,
kúur nyaa'étəm,	after a short time,
piipáa 'ashéntits xamshé kavatáyənya kamémt.	one person brought out the morning star.
Nyaathúum,	Then,
'anyáayk viitháwət,	it was light,
mattatsáaməly 'anyáayk 'amáttnyi.	everything was light on the earth.

Nyaathúum,⁶¹³	Then,
Kumastamxó,	as for Kumastamxó,
'atsaayúu 'amáy kwatháwənya,⁶¹⁴	as for the things that were up in the sky,
atháwk,	he took them,

veewém.
Aayáak,
ooyóovxaym,
'avá kwatiinyáam alyavák uuvát⁶¹⁵
'anyáanya ta'úlyk.

Nyáava awíim:
piipáanya iiwáanyts oopóoyək,⁶¹⁶
nyaamák,
nyiiwík a'ím,
kanáavək awét.

Kumastamxó
'atsaayúu 'ax'áa awéxaym,⁶¹⁷
nyaanyi av'óowk,
'avá kwatiinyáam atóly av'óowk.

Shamáany aatskyíttk 'et.
Alyathúutsk aatskyíttk.

Nyáava nyaawíim,
'anyaaxáapk apámk.

"Makyéts vathány máarək?"
'ét.
" 'Anyétsəts,"
a'ét.
Kwatsáanənyts uu'íitsk.
" 'Atsaayúu malyxó nyáanyi nyam'aakwíintsəxá.⁶¹⁹
Nyáanyənyts aauukwíly uu'its athúum."⁶²⁰
'Atsaayúu kaawíts aauukwíly nyaa'íim.⁶²¹
Nyáanyts atspáatsk.

he took them away with him.
They went along,
and they saw him,
he was sitting in the dark house

holding the sun in his hand.

This is what he did:
he frightened the people,

and after that,
he wanted to help them,
and he explained (things) to them.

Kumastamxó
did something to a cottonwood,
(so that) it grew there,
(so that) it grew in the middle of the dark house.

He cut the roots, they say.
He cut them using his power of thought.⁶¹⁸

When he did this,
(the cottonwood) fell towards the west.

"Who wants this?"
he said.
"We (do),"
they said.
The Quechans said it.
"We will wrap it in those feathers and things.
That is what is called the feathered staff."
Whatever thing (it was) is called the feathered staff.
Those (people) went out.

Kumastamxóts piipáa nyii'íim,	Kumastamxó said to the people,
"Mat'árvək!	"Outside!
Mat'árəly kaayémk!"	Go outside!"

Piipáa Kwatsáan 'ashéntəts,	There was one Quechan person,
'atsaayúu *Diegueño* a'ét,	and someone called a Diegueño,
nyáanyənyts,	that one,
'atsaayúu 'íim —	he is called something else now —
Kamayáats.	Kamia.
Nyáanyts xuuvíkəly uupúuvək,	Those two went in,
'avály uupúuvək,	they went into the house,
nyaawíim,	and then,
nyiioo'éeyk 'etá,	he taught them, they say,
'atsaayúu,	well,
'avá,	about the house,
'avá àree'óoy,	about the fiesta house,
'avá Kara'úk.	about the Kar'úk house.[622]

'Atsaayúu,	Well,
piipáa Kwatsáannya,	the Quechan person,
Paamavíts a'íim amúly,	he was named Paamavíts,
nyáanya nyiishíit av'áarkityá,[623]	and that is what they always name (his descendants),
'iipáa.	the man's.
'Aatskóoytsəts,	The old women,
nyáanyts Maavé a'ím uumúulyək.	they are named Maavé.

'Aayúu,	Well,
'ax'áats nyiiríish a'ím,	there were no cottonwoods,
'eethóots nyiiríish a'ím,	there were no willows,
'atsaayúuts makyí avám[624]	there was nothing anywhere
'oowéxats athúulya'émt;	for them to use;[625]
aaíimk,	(but) they did it anyway;
iiwáam atséwkm.[626]	they made it themselves.
'Avá matkyáaly atséwk,	They made a ramada,
avoonóoxaym,	and while they were doing it,
piipáanyts mat'ár oov'ótsk,	the people were standing outside,
xítsək a'ím,	they were lined up,

'anyáavi shathómpək,
ooyóovək.

Kumastamxóts a'íim,
"Nyamáam,
aavíirək,"
a'ét.

Piipáanyts láw a'ím ooyóovək,

ooyóovxaym,
'aványənyts 'ashéntik nyiivá
  lya'émk,
'aványts xavík nyiitháwk 'ét.
'Ashénti Kwatsáan nyiiwéeyk,
'ashénti Kamayáa nyiiwéeyk.[627]

Kumastamxóts nyiiuutsáam.
Kwa'aapáts avoonóom,
nyáany nyiishtúum,
Kamayáa nyavály aakxávək.[628]

Nyiioo'éeyk 'et.
Nyaayúu,
nyáany kwalyvíinya iiwáam
  uutsáaw a'ím.
Kwa'aapányənyts aayáak,[629]
pa'iipáany —
iiwáam pa'iipáanya
  nyiiuukanáavək 'et.
Nyiioo'éeyk.

Kumastamxóts a'íim,
"Pa'iipáa nyiikwanáam
  matsanályxa.
Nyaamatsanályəm,
vathány,
'avá vathíly moonóok,

*they were facing east,
and they were looking.*

*Kumastamxó said,
"That's all,
it's finished,"
he said.*

*The people turned their heads
  quickly and looked,
they looked, and suddenly,
there wasn't (just) one house
  there,
there were two houses, they say.
He had done one for the Quechans,
and he had done one for the
  Kamias.*

*Kumastamxó led them.
The Cocopas were around,
and he gathered them,
and he took them into the Kamias'
  house.*

*He taught them, they say.
Well,
he wanted them to make one like
  that for themselves.
The Cocopas went,
and as for the people —
they themselves explained it to
  people, they say.
They taught them.*

*Kumastamxó said,
"You will lose an important
  person.
When you lose him,
this (person),
you will go in this house,*

maatsuupílyxa.630	and you will honor him.
Muuthúutsxá631	That's what you'll do
vanyaayémǝm."	when he is gone."

***632

Nyamáam,	Finally,
tiinyáam.	it was dark.
Kumastamxóts,	Kumastamxó,
avány,	(he said it) to that one,
Ampótt Aasáarǝk Kwatiinyáam a'íim:	he said it to He Spills Dust at Night:
nyáany,	those (speeches),
tsooqwéra viikwatháwǝnya,	the speeches that were there,
nyáanyts vasháwǝxa,	he was the one who would take care of them,
a'íim.	he said.
Kumastamxóts 'atsaayúu shaavár 'atáytanǝm áayk.	Kumastamxó gave him many songs and things.
Nyaawíim,	Then,
Kumastamxóts kwatiinyáamnyǝm awíim 'anyáayk viitháwǝt.	Kumastamxó did something with the darkness and it became light.

Shoopóowk 'étǝma.	He knew, they say.
'Atsaayúu,	Well,
piipáa kwashíintǝnyts,	each person,
Kwatsáan kwashíintǝnyts kaawém 'atsawíi nyaa'íim,633	each Quechan intended to do things somehow,
nyaa'íim,	and so,
piipáa kwashíintǝny nyuukanáam,	he told each person,
"Máanyts mashoopóowk mathútya makyípa nyiimaaxwélyk mathúum makyík mamánk mathúum.	"You know which (tribe) you belong to and where you come from.
Nyáanya mashoopóowk.	You know that.
Nyáava miiwáanyts nyeepétt aly'émú,"	This (is something) you must not forget,"
a'ét.	he said.
"Miiwáanyts nyeepéttxaym,	"If you were to forget it,

muutar'úyk makyíly mawémxanya athúulya'emxa."	you wouldn't go to the right place."[634]
Piipáa alykwatanáknya a'íim — nyaaqásəm, 'avá kwatiinyáam alyaxávək, Kumastamxóts a'íim, "Avathúum: Xavatsáats 'akútsk,[635] xiipúk atspáam, nyáanya Xavatsáats 'íim 'ashék.[636] Athóxaym, Xavatsáatsənyts veeyémtəm athúm,[637] nyáany a'íim Xaanyé a'éxa. Mavatstsáanya tsáaməly nyáanya mashéxa."	He said to the leader — when he summoned him and he entered the dark house, Kumastamxó said, "It happened like this: Xavatsáats is eldest, she was born first, and I named her Xavatsáats. However, Xavatsáats left, and so, that's what she is called, she will be called Xaanyé (Frog). That is what you will name all your daughters."
Nyaa'íim, Pàxiipáats a'íim aqásk, nyáanya, nyiiootséts atséwəntík.	Then, he summoned Paxiipáats, that (person), and he made the (people) that he led.
"Mavatstsáats voonóom, nyáany Xiipáa ma'éxa, nyiimashíit." Mapísa, Xatalwénya, nyáany nyaalyavíim,[638] xatalwíik a'ét.	"When you have daughters, you will call them Xiipáa, you will name them (that)." Nowadays, he is Coyote, and when he acts like that, he is being like a coyote, they say.
Piipáa Kwalya'óots nyáany ashék,[639] Lya'óots a'íim. Nyáanyts 'aayúu a'íim a'et. Oov'óowəny. 'Akwé kamán,[640]	He named that person Piipáa Kwalya'óots, she is called Lya'óots. That means something, they say. Rain. That which comes from the clouds,

nyáany a'íim.	that's what it means.
Mapísa ashék 'ítya,	If they were to name her nowadays,
'Akwíik a'íim.⁶⁴¹	she would be called 'Akwíik (It Is Cloudy).
Paamaavíts a'íim;	(Another person) is called Paamavíts;
'atsaayúu 'aavé taaxán a'íim,	that means rattlesnake or something,
nyáanya.	that (name).
Paa Maavéts a'ím.	He is called Paa Maavéts 'Snake Person'.
Nyáanya,	That name,
'aavé taaxánəny nyaanyiimánk a'íim.⁶⁴²	it comes from that (word for) rattlesnake.
'Aavé amúlyk.	He is named Snake.
Piipáa alykwaaéevəntiny,	The next person,
nyáany Shakwapáas a'íim ashék,⁶⁴³	he named that one Shakwapáas,
ooshéeyk 'et.	he named him after (the red ant), they say.
Nyáanya,	That (name),
Tsamathúly Kwa'axwétta,	Red Ant,
nyáany a'íim.	that's what it means.
✴✴✴⁶⁴⁴	✴✴✴
Piipáantinya,	Another person,
nyáanya,	that one,
Matt'á a'ím ashék.⁶⁴⁵	he named him Mat'á.
Mapísa,	Nowadays,
nyaa'íim,	when they say it,
talypó uuítsəny.⁶⁴⁶	what they say is talypó (roadrunner).
'Atsaayúu,	Well,
Nyáanyi kamánk a'ét.⁶⁴⁷	that's where it comes from, they say.
Mat'á uu'ítsnya,	The one they call Mat'á,
Kumastamxóts amúly áayk 'éta,	Kumastamxó gave him his name, they say,
nyáany,	that one,
nyaavéshəm ayúuk.	when he saw him run.

Alyaaéevəntik siiv'óowm;⁶⁴⁸   (Another person) was next, standing over there;

nyáany,   and as for that one,
Alymúush a'íik 'eta.   he was called Alymúush (Screwbean), they say.

Nyiiv'óowəntim,   (Another one) was standing there too,
nyáanya,   and that one,
'atsaayúu,   well,
'Aqwáaq Nyatsaqwély uu'ítsnya,   he is the one they call Deerhide,
nyáanyi kamánk;   that's what (the name) comes from;
Shànykwa'áaly a'ím amúlyk.   he named him Shanykwa'áaly.

Nyiiv'óowəntim,   Another one was standing there too,
'atsaayúu 'ats'iipáyts siiv'óowm,   something like an insect was standing over there,

nyáany,   and as for that one,
'Astamuuxán a'íim ashék 'et.⁶⁴⁹   he named him 'Astamuuxán, they say.

Nyiiv'óowəntim a'ím,   (Another person) was standing there too, and so,

nyiiv'óowəntinyək aakxávət.   he was standing there too and he came in.

Kumastamxóts anák,⁶⁵⁰   Kumastamxó sat down,
alynyiithúutsk,   and he thought about it,
'atsaayúu a'íim 'itya.   and he said something, they say.
Kwashkyúu,   Kwashkyúu,
Kwashkuu,   (or) Kwashkuu,
nyáany a'éta.   that's what he was called.
Eethóony aashkwáaly 'axály katsáam,⁶⁵¹   (It means) put willow bark in water,
'anyáa shaaxúukəm,⁶⁵²   (for) ten days;
nyáany shamaxályək.⁶⁵³   that (is how) they soak it.

Piipáa viikwathíintínya,⁶⁵⁴   To the next person who came along,
Kumastamxóts a'íim,   Kumastamxó said,
"Xalypótt.   "Xalypótt.
Mavatsíiny maqásk,   (When) you summon your daughter,

nyáany ma'éxa."655
Xalypótt a'íim.
'Atsaayúu,
'aayúu 'anykór awíim,
aavíirək a'íim.

Piipáa 'ashéntəntíts avéshk
    viithíik nyiiv'óowk 'etá.656
"Nyam'ataxakyéevám?"
a'íik 'et.
"Kaváarək.
'Anyáats piipáa mootsétsnya
    Xakshíi 'a'étxa."657
'Atsaayúu 'ím 'íikəta,
'amáttənyts 'avérək a'ím.

Kumastamxó nyaa'íntik a'ím,
'atsaayúu 'avíi nyaa'étk,

'atsxavashúu nyaa'ét,658
a'íim oonóok,
nyáany nyiishíitk,
amúly nyiiáayk 'et.
Shiimúly.

Kumastamxóts piipáa
    kwashíintəny 'atsaayúu
    'axnáaly nyiiáayk 'et.
Nyaany awíim,
uutápənya oo'éeyk.

Awíim,
aashtuuváarxaym,
'atsiimátsk avoonóok 'et.

'Anyáavik,
'Avá 'anyáavik oov'ótsk 'ét,660

that's what you will say."
He said Xalypótt.
Well,
(it means) something is already done,
it means it is finished.

Another person came running and
    stood there, they say.
"Am I too late?"
he said, they say.
"No.
I shall call the people you lead
    Xakshíi."
That means something, they say,
it means hard ground.

Kumastamxó did it again,
he said (the names of) rocks and
    things,
he said (the names of) green plants,
he went on saying it,
and when he named them,
he gave them first names, they say.
And their clan names.

Kumastamxó gave each person a
    gourd rattle or something, they
    say.
That's what he did,
and he taught them the art of
    *throwing the gourd.*659
Then,
they sang, and right away,
(the others) were dancing, they say.

On the east,
they stood on the east (side) of the
    house, they say,

xáam kuuthútsənyts,
piipáa uushíitənyts.
'Aváatóly,
Kwaatsáanənyts matxávik
    oov'ótsk 'eta.
Kamayáanyənyts 'anyaaxáapk
    oov'ótsk,
Kwa'aapányənyts kavéely oov'ótsk,
Xattpáa 'Anyáats 'anyáavik oov'ótsk.
Kumastamxóts Xawáalyapáayəny
    a'íim,
'Axaxavashuupáayəny a'ím,
"Kaayémk,
matxávi 'anyáavi kaayémk!"
nyaa'íntik 'ím,
"Tsamawéevanyts nyáavi
    matxávik 'anyaaxáapk
    kaayémk kaayáak!" 'et.[661]
Kawíiya uu'ítsnya,
    ***[662]
"Nyáanyi 'anyaaxáapk
    kashathómpk kaayáak!"
Nyaa'íim,
nyiikamáanəny a'íik 'eta.
"Mátsa,
pa'iipáa nyáanyəm kavéely
    maayémxa.[663]
'Awétəm athúm,
nyáanyiimánk,[664]
'anyép alynyiimuuthúutsəxa,[665]
makyí nyamanyaváyk
    alymoonóom.[666]
Nyáava 'a'ím.
Piipáa kwanymé 'athúu 'a'ím
    vi'av'óowk."

Xamakxáaváts 'ashéntik,

the different ones,
the people of various clans.
In the middle of the house,
the Quechans stood on the north,
    they say.
The Kamias stood on the west,

the Cocopas stood in the south,
and the Maricopas stood in the east.
Kumastamxó said to the
    Hualapais,
and to the Havasupais,
"Go,
go to the northeast!"
and he also said,
"Chemehuevis go here to the
    northeast!" he said.

To the ones called Cahuillas he said,
***
"Head to the west there and go!"

Then,
he spoke to the others, they say.
"As for you,
you will go south with these
    people.
I do this, and so,
from now on,
you must think about me,
wherever you live.

This is what I say.
I am going to turn into a different
    person."

The Mojaves were the only ones

nyáanyi Kumastamxó
nyiivoo'óowənya nyáany
oov'ótsapatk.⁶⁶⁷
Xuumáar eekwévəts athúum,
vuu'átsk vaayáa athúulya'émtək
kwalyavíit.⁶⁶⁸

Marxókavékts Kwatsáan awíim,
Kamayáa awíim:
nyáanya veetsawém,
xiipúk veetsawém.
Nyaamák,
Kwa'aapáts athúum.
Xattpáa 'Anyáats vaayáatənti:
'anyáavi shathómpk vaayáak,⁶⁶⁹
shaly'áy aatsxuukyítsk,
'aayúu,
'avíi 'atáyts avatháwm,
nyáany aatsxuukyítsk.
Kwatsáants athúum
Diegueño 'et —
'atsaayúu a'ím 'ityá —
Kamayáa —
nyáanyts avaayáak,
'Avíi 'Avérá apámk 'et.⁶⁷⁰

Nyaapám,⁶⁷²
'atsaayúu,
'anyáavi kwaatsénənyts,⁶⁷³

'avíim kwaatsénənyts.

'Atsaayúu,
'a'íits nyoov'ótsk athúum athútya.
Nyáanyi anáak athúm.
Arii'óoy tsavóowk avoonóok.
Avoonóoxaym,
Kwa'aapányənyts apámk 'et.

*that stayed in the same place as
   Kumastamxó.*

*They were very young, and so,
they couldn't walk (yet), so it
   seemed.*

*Marxókavék did the Quechans
and he did the Kamias:
he took them away,
he took them away first.
After that,
it was the Cocopas.
The Maricopas went along too:
they went along heading east,
and they crossed the desert,
well,
there were many mountains,
and they crossed these.
It was the Quechans
and the Diegueños —
they call them something (else) —
Kamias —
they went along,
and they got to 'Avíi 'Avérá (Hard
   Mountain), they say.*⁶⁷¹

*They got there,
well,
the ones who descended on the
   east (did),
the ones who descended the
   mountain (did).
Well,
trees were growing there.
They stopped there.
They were holding a fiesta.
There they were, and all of a sudden,
the Cocopas got there, they say.*

Kumastamxóts nyáany áar aly'émk 'eta.⁶⁷⁴	*Kumastamxó didn't want that, they say.*
Matanyúuv nyaa'íim,	*They were going to fight,*
áar aly'ém.	*and he didn't want that.*
'Etəsáa,	*However,*
'atsaayúu nyiikyáam oonóok 'eta.	*they went about shooting things, they say.*
Kwatsáan nyiiwíim,	*They did it to the Quechans,*
Kamayáa nyiiwíim.	*and they did it to the Kamias.*
Xattpáa 'Anyáats	*The Maricopas*
Kwa'aapánya aakyéevək;	*were side by side with the Cocopas;*
oov'ótsk,	*they stood there,*
awínypatk oov'ótsk.	*and they did it too, standing there.*
Kumastamxóts 'aayúu matxá aspér atséwk 'ét.⁶⁷⁵	*Kumastamxó made a strong wind or something, they say.*
Awéxaym,	*He did, and right away,*
nyaakwévək 'eta.	*it was no good, they say.*
'Anóqəm,	*It was just a little,*
'atsaayúu 'anóqts— oov'óowts 'anóq.	*a little thing— the rain was little.*
Aasáarək 'et.	*He sprinkled it, they say.*
Awéxayk,	*He did, and right away,*
nyaa'íim,	*he said,*
" 'Anyáats 'atkavék,	*"I am going back.*
'Avíi Kwa'amée aly'ayémxa."	*I will go to 'Avíi Kwa'amée."*
Nyaa'íim,	*Then,*
Marxókavék nyáany a'íim,⁶⁷⁶	*he said that to Marxókavék,*
aatooqwérət.	*and (Marxókavék) followed him.*
'Avíi Kwa'améeny aváam nyaatsémk,	*When he had almost reached 'Avíi Kwa'amée,*
Marxókavékts 'atsarávək 'et.	*Marxókavék got sick, they say.*
Piipáanyənyts atháwk,	*The people took him,*
viiwáanyək,	*and they went along,*
'axányi kamémk 'eta,⁶⁷⁷	*and they brought him to the water, they say,*
wanymooyétstəm kwathútsəny.	*because they liked him.*

Yuma,	Yuma,
mapísa *Yuma* uu'ítsənya.	the place they call Yuma nowadays.
'Axányənyts aráwtánk 'et.⁶⁷⁸	The water was very swift there, they say.
Athótəm athúm,	It was, and so,
xookyéev 'íny nyeekwéevək a'ét.⁶⁷⁹	their attempt to cross was no good, they say.
Kumastamxóts nyiiv'óowk ayúuk av'óowk 'etá.	Kumastamxó stood there watching, they say.
Matháavəm ooyóovək,	He saw that it was difficult,
vanyaawíim:	and he did this:
'axány tatsénk 'eta.	he made the water go down, they say.
Nyaawíim,	Then,
pa'iipáa Marxókavék apáyk viiwáak 'eta.⁶⁸⁰	the people went along carrying Marxókavék, they say.
Aatsxuukyítsk,⁶⁸¹	They went across,
'Avíi 'Avoolypó nyaaváamk.⁶⁸²	and they got to 'Avíi 'Avoolypó (Housepost Mountain).
Marxókavékts a'íim,⁶⁸³	Marxókavék said,
" Vathány 'iiwáam 'anyamátt-ts athútya.⁶⁸⁴	"This is our own land.
Nyáavi 'anytsuuváayəxa.	We shall live here.
'Iimáattəny katapómk	Burn my body
'avíi vikavátsnya,"	at the mountain that is here,"
nyaa'íim,	he said,
apúyk 'eta.	and he died, they say.
Tsakwshányənyts avík shathómpk,	His head was facing in that (direction),
kavéely shathómpk.	it was facing the south.
Nyáanyəm ootanyék 'et,	That's where they cremated him, they say,
nyáanyi⁶⁸⁵	there,
'avíiny.	(at) the mountain.
'Amó Kwata'órv uu'íts athúuk 'et.⁶⁸⁶	It is 'Amó Kwata'órv (Cumulus Clouds on Top), they say.⁶⁸⁷
'A'áw Aráak Aakyáam.	(Or) 'A'áw Aráak Aakyáam (Blazing Fire Encircles It).

Nyáany 'avíinyts avatháw alyaskyíik 'axwéttk 'eta, 'atsaayúu, kwaráa nyiimánəm.	There are still rocks there, and they are red, they say, well, because of the flames.[688]
Piipáanyts matsats'íim nyiixúu 'et. "Áa! Apúyk! Apúyk!" 'et. Nyáanyəm, Kukwiimáatt a'íim, Kumastamxó a'íim, nyáanyəm Marxókavék nyaa'íntik.[689]	The people wept and made a ruckus. "Ah! He is dead! He is dead!" they said. With that, they meant Kukwiimáatt, and they meant Kumastamxó, and with that they meant Marxókavék too.
Piipáanyənyts Marxókavék ootanyék 'et, 'avíi 'amáynyi. Kwatsáants nyáasily aayémk. Marxókavékts aatsooyóoyəm[690] 'atsaayúu nyiikwanáam awítsk 'et.[691] Nyaany nyiioo'éeyt. Nyiiuukanáavtank aavíirk awitya, nyuu'íits.	The people cremated Marxókavék, they say, at the top of the mountain. Quechans go over there. Marxókavék shows them how to do great things, they say. That's what he teaches them. He really tells them everything,[692] they say that.
'Iitspátsəts vathány 'avíiny aatsuukúulytiyum. 'Anyáa tsuumpápəm vaayáak,[693] 'amáyk kayáamk, 'amáy alyapámk, 'amáy nyáanyi, 'aayúu, shamáts ooyóovək 'et. Shamáak ooyóovək mattapéek, Marxókavékts nyii'íik 'eta.[694]	Men have always climbed this, the mountain. They go on for four days, they head towards the top, they reach the top, and there at the top, well, they see dreams, they say. They dream and see many things, and Marxókavék says (something) to them, they say.
"Kaawíts máarək?" nyaa'íim,	"What do you want?" he says,

awíi kwa'átsk 'et:	and he does just as he is supposed to:
nyiiáayk.	he gives it to them.
Pa'iipáa kwas'eethéets 'atáyk[695]	Many doctor people
nyáasi aayém av'áarkitya,	go over there, they say,
'Avíi Kwa'amée uu'ítsnya.	(to) what is called 'Avíi Kwa'amée.
Nyáanyəm,	By (doing) that,
'atsvée — Kumastamxó ooyóov 'ím.	they intend to see whoever it is— Kumastamxó.
Shamáts tsuumpápəm aayáanyk apámk athútya.	They go on for four days, until they get there.
Shaavár makyík nyiiáay lya'émk,	He never gives them songs,
nyiioo'éey lya'émk 'et,	he didn't teach songs, they say,
'Amó Kwata'órəv.[696]	(at)'Amó Kwata'órv.

Kumastamxóts a'ím,	Kumastamxó said,
"Nyaanymáam,[697]	"That's all,
aavíirək,"	it is finished,"
a'íik 'et.	he said, they say.
Nyáanyi av'óowk,	He stood there,
alynyiithúutsk,	and he thought,
" 'Amátt aly'axávxa,"[698]	"I will go into the earth,"
a'íim,	and he said,
nyáany a'íim;	that's what he said;
aatsuumpápk 'eta:[699]	he (said) it four times:

" 'Amátt aly'axávək,	"I am going into the earth,
aly'axávək,	I'm going into it,
aly'axávək.	I'm going into it.
'Aayúu 'amátt nyaakuupáyk,	(This) thing is entirely earth,
nyáany 'ashéntəm 'ayúuxa.	that's the one (thing) I will see.
Nyáany 'ashéntəm 'ayúuxa.	That's the one (thing) I will see.
Nyáany aly'axávək,	That's what I'm going into,
'atsaayúu 'axá nyamooyémǝny,	the path of the river,
arúv nyam'ayém,	I will go along where it is dry,
maxáktan 'axávəxá,"	I will go into the area below,"
a'íim,	he said,
aashváarək.	he sang it.

Xiipúktank,	The first time,
vathány aashváarəm,	this is what he sang,
eeméts 'amátt alyaxávək,	and his feet went down into the earth,
a'ét.	they say.
Nyaa'íntim,	When he sang it again,
miisíly aváamk,	it came up to his thighs,[700]
nyáanyily 'amátt alyaxávək 'et.	and he went into the earth there, they say.
Nyaathúntim,	When he did it again,
nyaaxamókəm,[701]	the third time,
malyaqényənyts 'amátt axávək 'et.	his throat went into the earth, they say.
Nyaathúntik,	When he did it again,
nyáanyamáam,	that's all,
athúts aatsuumpápk athúm,	he did it four times, and so,
'amátt alyaxáv.	he went into the earth.
Makyík thomayúuv aly'ém.	He was not visible at all.
Nyáanyily,	In there,
'amátt alyavák uuváanyək	he went into the earth and stayed there
shamáts tsuumpápk 'et.	(for) four nights, they say.
Nyaathúum,	Then,
takavék atspákəntik 'et,	he came up again, they say,
nyaanyiiv'óowk.	and he stood there.
Nyaa'íim,	He said,
" 'Anyáats 'akúulyúm,"	"I am going to climb,"
a'íim,	he said,
iisháalyəny ootameramérək,	and he held his arms out straight,
oov'óowəny,	and he stood there,
aashváarək 'et.	and he sang, they say.
" 'Anyáats 'atáqshək,	"I jump,
'atáqshək,	I jump,
malyxóts,[702]	wing feathers,
'iimáatt malyxóts,	my body's wing feathers,
'iisháalynya malyxóts,	my hands' wing feathers,
'iimáatt malyxóts,"[703]	my body's wing feathers,"

a'íim,	he said,
aashváarək 'et.	he sang it, they say.
Nyaathúum,	Then,
ayérək viiyáatəsáa,	he went flying off, but
'axótt aly'émk,	he didn't do it well,
a'ét.	they say.
'Atsaayúu,	Well,
shaavárəny nyaa'íim aatsuumpápk,	when he sang the song he did it four times,
nyaawíim,	and then,
malyxónya awíim aatsuumpápk 'eta.	he spread his wings four times, they say.[704]
Ayér a'ím.	He wanted to fly.
" 'Anyáa,	"As for me,
'anyép ooshéeyk a'ím:	(this) is what they will name me:
'Ashpáa Kwanyíily 'a'éxa.	I will be called 'Ashpáa Kwanyíily (Black Eagle).
'Anyaaxáapk,	In the west
'Ashpáa Kwanyíily 'a'íim,[705]	I (will be) called Black Eagle,
'anyáavik,	and in the east
'Ashpáa 'Atsíi Kwatssáa,[706]	'Ashpáa 'Atsíi Kwatssáa (Fish-Eating Eagle),
kavéely,	and in the south
'Ashpáa Xamáaly."	'Ashpáa Xamáaly (White Eagle)."

PART IV:
THE MIGRATION OF THE YUMAN TRIBES

*Told in the Quechan Language
by George Bryant*

DOI: 10.11647/OBP.0037.04

The Migration of the Yuman Tribes

Kwatsáan uu'ítsənyts,	The ones called Quechan,
piipáats,	the people,
'anykór amánk athútya.	they began long ago.
'Atsaayúu,	Well,
matxávik,	from the north,
nyáanyəm vaathíik,[707]	they came from there,
makyík aathíik athútya.	they came from somewhere.
Athótəsáa,	However,
'axá sa'ílyts avathíkəm,	the ocean is there,
nyáany amákəly.	and it was beyond that.

Tsíin Nyatsamáatt-ts siitháwk athúuk 'et.	Asia is over there, they say.
Nyáasi kaathómk vanyoonóom,	They were doing whatever it was over there,
'axá sa'ílyənyts nyaaxatsóorəm,	and the ocean was frozen over,
athúm,	and so,
'atsaayúu,	well,
xanapáatsk viitháwəm,	there was ice,
athúm,	and so,
aatsxuukyítsk athúuk 'etəma.	they went across, they say.
Aatsxuukyítsk athúm,	They went across, and so,
nyaanyiimánk vaathíik athútya.[708]	they started there and came this way.
'Amátt ooyóovək vaathíik,	They saw land and they came this way,
aatsénk vaathíik,	they came down,
athúm,	and so,
kaa'íts	some of them
'anyáavik shathómp,	headed to the east,
kaa'íts 'amátt atóly shathómp,	and some of them headed to the middle of the continent,
'ís	but
'anyétsəts,	we (Yuman people),
va'aathíik athútya.	we came this way.
'Aatsénk av'aathíixaym,	We came down and headed this way, and right away,
'axá sa'ílyənyts avathík,[709]	the ocean was here,
iisháaly 'axáan avák,	it was on the right,
athúum,	and so,
'avíits athúum,	there were mountains,

iisháaly kwasár nyáanyik amánək athúm,	they rose up there on the left side, and so,
atsénək viithíik 'ítya.	they went up, they say.
'Atsaayúu,	Well,
'a'íits oov'ótstiyum.	there used to be trees there.
'Atsaayúu,	Well,
'amátt xatsúur alyoov'óts,	they grew in cold places,
nyáany,	those (trees),
nyáany ooyóovək	and (the people) saw them,
vaathíik	and they came this way,
vaathíik,	they came this way,
alyaatsénk.	they came down.
Aashmátsk,	They slept,
vaathíintik	and they came this way again,
aatsénk athúm,	they came down, and so,
'akórtan ayémǝm,	a really long time passed,
vaathíik athútya.	and they came this way.
Nyaathíim athúm,	They came, and so,
viithíik viithíik,	they came and came this way,
viithíik,	they came this way,
kaawíts? —	and what was it? —
'axá sa'ílyənyts 'amátt alyaxávək vaa'ée 'ím,	the salt water came into the land, like this,[710]
nyáany aamáarək,[711]	and it flooded that (land),
athúm,	and so,
nyáanyi apámk,	they got there,
nyáanyi atíivək 'et.	and they settled there, they say.
Nyaathúum,	Then,
vuu'átsəntík,	they traveled again,
avaathíik vaathíik athum,	they came and came this way, and so,
'atsaayúu,	well,
'amátt-ts matxávik avák,	there was a place in the north,
'avíits 'anyáavi amánk,	the mountains were in the east,
matxávik avák athúm,	and it was in the north,
nyáany.	that place.[712]
'Atsaayúuts athúuk 'etəma.	There was something there, they say.
'avíits shipshípk nyiiv'óowk 'eta.[713]	A sharp-pointed mountain was there, they say.

Va'aayáanyək,	As we went along,
'amáytants,	the very top,
'atsaayúu,	well,
'asáyk athúm,	it was foggy, and so,
nyáany aakwíinək,⁷¹⁴	it was wrapped in that (fog),
athúm,	and so,
'Asá Kwapáy a'ím ashét.	they named it 'Asá Kwapáy (Fog Bearer).⁷¹⁵
Nyaanyiimánək,	Starting then,
nyaanyiitíivək avatíiv,⁷¹⁶	they settled there,
nyakór ayém,	and a long time passed,
'axóttəm nyaayuuk,⁷¹⁷	and when they saw that it was all right,
avaathíintik 'etəma.	they came this way again, they say.
Avaathíintik,	They came this way again,
vaathíintik,	they came this way again,
nyáavi,	and at this point,
'atsaayúu,	well,
shaly'áyts mattapéek 'eta.⁷¹⁸	there was a lot of sand, they say.
'Amátt shaly'áyts athúm,	The land was sand,
nyáasi athík athúm,	there it was, over there, and so,
nyáany aatsxuukyítsk avaathíik.	they went across that (sand) and came this way.
Nyáany aatsxuukyítsk	They went across that (sand),
vanyaathíik,	and when they came this way,
'atsaayúu,	well,
apámantík 'ítya.	they got there, they say.
Vathí,	Here,
mapíistəm,	nowadays,
'atsaayúu,	well,
'avíi nyaanyiiv'óowm,	there is a mountain standing there,
nyáany avathík athum,	that's where it is, and so,
vatháts athútyá.	this is it.
'Axá viikwáamənyts,	The water that passes by here,
nyáanyts aviiyáak,	that (water) went along,
uuqáarək voonóonyək,	and it eroded (the earth), forming a canyon,⁷¹⁹
nyáany,	and as for that,

'amáy nyiitíivək 'et.	they settled up there, they say.
Nyáanyts nyatsuuváayk athútya.	They are the ones who live (there).

Piipáats 'atáytants athótk,[720]	There were people, a whole lot of them,
aaíim matt-takyéevək vaathíik 'etəma.[721]	and they happened to be together, they say.
Vaathíinyək,	They came this way, until
nyáanyi atíivək.	they settled there.
Aashmátsk athótk,[722]	They slept, and so,
nyatsuuváayk voonóom,	they were living there,
piipáanyts nyamáam,	and the people were coming to an end,
mattshatpótt a'ím vanyoonóom,	they were getting ready to split up,
avaayáak 'éta.	and they went along, they say.[723]
'Ís	However,
piipáats siitíivəntik 'éta.	there were people over there too, they say.
Siitíivəntik,	They were over there too,
nyáany,	and as for that,
nyáanya,	as for that,
avíly	into this (place),
kwaanáqily aatsénəxáym,	they went down into the valley,[724] and right away,
'axányənyts tama'órək vaa'íim,	water filled it up like this,
viitháwm,	and here they were,
aamáttk athúm,	and (water) covered everything, and so,
aamáttk athúm,	it covered everything, and so,
nyáany,	as for that,
ooyóovək avoonóok.	(the people) were looking around.
"Xaméra 'axóttíik," nyaa'ím,	"It might be better later on," they said,
"Aly'aatsénəntixá."	"We'll go down again (later)."
A'íi voonóok athúuk 'etəma.[725]	They went on saying that, they say.
Avathúum nyaathúum.	It was like that.
Nyikamáanənyts avaathíik 'eta.	The rest of them came this way, they say.
Oov'ótsxa.	They were going to stop.
Oov'ótsk,	They stopped,
avaathíik 'et.	and they came this way, they say.
Vuu'átstəntik,	They traveled again,
avaathíinyk,	they came this way,
avaathíiny,	they came this way,

nyáavi apák 'etəma.	and they got here, they say.
Nyáavi apák athúum,	They got here, and so,
'amátt nyáasi atíivənyək.	they stayed in that place over there.
Nyaasiitíivnyək,	They stayed over there,
'axáts asáttk vanyaayáam,	and the water started going down,
nyáanya,	and (at) that point,
alyaatsénəm 'ím.	they intended to go down into (the valley).
Xáam Kwaatsáan 'et.	They were Xáam Kwaatsáan (Those Who Descended by Means of Water), they say.
Kwatsáan nyii'íim,	They call them Quechan,
mapísa Kwatsáan a'étk,	nowadays they are called Quechan,
avathíkəm,	and here they are,
nyáanyəm,⁷²⁶	but at that (time),
Xáam Kwaatsáants athúuk 'etəma.⁷²⁷	they were Xáam Kwaatsáan, they say.
Vaathíik,	They came,
vaathíik,	and they came,
vaathíim,	they came this way,
nyáavi,	and at this point,
'axá kwaakwíinnya,	(at) a bend in the river,
matxávik amánk,	they started in the north,
aviithíinyək aváak,⁷²⁸	and they came until they got here,
nyáavi athúum.	it was right here.
Viiyáanyək,⁷²⁹	They went along,
akúulyəntik 'eta.⁷³⁰	and they went back up, they say.
Athúum,	So,
nyáavi,	at this point,
xaméra,	later on,
athúum,⁷³¹	it happened,
'akór alyayém,	a long time passed,
nyáanyi,	and at that point,
Xáam Kwaatsáants nyiiuu'íitst,	they called them Xáam Kwaatsáan,
nyáanya,	and that (valley),
nyáany nyatsuuváayk 'ítya.	that's where they lived, they say.
'Ís,	But,
vatháts,	these (people),
matxávik shathómpk vaayáak,⁷³²	they headed to the north and went along,
piipáa 'atáy alyaskyíits avathúm,	they were still a lot of people,
nyáanyi,	and at that point,

avaayáak vaayáany,	they went and went,
nyáasi,	and over there,
nyáasi atíivəntík 'eta.	they settled over there, they say.
'Amátt,	The place,
nyáasa,	that one over there,
matxávik avák,[733]	it was in the north,
'axányts atsénk viithíik.[734]	and the water was coming down and coming along.
'Axá kwaráawənyts —	The running water —
'Axá 'Axwétt,	'Axá 'Axwétt (Red Water, the Colorado River),
'Axá 'Axwétt a'ét,	it's called Red Water (the Colorado River),
nyáanya.	that (running water).
Nyáanya,	As for that,
mapísa xáak athúum,	nowadays it's different,
'atsaayúu,	(that) thing,
aapéttk,	they closed it off,
kaawémk avathót.[735]	they did it somehow.
Kwatsáants	The Quechans
saayáaxayk,[736]	went along, over there, until
nyaanyiitíivək 'eta.	they settled there, they say.
Vathík atíivəm,	They settled here,
'akórtan ayémk,	and a really long time passed,
viitháwxaym.[737]	while they were here.
Piipáanyts thúutt nya'íim,	The people increased (in population),
nyaayúuk,[738]	and when they saw this,
aatsxuukyítsk 'etəma.	(some people) went across, they say.
Aatsxuukyítsk athúm,	They went across, and so,
amák atíivapátxá a'ím,	they decided that they would settle back there,
vaayáak 'eta.	and they went along, they say.
Mattashtúum,	They volunteered (to go),
vaayáak,	and they went,
nyáasi,	and over there,
aaxkyéenyik atíivək.	they settled on the other side.
Athúum,	So,
siitíivəm,	they settled there,

nyáanya,	and as for that,
nyaanyiimánk,	from then on,
shiimúlyk 'ítyá:	that has been their name, they say:[739]
***[740]	***
'Axám Aakxáv 'eta.[741]	'Axám Aakxáv (They Went Through Water), they say.
Xamaakxáv a'íim,[742]	They are called Xamaakxáv (Mojave) (for short),
a'íim 'ítyá.[743]	they are called (that), they say.
'Axám aakxávək,	They went through water,[744]
nyáasi aaxakyéevək,	they went across to that (side) over there,
nyáasi atíivapat,	and they, for their part, settled over there,
avoonóonyk,	and there they were, until —
avoonóok,	there they were,
thúutt nyaa'ím,	and when they increased (in population),
mattashtúutəntik vaayáak 'etá.	(some of them) volunteered to go, they say.
Piipáa nyáanyts mattashtúum,	Those people volunteered,
vaayáak vaayáak,	they went and went,
'amáytan aatsuukúly.	and they climbed up really high.[745]
Nyáany a'íim.	That's what they say.
'Axám aatsuukúlyək a'ím 'eta.	They were going to go upstream, they say.[746]
'Atsaayúu a'íim 'ítyá.	They were called something, they say.
'Axáts aráawk atsénk viithíim,[747]	They came down the rapids and came this way,
nyáany	and as for that,
kwaa'úurnyəm aayáak,[748]	they went along the bank,
vaayém.	and they went away.
'Axám aatsuukúlyk 'eta.	They went upstream, they say.
'Axály oonóok uuthúuts aly'ém.[749]	They weren't in the water.
'Amáttnyi athúum,[750]	It was on land,
'axánya tsanyók siiyáak 'etá.[751]	they went along following (the course of) the river, they say.
'Amátt.	(On) land.
Saayáak vaayáak awím,	They went along over there, and so,
kwanyamély apámətík 'etá.[752]	they reached another (place), they say.
Apámxáym,	When they got there,
vathí,	right here,

'anyáavik ooyóovxaym,
'avíits viiyáanyək,⁷⁵³
nyáanyi uuqáarək siivám ooyóovk awim,⁷⁵⁴
" 'Anyétsəts,
nyáasi 'aayémxá,"
a'íik 'eta.

A'íim,
mattashtúuntik,
siiwáanyək —
saayáanyək —
'atsaayúu ooyóovək 'eta.
'A'íits 'almétstank oov'ótsəm,
nyáanya,
nyáany kaa'émk ashé:⁷⁵⁵
Xawáaly 'éta.
Xawáaly a'íim ashék awim,

nyáany maxák nyiitíivək awim,
nyatsuuváayvək.⁷⁵⁶
Nyáany,
nyamúlyəny,⁷⁵⁷
amúlya áayk 'etəma,
nyáanya.
Pa'iipáa avkoonóonya,
amúlyənyts a'ím:
Xawáalyapáay a'íik 'et.⁷⁵⁸

Xawáalyapáay a'íim,
nyáanyənyts.
Nyáanyiitíivək,
alyaskyíik avatíivxa.

Athótəm athúum,
'akór alynyaayém,
piipáats mattashtúuntik saayáak 'eta.

when they looked towards the east,
the mountains went along,
and they saw that there was a canyon over there, and so,
"We (are the ones),
we will go over there,"
they said, so they say.

So,
(some people) volunteered again,
they went ahead, over there, until —
they went along, over there, until —
they saw something, they say.
There were tall trees standing there,
and those (people),
they named them somehow:
Xawáaly (Pine), they say.
They named them Xawáaly (Pine), and so,

they settled under those (pines), and so,
they lived there.
As for that,
as for their name,
(the trees) gave them their name, they say,
those (people).
The people that were around there,
it became their name:
they are called Xawáalyapáay (Pine Tree People), they say.

They are called Hualapai,
those (people).
They settled there,
they are still (there) and and they will be there.

It happened, and so,
when a long time had passed,
people volunteered again and went on, they say.

'Axány tsanyók siiyáak,
xáam aatsuukúlyəntik
　vaayáaxaym,
'amáy aatsuukúlytəm athúm.
'Axányts maxáktan athík,
avathíkəm,
ooyóovək 'eta.

Tsapéevək avathík kwalyavíit-sa,⁷⁵⁹
mattapées athótk athum,
nyáany,
ooyóovək athúm.

'Amáy tan athúm,⁷⁶⁰
aqáarək viithík,
'aqáqəny kwaqáqənyts mattapéek
　awim,
makyík alyootsénəmxats
　athúulya'émtəm,
kaathomk alyuuváak;⁷⁶¹
" 'Aaíimk nyii'atíivək.
'Amáy vathí 'atíiv aly'a'émtəka?"
　a'ítya.
A'íim,
athúuk 'etəma.
'Amáy nyiitíiv athúm,

oonóoxaym,
piipáa kaa'íts vaayáak,
athótk ooyóov 'étk athúm,
avaayáaxaym,
'oonyé lyavíik atsénk,
'axály atsénk athúuk 'etəma.
'Axály atsénk athúum,
nyáanyi,
aatsxuukyítsk,
aakavék athúuk 'ím,⁷⁶²
avoonóot.⁷⁶³

They went along following the water,
they went upstream again and went
*　along, and soon,*
they had climbed up high.
The water lay well below them,
there it was,
and they looked at it, they say.

It seemed small, but
it must have been tremendous,
that (valley),
when they saw it.

It was very high up, and so,
(the land) was deeply eroded, lying here,
there were lots of canyons and split
*　places, and so,*
there was no way they could go down
*　into it,*
and they went on doing what they could;
"Let's just settle down.
Why don't we settle here in the high
*　place?" they said.*
So,
that's what they did, they say.
They settled there in the high place,
*　and so,*
there they were,
and some of the people went off,
they intended to look around, and so,
they went along, and suddenly,
something like a road went down,
it went down to the water, they say.
They went down to the water,
and at that point,
they crossed,
and they went back, they say,
and there they were.

Nyáanya,
mattkwashéntəts ayéxaym,⁷⁶⁴
vathí kwáamənyts,
nyáanyts athúm.
Avuuthúuts,
ooyóovək voonóonyək,
'axótt kwalyavíish a'íim.⁷⁶⁵
'Axá nyiimánk aapáyk,
vaa'ée a'íim,
'amáytan,
'amátt-ts siitháw,⁷⁶⁶
nyáanya,
nyáany atíivətxá.
Uu'íitsk athúm,
'a'íi kaawíts awíim,
ashtúum,
'atáyk athúm,
'axányts apáyk
nyáanyi aapáxm,⁷⁶⁷
nyáany ashtúum,
'avá uutsáawk.
'Avá uutsáawk avoonóonyək,
aatsavérk athum.
Nyáanyi nyatsuuváayk,
nyáanyi atíivək aashmátsk a'ávək
  awim,
nyatsuuváayk,
nyiitíivəm,
nyaathótəm athúm.⁷⁶⁸
Nyáanyi,
nyiikwatíiv nyáanyənyts,
xó—
avoonóoxaym,
'atsaayúuts avatháwk 'et.
'Avíits.

'Avíits avatháwk,⁷⁶⁹
'axányts nyamayémk,

As for that,
the same (group) went along, and suddenly
the ones that had passed by here,
they were the ones.
They did that,
they went on looking,
and it seemed to be all right, they said.
It sloped up from the water,
it was like this,
and way up there,
there was a place,
and that (place),
that was where they would settle.
They intended to, and so,
they used wood or something,
they gathered it,
there was a lot of it,
the water had carried it
and placed it there,
and that's what they gathered,
and they built houses.
They went about building houses,
and they finished.
They lived there,
they settled there and they slept
  anywhere, and so,
they lived (there),
they settled there,
it happened.
At that point,
the ones who settled there,
oh!—
they were there, and suddenly
there were things there, they say.
Mountains.

Mountains were there,
and the water went around them that way,

nyamayémk voonóonyək,	it went around that way, until
kwaskyíi vatáytan lyavíik a'íim,	there was something that looked like a really big bowl,
nyáanyily kwiixáalyts vanyaathíim,	and into that the flood came,
'axányts alytam'óorək athúm,	and water filled it up, and so,
nyaasáttəm,	when (the water) receded,
'amátt alykwatháwənyts asáttapatk 'eta.	the dirt that was in it receded too, they say.
Alyatséntəm athúm.	It went down (to the bottom).
'Axányənyts atóly atháwk a'eta,[770]	Water remained in the middle (of the rock), they say,
'avíi uutskúpənya.	(in) holes in the rock.
Nyáany,	As for that,
nyáanyi alyatháwəm,	there is was,
ooyóovxaym,	and when they saw it,
xavashúutánk 'eta.	it was really blue, they say.
Nyaanyiimánək xó—	Starting there, or—
'atsaayúuts athúuk 'ím 'itya.	there was a reason for it, they say.[771]
'Amáyəly ayúuxaym,	(Blue) could be seen in the sky, and as a result,[772]
'axányily axávək,	it went into the water,
'axányily athúu kwalyavíik,	it seemed to be in the water,
xavashúu kwalyavíim,	(the water) seemed to be blue,
ooyóovk athúm;	and they saw it;
avoonóok a'ét.	there they were, they say.
Nyaathótəm athúm,	It happened, and so,
'Axá Xavashúu a'íim,[773]	they are called 'Axá Xavashúu (Blue Water),
amúlyk 'eta.[774]	they are named (that), they say.
Piipáanyənyts nyiitíivəntim,	The people settled there,
'Axá Xavashúupáay a'íi uumúulyk,[775]	they were named 'Axá Xavashuupáay (Blue Water People),
nyaanyiimánk,	and that's where they came from,
nyáany ashék 'ítya.[776]	and that's what they named them, they say.
'Axá Xavashúupáay uu'ítsa.	Havasupai is what they are called.
Athótəm athúm,	It happened, and so,

nyáanyi,	at that point,
nyáanyiitíivapatk awet,	they, for their part, settled there, and so,
avatíivək 'ítyá.	they settled there, they say.
Alyaskyíik avatíivək.	They are still there.
Nyáanya athúum:	That's what happened:
'axóttk avatíiv.[777]	it was good and they settled there.
'Ís,	But,
nyiikamáan,[778]	as for the rest of them,
nyáany lyavéenyapátk,	they were the same too;
nyáany nyuutíivəny,	the place where they settled,
wanymooyétsk 'et.	they liked it, they say.
Athúum.	They did.
Nyáanya.	That (place).
Nyiitíivək athúum,	They settled there,
nyaanyiimánk.	starting then.
Kànyaa'íim,	Sometimes,
aatsénk,	they (would) go down,
maatsawíts avatíivəm ooyóovəxa.	and they would see their relatives settled there.
Aatsuukúlyxa.	They would climb (back) up.
Nyaatsuukúlyəntík,	When they climbed up again,
nyáasi,	to that distant place,
apám,	they got there,
piipáa maatsawíts soonóom,	people they called relatives were there,
ayúuk,[779]	and they saw them,
a'íim,	and so,
kanáavək,[780]	they told them about it,
avoonóok,	there they were,
nyaa'íim,	and then,
vaathíik,	they came this way,
nyáavi aatsénk,	they came down here,
vaathíinyək —	they came this way, until —
vaathíiny,	they came this way, until
nyáavi apák.	they got here.
Piipáa avkwathíkəny ayúuntik 'eta.	They in turn saw the people that were here, they say.

Nyamáam,	Anyway,
xuumáarənyts tsapéek,	there were a lot of children,
xó —	or —
piipáanyts mattapéek,	there were a lot of people,
athúum,	there were,
'ís,	but
nyaavoonóoxáym,	while they were here, suddenly,
athúum.	it happened.
Athúum athúm,[781]	It happened, and so,
nyáanyts athúum.	that's what happened.
Nyáavəm kwatíivənyts alyaatsénk 'etá,	The ones who had settled there came down, they say,
Xáam Kwaatsáanənyts.	the Xáam Kwaatsáan, (Those Who Came Down by Means of Water).
Xáam Kwaatsáan 'eta.	The Xáam Kwaatsáan, they say.
Kwatsáan 'ét,	They are called Quechan,
mapísa.	nowadays.
'Ís	But
nyáasəm alyaatsénk,	they came down from that distant (place),
kaawíts nyatsuuváayapatk,	and they lived somewhere (in that area) too,
nyáanyiitíivəm,	they settled there,
nyáany ooyóovək,	and (other people) saw that,
a'íim a'íik 'eta.	and they called them (by that name), they say.
Piipáanyts avuuthúutsəsh.	The people did that.
Xáam aatsénk,[782]	They came down by means of water,[783]
'atsaayúu,	and, well,
nyáanyi,	at that (place),
nyáanyi nyatsuuváayk avoonóonyək;	they were living there;
"Alynyaa'atíivúm," a'im.	"We will live here," they said.
"Av'athík 'athósh, 'anyétsəts."	"Here we are, we are the ones."
'Ís,	However,
siikwaayáanya,	the ones who kept going,
a'íintim,	they were called something else,
Xamakxáavəts a'étk,[784]	they were called Mojave,

'Axá Xavshuupáay 'etk,	they were called Havasupai,
Xawáalyapáay 'éta,⁷⁸⁵	they were called Hualapai,
Xawáalyapáay,	Hualapai,
nyáanya.	those (people).
Nyáany,	As for that,
mattatsáaməly,	all of them,
mattamaawíik avathík 'ítya.	they are related to each other, they say.
Athótəm,	So,
athúu lyaskyíik viitháwtəsáa,	it's still the same, but
kór ayémk vanyaatháwm,	they have been there for a long time,
a'ím	and so,
nyáany,	that's it,
nyáany a'íim,	that's what they say,
katsuunávək oonóo aav'áarəm.	they have always explained it (in that way).
Makyík ma'áv alyma'ém,	You never hear (the story) any more,
táam,	it's gone,
sáa	but
avathík,	it happened that way,
avathík athótəm athúm.	it did happen that way.
Nyaanymáamtək athútya.	That's all.

[Footnote reference: 785]

Notes

1. A false start is heard here: *'Amattáam nya— nyakór*. The term 'false start' refers to an interruption in the flow of speech after which the speaker restarts and usually rephrases his utterance. False starts occur frequently in natural speech and indicate that the speaker is thinking and formulating his utterance while he speaks. They are noted here in order to account for minor discrepancies between the spoken and written versions of the narrative.
2. A false start is heard here: *thóm—iimáatt-ts thómayúuv aly'ém*.
3. *'Ashútsíi* was changed to *'ashútsáa* upon review.
4. *'Antséníi* was changed to *'antsénáa* upon review.
5. Mr. Bryant suggests *kaa'íts nyáany lyavíim a'ét* as an alternative formulation of this line.
6. *'Atkavék* was changed to *'atkavékxá* upon review.
7. This line literally means 'nothing was visible at all, but'.
8. This line literally means '(someone) went about explaining things to him, they say'.
9. This line literally means, '(someone) said that, (someone) told him about it, they say'.
10. A false start is heard here: *'atsaayúu 'axóttk—'uuxúuttk viitháwm*.
11. *Aví aa* was changed to *nyáavi* upon review.
12. This line is heard in the recording as *xaméer 'atséwəm*; it was changed upon review.
13. *Alyoonóok* was changed to *alyuuváak* upon review.
14. A false start is heard here: *náa shaakwíink vaawée vaawée awétk*.
15. A false start is heard here: *'amátt—'axá vathány*.
16. *Nyiitháwk* was changed to *nyiitháwt* upon review.
17. Mr. Bryant suggests *'atsaayúu 'a'íits aatspáatsk athúuk a'ét* 'trees and things emerged from them, they say' as an alternative formulation of this line.
18. Mr. Bryant suggests *'ax'áats athúntik* as an alternative formulation of this line.
19. *Uuváa* was changed to *uuváak* upon review.
20. *A'íim* was changed to *uu'íts* upon review.
21. A false start is heard here: *nyaa—nyáanyts*.
22. The word *alya'émk* was inserted upon review.
23. This line is heard in the recording as *'akórtan alyayém nyaa'ávək. alyayém* was changed to *lyavíik* upon review.
24. This line literally means 'it seemed like a long time, and when he experienced it'.
25. The expression *iiwáanyts apúyk* literally means 'his heart died'; its idiomatic meaning is 'he was alarmed'.
26. This line is heard in the recording as *ayáalypátk*; it was changed upon review.
27. A false start is heard here: *'Axám— 'axám áamk*.
28. This line literally means '(someone) told him things, they say'.
29. This line literally means '(someone) told him this as well, they say'.
30. *Eethónyi* was changed to *eethónyily* upon review.

31 Mr. Bryant suggests *eethóts atáarək* as an alternative formulation of this line.
32 This line is heard in the recording as *'Asákwiimáatt 'atsaayúu tsáaməly alykwaskyúitanəny nyáanyts athúum*; it was changed upon review.
33 This line literally means 'all of *'Asákwiimáatt*'s things still existed, they say'.
34 *Viitháwxaym* was changed to *viitháwxayk* upon review.
35 *Siiyáa* was changed to *siiyáat* upon review.
36 *Kukwiimáatt* was changed to *Kukwiimáatt-ts* upon review.
37 This line is preceded by an indecipherable false start.
38 Mr. Bryant uses the names *Kukumáatt* and *Kukwiimáatt* interchangeably to refer to the Creator. To avoid confusion, the name of the Creator is regularized as *Kukwiimáatt* in the English translation.
39 This line is heard in the recording as *pa'iipáa nyaanyi atíiv 'ím*; it was changed upon review.
40 *Kwatáarəny* was changed to *kwatáarənyts* upon review.
41 A false start is heard here: *xáak athúuts—uuthúutsk 'étəma*.
42 This line is heard in the recording as *'axá shaakwérəny athúum*; it was changed upon review.
43 *'Axá shakwíints* was corrected to *'axám shuukwíints* upon review.
44 This line is heard in the recording as *'axa—'axá kashaakwíin nyáanya sharéq 'íinyək*. It was changed upon review.
45 *Nyáanya* was changed to *nyáanyi* upon review.
46 This line literally means 'things were small'.
47 This line literally means 'as for those that were located in the sky, they were small'.
48 This and the following line were suggested on review. They replace three lines heard in the recording: *'amátt atsénk, aatsénk, 'amáttnyi aatsén* 'they fall to the ground, they fall, they fall to the ground'.
49 This word was originally recorded as *Pa'iipáa Eethó Kwatáarənyts*; the subject case marker was deleted upon review.
50 *Kwa'íts* was changed to *kwathútsəny* upon review.
51 The word *kwathútsəny* was inserted upon review.
52 A false start is heard here: *Nyam—nyáany 'ashoopóow aly'a'émtəká*.
53 Mr. Bryant suggests *nyaaviimánk athúuk 'etá* as an alternative formulation of this line.
54 This line literally means 'those that he was to do were there too'.
55 Mr. Bryant suggests *mattxatsváak aatsuumpápəm atséwk* 'he made four couples' as an alternative formulation of this line.
56 *Kamayáa* or *Kamia* is the Quechan name for Kumeyaay people.
57 Several lines of false starts have been omitted here.
58 Upon review, Mr. Bryant suggested replacing *xavíkəm* with *taxavíkəm*.
59 This line is heard in the recording as *nyáanyi makyík áar aly'émpak*; it was changed upon review.
60 Mr. Bryant suggests changing this line to read *makyík 'akór alya'ém siiváxáym*.
61 Mr. Bryant suggests replacing this line with *nyaaváamk*.
62 In the recording this line is unclear but sounds like *kanáavxa*; it was clarified on review.
63 A false start is heard here: *Kukwiimáatt-ts 'atsaayúu 'atáyəm ats—atséwk*.
64 A false start is heard here: *nyaa—nyaanyiimánək*.
65 Mr. Bryant suggests *'anyáa kwashíintəm* as an alternative formulation of this line.

66 A false start is heard here: *Kwiimáatt—Kwakwiimáatt-ts shoopóowk 'etá.*
67 Upon review, Mr. Bryant suggests replacing *'anyáa,* which is rarely used with the meaning 'me', with the more common form *'anyép* 'me'.
68 Two lines of false starts are omitted here.
69 *Kwas'eethéeny* was changed to *kwas'eethéets* upon review.
70 A false start is heard here: *'atsaayúu kwas—kwas'iitsthíts viikwatháwnya.*
71 Upon review, Mr. Bryant suggests replacing *avkoov'óowənyts* 'the rain (subject case)' with the more common form *oov'óowts* 'rain (subject case)'.
72 A false start is heard here: *Nyaa—nyáanyəm.*
73 A false start is heard here: *uumárəny—aamárəntík a'íim 'itya.*
74 A false start is heard here: *'ats—uuváxayk.*
75 False starts are heard here: *'ats—Kwatsáan 'iipáany nyáanyi nyaalyaa—aatsoonóoy aly'émk 'etá.* Upon review, Mr. Bryant suggests replacing *aatsoonóoy* 'he abandons him' with *namák* 'he leaves him'.
76 This line is heard in the recording as *nyi—nyáany xáak uuváam athúm;* it was changed upon review.
77 This word was inserted upon review.
78 *Amúlyts* was changed to *amúlyk* upon review.
79 This line literally means, 'some were alive, they were over there in turn'.
80 False starts are heard here: *nyáany awíi—aly—awíiməm uuthúutsk 'etəma.*
81 A false start is heard here: *aváts xáak awi—xáak avám.*
82 A false start is heard here: *Nyáany Kwatsáan xiipan—xiipúkts athúum 'ityá.*
83 A false start is heard here: *míim—awíim siiwáak 'etá.*
84 *Kwiixáalyk* was changed to *kwiixáalyts* upon review.
85 A false start is heard here: *sii—'Aqáaqts siivám.*
86 A false start is heard here: *Nyaa—nyaa'íim.*
87 Two lines are omitted here in which Mr. Bryant explains (in Quechan) that he is about to move on to the next part of the story.
88 *Uu'ítsənyts* was changed to *uu'ítsənya* upon review.
89 *Nyiitsáawəntík* was changed to *nyiitséwəntík* upon review. Mr. Bryant suggests *nyiiuutsáawəntík* as another alternative.
90 A false start is heard here: *nyaa—nyáanyiimánk awítsxá.*
91 This line is heard in the recording as *pa'iipáts.* It was changed upon review.
92 This line is heard in the recording as *kwatsatkyáavək;* it was changed upon review.
93 This line literally means 'That one led them first, they say'.
94 *Shiimúly* was changed to *shiimúlyts* upon review.
95 *Mat'á* is heard in the recording with a long vowel—*Mat'áa;* it was changed on review.
96 At this point the text has been revised considerably in order to clarify matters of fact. Fourteen lines have been deleted and replaced with ten new lines which Mr. Bryant composed upon review.
97 This is the last line of the revision mentioned in note 96. Henceforth the text follows the the recoring.
98 The word *a'ím* 'they were called' was inserted upon review.
99 A false start is heard here: *xan'aapuk—xan'aapúuk 'íkəm.*
100 This line literally means 'snakes were like that, they say'.
101 *Nyáany* was changed to *nyáanyts* upon review.
102 This line is heard in the recording as *'aavé 'atskwatsakyíwəny;* it was changed upon review.

103 This line is heard in the recording as *'aayúu matxávil xwérər awétk*; the word *atáp* 'he threw him' was added upon review.
104 This line was added upon review.
105 Upon review, Mr. Bryant suggests *xáam uuthúutsk athúuk 'éta* 'they are different kinds, they say' as an alternative formulation of this line.
106 This line is heard in the recording as *nyaanyiimánk awím*; it was corrected upon review.
107 A false start is heard here: *xuumáar nyii—nyiivasháwk uuváxaym*.
108 A false start is heard here: *'atsaayúu 'aave kwa'ats—kwa'atsláytsəny nyii'aqáasəm*.
109 Several lines of false starts are heard in the recording but are omitted here.
110 A false start is heard here: *nyaa—nyaa'aláaytanəm*.
111 Mr. Bryant suggests changing this and the preceding line to *xuumáyts athútyá, nyáany xuumáyts athúuk a'ét* 'he was his son, he was his son, they say'.
112 A false start is heard here: *saa—xatsúurək nyiináamk viitháwm*.
113 *'Avuuyáanyi* was changed to *'avuuyáany* upon review.
114 This line literally means 'things have been there, and they are always seen, they say'.
115 *Alyavám* was changed to *alyaváamk* upon review.
116 This line literally means 'a day was one and it arrived and so'.
117 A false start is heard here: *Sanyts—sanyts'áakts nyáany lyavée av'áarəm mayúuk*.
118 *Av'áartək* was changed to *av'áartəm* upon review.
119 *A'éxáym* was changed to *uuváaxaym* upon review.
120 This line literally means 'he was dying, he was experiencing it, he was doing it slowly'.
121 A false start is heard here: *viiya—viithíknyək*.
122 *'Atsatsuunyúuts* was changed to *tsuunyúuts* upon review.
123 *Lyavíik* 'he resembled him' was changed to *lyavíi a'ím* 'he wanted to resemble him' upon review.
124 A false start is heard here: *nyaany—nyaanyiimánk*.
125 Upon review, Mr. Bryant suggests replacing *a'ítsk* 'they (collective plural) say' with the distributive plural form *uu'íitsk*.
126 In the recording, this word sounds like *taspérək* 'he tightens it', but *kaspérək* 'be strong!' makes more sense in the context.
127 A false start is heard here: *Matt—mattkuutar'úytsək*.
128 *'Anyáavi* was changed to *'anyáavik* upon review.
129 A false start is heard here: *asho— asóok 'ét*.
130 *'Axáyk* was changed to *'axáyts* upon review.
131 It is not clear why the plural form *aatspáats* is used here (and again three lines hence) rather than the non-plural form *atspáam*.
132 A false start is heard here: *'ats—Xatalwényənyts*.
133 A false start is heard here: *'ats—'atsaayúu kamánk athúuk 'etá*.
134 A false start is heard here: *uuwíts—'atsuuwítsnyá*.
135 This word is hard to hear in the recording; it was clarified upon review.
136 The narrative is interrupted here for technical reasons (so that a cassette tape may be turned over).
137 A false start is heard here: *Kumastamxóts nyáanyi tsiimaa—tsaamánək*.
138 A false start is heard here: *nyáanya 'ats—'atsaráav mattkwatspée athúuk 'etəmá*.
139 This line literally means 'it was a terrible sickness, they say'.
140 Upon review, Mr. Bryant suggests *'Aavé taaxánts nyaaváamǝm* as an alternative

formulation of this line.
141 This line is heard in the recording as *Kukwiimáattənyts atháwk tapúyk 'et*. It was corrected upon review.
142 *Nyáanyi* was changed to *nyáany* upon review.
143 *Nyiimáattəny* was changed to *iimáatənyts* upon review.
144 *Uu'ítsəny* was changed to *uu'íts* upon review.
145 This line is heard in the recording as *'amáttnyily axwélyk* 'he dug in the ground'. It was changed upon review.
146 Mr. Bryant suggests *'axányts nyamayémk athúuk 'eta* 'water has flowed through there, they say' as an alternative formulation of this line.
147 A false start is heard here: *nyaalyavíintits viiva—viithíkəm atháwk awím*.
148 A false start is heard here: *nyáany—nyáanyi amáarək*.
149 Mr. Bryant suggests *'Axá Aráw Kwa'axwéttənyts* 'It is the Colorado River' as an alternative formulation of this line.
150 A false start is heard in this line: *Kwatsáan nyamátt atóly—atóm viikwáama*.
151 Mr. Bryant suggests *'atsíi xáam uuthútstan atséwk* 'he made different kinds of fish' as an alternative formulation of this line.
152 A false start is heard here: *'axányi xany—xiipáan avkwathíkəny*. Mr. Bryant suggests *'axály avkwathíkənya nyiitséwkəntík a'eta'a* 'he made those which are in the water, they say' as an alternative formulation of this line.
153 This line literally means 'the ones that are located near the water'.
154 A false start is heard here: *'axály'—axály avkwathíkənya nyiitséwk voonóok 'ityá*.
155 This line literally means 'he went about making those that are located in the water, they say'.
156 A false start is heard here: *'Atsíi kwa—kwarts'áakənyts*.
157 Mr. Bryant suggests *nyáasily oonóok avoonóonyək* 'they were over there, moving about, until' as an alternative formulation of this line.
158 A false start is heard here: *'avíits viiva—viivám*.
159 *'Atsaayúuts* was changed to *'atsaayúu* upon review.
160 A false start is heard here: *nyáany—nyáany atséwk 'etəma*.
161 Two lines of false starts are heard in the recording but have been deleted here.
162 *Oovar'é* was corrected to *alyoovar'é* upon review.
163 This line literally means 'he did it (so that) it was like a church'.
164 Mr. Bryant suggests *nyáanyily uuthúutsk a'íim* 'intending them to be in it' as an alternative formulation of this line.
165 A false start is heard here: *a'íi—a'íim a'íikəta*.
166 Mr. Bryant suggests *kaawíts xáam kuuwítsnya nyáanya awíntík* 'they did different things in turn' as an alternative formulation of this line. The function of *nyáanyəm* in the original version is not clear.
167 A false start is heard here: *'a'áw awíim 'ats—ootséwxanya*.
168 Upon review, Mr. Bryant suggests that *xatsóorək* 'it is winter' might be more appropriate here than *xatsúurək* 'it is cold'.
169 *Mootséwnyəm* was changed to *mootséwnya* upon review.
170 Mr. Bryant suggests *nyáanya piipáanyənyts nyiimashíitəxa* as an alternative formulation of this line.
171 The word *shiimúly* was added upon review.
172 A false start is heard here: *pa'iipáa nyii— xáak tsawémk 'etá*.
173 This line was inserted upon review.
174 A false start is heard here: *Kwats—Kwatsáan pa'iipáa nyiikwanáamts*.

175 Mr. Bryant suggests *kwara'áktants athúum* 'he was a very old man' as an alternative formulation of this line.
176 A false start is heard here: *'Axá—'amáttəny alyaxávək 'et*.
177 A false start is heard here: *nyakónyənyts nyáanyi kamánk ats—atspák awityá*. Mr. Bryant suggests replacing *awityá* with *athútyá*.
178 A false start is heard here: *'atsaayúu tsáaməly oo—kwatséwənya*.
179 This line literally means 'days were four'.
180 Mr. Bryant suggests *pa'iipáany nyiiyúuk nyiiuutar'úy a'ím avuuváak athót* 'there he was intending to watch over and take care of the people' as an alternative formulation of this line.
181 The first portion of this narrative was recorded on Tapes 6 and 7; see the Introduction and note 343 for discussion.
182 Mr. Bryant suggests replacing *a'ím* with *a'ét*.
183 The words *amánk athót* were added upon review.
184 Two lines were omitted upon review.
185 Mr. Bryant suggests replacing *'ashénits* with *'ashéntəntíts*.
186 Mr. Bryant suggests omitting the evidential suffix *-sh* here.
187 A false start is heard here: *eethótsəny—eethónya uutstáaq 'et*.
188 This line is heard as *Kwara'ák Kwatáar—Eethó Táar a'ím 'ityá*. Mr. Bryant rephrased it and added vocative case marking upon review.
189 A false start is heard here: *Kukwii—Kukwiimáattənyts*.
190 This line is heard as *nyiioov'óowk*; it was changed upon review.
191 This line is heard as *oov'óowənya*; it was changed upon review.
192 This line is heard as *'atsaayúuny ataspák*; it was corrected upon review.
193 Several false starts are heard here.
194 This is an old expression and is no longer used in modern Quechan. Mr. Bryant used it here because it appears in Harrington (1908).
195 Mr. Bryant suggests *iiwáam awíim* 'he did it on his own' as an alternative formulation of this line.
196 Mr. Bryant suggests adding *a'ét* at the end of this line.
197 *Awíi lya'ém* was replaced with *a'íi lya'ém* upon review.
198 Two indecipherable lines are omitted here.
199 A false start is heard here: *vathány— 'amáynya 'atawáamk*.
200 *Nyaaváany* was changed to *nyaaváamk* upon review.
201 A false start is heard here: *nyáany a'íik—'atsaayúu*.
202 Mr. Bryant suggests *Eethó Kwatáarənyts nyaawíim* 'if the Blind One did it' as an alternative formulation of this line.
203 Kamia is the word Quechan people use to refer to the Kumeyaay (Diegueño) people.
204 In this line and two lines hence, *Páa 'Anyáa* was changed to the more formal *Xattpáa 'Anyáa* upon review.
205 Upon review, Mr. Bryant suggested replacing *takyévək* with plural form *tatkyáavək*.
206 *A'ím*, very faintly heard, was replaced with *a'ét* upon review. Mr. Bryant also suggests replacing *eemé kwaly'ooxóony* with the unsuffixed *eemé kwaly'ooxóo*.
207 This and the previous line literally mean 'The Blind Person's heart was not good (as) he stood there'.
208 This line literally means 'as soon as he wants to pick them up he does so'. The Blind Person is arguing that there are advantages to having webbed fingers.

209 *Taráavxáym* was corrected to *taaráavxáym* upon review.
210 A false start is heard here: *Piipáa Kwatáara—Eethó Kwatáarənyts siiv'óowm*.
211 This line is heard as *masuuráyəny péem*; it was changed upon review. Subject case marking is expected but is not heard.
212 *A'exáym* was changed to *awéxáym* upon review.
213 Mr. Bryant suggests *nyáanyts athúuk a'ét* 'that's what happened, they say' as an alternative formulation of this line.
214 This line literally means 'this is that which takes place'.
215 *Nyáany* was changed to *nyáanyi* upon review.
216 *Nyáava* was corrected to *nyáavi* upon review.
217 In the recording, this line sounds like *s a'ét*; it was clarified upon review.
218 Here and two lines hence, *Páa 'Anyáa* was replaced with the more formal *Xattpáa 'Anyáa* upon review.
219 A false start is heard here: *makyík Páa 'Anyáany kavée—kavéely ooshathómp aly'émk 'eta*.
220 This line literally means, 'When his saying it was four'.
221 A false start is heard here: *Nya—piipáa nyáanya amúly áayk 'et*.
222 Mr. Bryant suggests *makyáany uu'ítsəny* as an alternative formulatioin of this line. *Makyáa* is the plural form of *makyí* 'who, which one'.
223 A line in English has been omitted here.
224 A false start is heard here: *Xattpáa— Xattpáa 'Anyáa a'íkəta*.
225 A false start is heard in this line: *Kukwiimáattənyts sanyts'áak nyii—nyiiáaylya'émk 'et*
226 A false start is heard here: *'anyétsa—'anyétsa awíim*.
227 A false start is heard here: *xáak—xáak awíim atséwk awím*.
228 This line literally means 'he did it differently, he made it'.
229 *'Atskakwek a'ávəxa* was corrected to *'atskakwékm 'a'ávəxa* upon review.
230 A false start is heard here: *'aatskóyts—mashtxáats iiwáam makyík xuumáar ayúu aly'émk*.
231 A false start is heard here: *nyaa—mayáak*.
232 The last word of this line is heard as *alya'émxa*; it was changed to *alyma'émxa* upon review.
233 This and the following two lines literally mean 'it is you, and it is that one, and you will never be in the same place'.
234 A false start is heard here: *xáam—xáak athíik atspák*.
235 This and the following line literally mean 'your meals would be many, they (would) be six'.
236 A false start is heard here: *ée—a'ávtəsáa*.
237 A false start is heard here: *Kukwiimáatt-ts sa—mashxáyəny a'íim*.
238 The last word of this line is heard as *alya'émk*; it was changed to *alyma'émk* upon review.
239 A false start is heard here: *piipáa—Kukwiimáatt-ts matxávi shathómp*.
240 A false start is heard in this line: *'atsaayúu sha—shakw'iiláa atséwk 'et*.
241 *A'íim* 'he said' was corrected to *awíim* 'he did' upon review.
242 *'Oowéxa* was changed to *'oowéxanya* upon review.
243 *Nyoo'éey* was corrected to *nyoo'éeyxa* upon review.
244 Mr. Bryant suggests *nyáany 'anymawéeyk mawéxa* 'you will do that for me' as an alternative formulation of this line.
245 *Alya'ém* is just barely audible.

246 *Eethó* 'eyes' was changed to *meethó* 'your eyes' upon review. A false start is heard in this line.
247 A false start is heard here: *'axányənyts takavék ats—atsénk*.
248 Mr. Bryant suggests *nyiiv'óowk a'ét* 'they stood there, they say' as an alternative formulation of this line.
249 A false start is heard here: *nyaa'awém—makyík nyuu'áav aly'émk*.
250 This line literally means 'he walked, he came, and he went, they say'.
251 False starts are heard in two places *'avá kw—'avá kwatiinyáamənya 'atséwx—'atséwxa*.
252 A false start is heard here: *ii—iimaattk uuthíik*.
253 A false start in English, little red—, and a line in Quechan, *xóo* 'or', are omitted here.
254 *Xanapúuk* is Mr. Bryant's interpretation of the word *xanapúk* which Harrington cites at this point in the story. In fact, *xanapúuk* does not mean 'piss ant' but instead is variant of *xan'aapúuk* 'water snake'. The word for 'piss ant' is unknown.
255 Mr. Bryant suggests replacing this and the preceding line with a single line: *'ax'áa kaayúmǝxáyk* 'he had no cottonwood yet'.
256 This line literally means 'he never asked for anything'. Upon review, Mr. Bryant suggested *makyík awíkts a'ím kwakyáav aly'émk 'eta* 'he never asked for them to help him, they say' as an alternative.
257 Mr. Bryant suggests *nyáanya piipáats athúuk a'ét* 'that was a person, they say' as an alternative formulation of this line.
258 *Nyiitaxrámpk* was changed to *alytaxrámpk* upon review.
259 This line is heard as *makyík shalyamák kwatháwnya nyav'áa lya'ém*; it was changed upon review.
260 The narrative is briefly interrupted at this point.
261 There is a brief digression into English at this point.
262 *Kaawíts kwa'anyáaw* literally means 'things which are hidden'.
263 False starts are heard here: *'anyáats—oh—máanyts—'atsaya—piipáa Kwatsáanənya matsúyly 'aaly'éta*. Mr. Bryant suggests changing *'aaly'éta* to *'aaly'étka*; the significance of the change is not clear.
264 A false start is heard here: *nya'ootséwxanya— 'ootséwxáyənya*.
265 A false start is heard here: *makyík pa'iipáa kuukanáav aly'ém—alyka'émk*.
266 After two more lines (which have been omitted here), the tape comes to an end.
267 Mr. Bryant suggests *amúly áayk 'et* 'he gave her a name, they say' as an alternative formulation of this line.
268 A false start is heard here: *xuumáyts—xuumáyts athúuk 'et*.
269 *Kumastamxó* was changed to *Kumastamxóts* upon review.
270 Mr. Bryant suggests *'anyáayənya 'amáynyi atséwətk awityá* 'he made light in the sky' as an alternative formulation.
271 This line literally means 'Marxókavék made the thing, the sun, give off light'.
272 A false start is heard here: *makyík 'ats—eethóny ta'axótt aly'émxá*.
273 Two lines consisting of false starts are omitted here.
274 *Kawíiya uu'íts* [pause] *nyaawíim* was replaced with *Kawíiya uu'ítsnya awíim* upon review.
275 Mr. Bryant suggests *awíntik avoonóowú nyaa'íim* 'if he is going to do it again' as an alternative formulation of this line.

276 This line literally means 'if he goes on doing it again'.
277 This line is hard to hear; it was clarified upon review.
278 A false start is heard here: *'aayúu tsáaməly masheethée—masheethéevət*.
279 A false start is heard here: *Kukumáatt-ts 'avá kwanyúilya—kwatiinyáamənya alyavák siivát*.
280 A false start is heard here: *'aayúu kaawíts tsuu—aatspáatsk oov'óts 'ím*.
281 Mr. Bryant suggests replacing *taaxán* with *taaxánk*.
282 This line is heard as *piipáa kwashúintənyts shtuutúutk 'etəma* 'each person got (something)'; the phrase *'a'íi 'ashéntəm* 'one stick' was added upon review.
283 *Kumastamxó* was changed to *Kumastamxóts* upon review.
284 Three lines consisting of false starts are omitted here.
285 As recorded, the word for 'prickly pear' sounds like *'aa'áa*; it was corrected to *'a'á* upon review.
286 A false start is heard here: *nyáanya Xattpáa Nya—'Anyáa nyiiáayk 'et*.
287 This line literally means 'to the one Maricopa'.
288 Mr. Bryant suggests *nyáany nyii'áayk 'eta* 'I give that to them, he said' as an alternative formulation of this line.
289 Mr. Bryant suggests *'anyáats 'awéxa* as an alternative formulation of this line. As it stands in the text, the line gets its irrealis interpretation from the suffix –*xa* which appears two lines hence.
290 *Nyaayúum* was changed to *nyaayúu* in this and the following line upon review.
291 Several lines consisting of false starts are omitted here.
292 Mr. Bryant suggests *pa'iipáats athíts 'amátt arúv awíi nyaa'íim* as an alternative formulation of this line.
293 The November 10, 2003 recording session ends here.
294 *Nyáanyəm a'íim* was changed to *nyaa'íim* upon review.
295 False starts are heard here: *makyík—makyí 'anyáay—makyí avá lya'émxá*.
296 This line literally means 'he did it and made it, they say'.
297 A false start is heard here: *Kukwiimáatt-ts nyaa—'amátt ka'ák aatsuumpápk 'et*.
298 A false start is heard here: *Kumastamxóts 'avá—'avá tiinyáamənya alyuuváak*. *Tiinyáamənya* was changed to *kwatiinyáamənya* upon review.
299 *Marxókavék* was changed to *Marxókavékts* upon review.
300 This line is heard as *Marxókavek—kavékts xáak 'atséwəntík 'eta*. *Xáak* 'in a different way' was changed to *'atsaayúu kwanyamé* 'something else' upon review.
301 A false start is heard here: *axtalwé—xatalwényənyts a'íim*.
302 *'Axály Mattnyakótt* and *'Axály Mattnyakót* are alternative forms (one with dental *t*, one with alveolar *tt*) of the same name. Mr. Bryant is not sure which is correct.
303 A false start is heard here: *Shakílykíly Kamáa—Nyamáa vaa'ét*.
304 Mr. Bryant suggests replacing this line with *nyáanyəm tsaqwérək a'éta* 'at that point he spoke, they say'.
305 This line is heard as *Nyáany 'amáyənyíi a'ím 'ityá*; it was changed upon review.
306 A false start is heard here: *ooshétsənyts 'í—'Aqáaq a'ét*.
307 The distributive plural form *uuthúuts* implies that each feather became something different: a different species of bird, Mr. Bryant explains.
308 *Kumastamxó* was changed to *Kumastamxóts* upon review.
309 This line is heard as *'axáts aví veeyémxaym* 'the water went away from here, and suddenly'. It was changed upon review.

310 A false start is heard here: 'amáyny—'amáynyəm áamk athúuk 'etəma.
311 A false start is heard here: nyii—nyiivátəm athúum.
312 This line is heard as takavék ookavék athúum 'he went back, he brought it back'; it was changed upon review.
313 This line is heard as vuuthíik nyaa'ávək; it was changed upon review.
314 A false start is heard here: 'amáattnya—'amáttənyts athúuk 'etəma.
315 The subject case marker -ts is unreleased and hard to hear. Its presence was confirmed upon review.
316 Tarúvək was corrected to arúvək upon review.
317 This line is preceded by a false start: vathí—nyaa—.
318 A false start is heard here: Nyáanyi—nyáanyəm atspák 'et. Mr. Bryant suggests nyáanyəm athíik atspákək 'et as an alternative formulation.
319 This line is heard as Aványa, aa, aatooqwérəlyts aly'ém 'ím. It was changed upon review.
320 A false start is heard here: Kukwiimáatt-ts mattapúy 'ím oonóo—uuváak athópəká.
321 Several lines of false starts have been omitted here.
322 A false start is heard here: Xavsúum Kuly—Xavashúum Kulyíits thomtaayúuk a'éta.
323 False starts are heard here: 'ats—'ats—Xavashúum Kulyíi uu'ítsənyts.
324 This line is heard as iiwáa—iiwáanyts a'íikəta; it was corrected upon review.
325 A false start is heard here: math—máany matháwk.
326 This line is heard as xuumáar matsáaw—matséwtsəxá. It was changed upon review.
327 Mr. Bryant suggests uu'íitsk a'éta 'they said, they say' as an alternative formulation of this line.
328 At this point in Harrington's (1908) narrative, a passage in Latin describes how children are conceived. We have omitted this passage.
329 The word 'anyép 'my' was added upon review. Even with this addition the syntax of the line remains uncertain; Mr. Bryant also suggests máany nyaxuumáyts nyaathúuva 'you are my son' as an alternative formulation.
330 This line is heard as nya'axuumáyk 'ityá, but Mr. Bryant firmly corrected it to nyaxuumáyk 'ityá upon review. He proposes 'anyáats nyaxuumáyk 'athutyá 'I call you son' as an alternative formulation.
331 Matxányanyts 'the wind (subject case)' was replaced with matxánya 'the wind (object form)' upon review.
332 This line is heard as makyík veeyém aly'ém; it was changed upon review. Mr. Bryant suggests tsayém 'íinyək kaváarək 'he tried to loosen it but it didn't happen' or tsayém 'íinyək nyeekwévək 'he tried to loosen it but it was no good' as possible alternative formulations.
333 A false start is heard here: maa—kwakapáarnyi atsáam.
334 An indecipherable line is omitted here.
335 This line is heard as nyamáap mapúyxa 'aaly'étk 'I think you will die'. It was changed upon review.
336 This line literally means 'he will not die'.
337 This line literally means 'the snake caused its rattles or something to make noise, they say'.
338 This and the following line literally mean 'and they reappeared. He wanted them to reappear'.
339 This line is heard as kúurtan nyaawím. It was changed upon review.

340 A false start is heard here: *max—nyaa—maxák kayáamk viiyáanyək.*
341 As mentioned in the Introduction, when this project was begun, narration was at first transcribed by hand. After two days of work, Mr. Bryant consented to have the story recorded, and Tape 1 commences at the point in the narrative marked by this note. The reader is advised that from this point forward, the narrative represents Mr. Bryant's early efforts at retelling the Creation story, and it accurately reflects the difficulty of the task. Between this point and the point marked by note 359, Mr. Bryant's retelling of "A Yuma Account of Origins" was formulated one line (or, in some cases, one sentence) at a time rather continuously, and, as is entirely natural under the circumstances, is characterized by false starts and rephrasings and is punctuated after almost every line with discussion of how the events reported in the turgid prose of Harrington (1908) might best be retold in the Quechan language. To avoid an unmanageable proliferation of endnotes, the many false starts, rephrasings, and discussions in this portion of the narrative are noted here once and for all. By the time he reaches the point in the narrative marked by note 359, Mr. Bryant has become a master of the difficult task of retelling, and the narrative proceeds in a relatively continuous manner from there forward.

After retelling the Creation story to the end, Mr. Bryant graciously retold the early portion for a second time for the purpose of recording. The material that precedes the point in the narrative marked by this note thus represents his later work and is (for the most part) continuous narration.
342 This line is heard as *máanyts 'atsnyamarávəm*; the word *miiwáam* was added upon review.
343 *Alyaakxávək* was changed to *alyaatsakxávək 'et* at the time of recording.
344 This line is pieced together from discussion.
345 At this point in the narrative there is an interruption and Tape 1 is turned from Side A to Side B.
346 *Nyawíim* was changed to *awíim* upon review.
347 This line is heard as *kwarávəny nyiivák.* The subject case marker *-ts* was added upon review.
348 Mr. Bryant suggests *'aavé tsuukyíwnyəm apúyt* 'he died from the bite of the snake' as an alternative formulation.
349 Mr. Bryant suggests *makwas'eethée aváats* as an alternative formulation of this line.
350 Mr. Bryant suggests *vuu'átsəny lyavíit* as an alternative formulation of this line.
351 Once again, Mr. Bryant suggests *vuu'átsəny lyavíit* as an alternative formulation of this line.
352 This line literally means 'a whirlwind arrived'.
353 Mr. Bryant suggests *awityá* as a substitute for *athutyá.*
354 *'A'ím* was changed to *'athúuva* upon review.
355 The narrative is interrupted here.
356 The term *mashtaxáay* 'girls' is used because young ladies in question have not yet given birth. A few lines hence, after having given birth, they are referred to as *sanyts'áak* 'women'.
357 This line is heard as *Xavshúu Kamuulyíi tsakuukwíitsk 'eta*; it was changed upon review.
358 This line literally means, 'on a day that was one'.
359 Narration becomes relatively continuous at this point.

360 *Wanymooyém* was corrected to *wanymooyéts* upon review.
361 *Xuumáark* was corrected to *xuumáarts* upon review.
362 *Aly'émantixá* was corrected to *alyma'émantixá* upon review.
363 This line is heard as *makyík piipáa—makyík 'iipátsa mashtoopóow alynyaama'émam*. It was changed upon review.
364 A false start is heard here: *Kukwiimáatt pa'iipáa—Kukwiimáatt-ts pa'iipáa tsuumpápam atséwtantik*.
365 A false start is heard here: *Kumastamxóts pa'iipáa kaa'íts— pa'iipáa kaa'íts ashtúum*.
366 A false start is heard here: *Mootséwanyts 'axótt aly—alya'ém*.
367 This and the preceding line literally mean, 'Kukwiimáatt's heart was bad, it was bad, they say'.
368 This line literally means 'it rained on top'.
369 A false start is heard here: *'anyáavik— 'anyáavi aaxweshaxwéshk awémk a'ét*.
370 This and the following line literally mean 'they dealt with possessions that were many, they dealt with them, but'.
371 Side B of Tape 1 comes to an end at this point.
372 This line was not recorded; it was added upon review.
373 A false start is heard here: *'axányik athíim—'axányik amánam*.
374 A false start is heard here: *'atsuuyuu—'atsaayúu Eethó Kwatáarany ootséwany*.
375 Mr. Bryant makes several false starts before settling on this formulation of this line.
376 A false start is heard here: *Iisháalyts—iisháalyanyts eemétsanyts shuunápanáapk a'ét*.
377 This line is preceded by two false starts.
378 This line is heard as *Kumastamxóts 'iipá uxwíip awi—axwíip awím*. It was changed upon review.
379 *'Iipány* was changed to *'iisávany* upon review.
380 A false start is heard here: *pa'iipáa nyii—nyiiaatsooyóoyk 'eta*.
381 This word is heard as *'Avíi vatáynyts 'amáttk athíik vii—viithíik 'et*. It was chanaged upon review.
382 This line is heard as *'amáttanyts akúulyk vaa'íim* 'the ground rose up like this'; it was changed upon review.
383 This line was added upon review.
384 This line was added upon review.
385 This line is heard as *'amáy atháwk*; the word *kayáamk* was inserted upon review.
386 This line literally means 'when he had not yet done it'.
387 There is a brief interruption here.
388 Several false starts and some discussion are heard at the beginning of this line.
389 False starts are heard here: *shaaxúuk aatsuumpáp — 'anyaa— 'anyáa shaaxúuk aatsuumpáp kayáam*. Upon review Mr. Bryant suggested replacing *kayáam* 'it goes on for a certain period of time' with *aváam* 'it continues for a certain period of time and then stops'.
390 This line is heard as *akwévam*; it was changed after a brief discussion at the time of recording.
391 This line was pieced together from several attempts and surrounding discussion.
392 This line is preceded by several false starts and some discussion.
393 Some discussion follows this line. Mr. Bryant suggests *Xavatsáats shiimúly*

kamánk as an alternative formulation.
394 A false start is heard here: Kukwiimáatt-ts aa nyamxavik—or nyaavée—kaayúumk.
395 False starts are heard here: Vatsíik—vats— vatsíits uuváak 'eta. Some discussion follows.
396 This line is heard as Eemé Xavashúu Kwalàpaláp; it was changed upon review. Some discussion follows.
397 Green Sole-of-the-Foot is better known as Frog.
398 This line literally means 'she was like Kukwiimáatt'.
399 This line was pieced together from several attempts and some discussion.
400 A false start is heard here: 'amátt—'amátt axávək.
401 This line is heard here as atsérəq tsuumpápk anáalyk 'eta. It was changed upon review.
402 A false start is heard here: xiipík—xiipúk uuthútsnya lyavíik.
403 A false start is heard here: 'axányi—'aványi alyaxávək.
404 A brief interruption follows this line.
405 This line literally means 'he came along saying "Aah! Aah!" they say.
406 A false start is heard here: Kaawíts— kaawíts 'aláayám?
407 This word was added upon review.
408 A false start is heard here: atóly—'iimáatt atóly aráavək.
409 A false start is heard here: iiwáam—iiwáam uuwítsənya awét.
410 Mr. Bryant suggests 'atsuuráványts thúutt a'íik 'eta 'his sickness got worse, they say' as an alternative formulation of this line.
411 One line is omitted here.
412 The narrative is briefly interrupted here. One line which precedes the interruption has been omitted.
413 Mr. Bryant suggests pa'iipáanyənyts as an alternative to pa'iipáa nyts.
414 This line is pieced together from several attempts.
415 Some discussion takes place here.
416 A false start is heard here: 'apénənyts—'apénts nyuu'áaly ashtúum.
417 A false start is heard here: Kukwiimáatt-ts Kumast—Kukwiimáatt-ts Kumastamxó aqásk a'ét.
418 A false start is heard here: Xuumárá—Xuumaréy! While the vocative case marker was -a in the 1930s (Halpern 1946a: 210), both -a (or -aa) and -éey are used today.
419 Vi'ayém was replaced with vi'ayémúm upon review.
420 'Ayém was replaced with 'ayémúm upon review.
421 This line is preceded by several false starts.
422 Xatalwé was changed to xatalwény upon review.
423 Some discussion takes place here.
424 A false start is heard here: Xatalwényənyts iiwáany kwatsítsk ve—kwatsíts a'íim shoopóowk.
425 This line is preceded by several false starts.
426 This and the following paragraph follow Harrington (1908:338). According to Mr. Bryant, however, it was not Wren but Kukwiimáatt himself who told Coyote, "Nyép 'iiwáa matháwk, matsanyóxa. You will (figuratively) take my heart, you will follow (its example)," and it was Kukwiimáatt's heart that Coyote took.
427 A false start is heard here: Xantavtsíip—Xanavtsíipts alynyiithúutsk 'et.

428 This line was pieced together from several attempts.
429 A false start is heard here: *'Atháwk 'axá—'axály 'atápuum?* Side A of Tape 2 comes to an end at the end of this line.
430 This line was added upon review. Another line was omitted.
431 *'Atsaráak* was corrected to *'ataráak* upon review.
432 Several false starts are heard here: *nyáasi nyamayúuxa— oov'ótsəm nyamayúuxa—mayúuxa.*
433 Several false starts are heard here: *'Apénts—'apénts—'apénts tatkyíttk.*
434 A brief discussion follows this line.
435 A false start is heard here: *iiyáany—eethóom awíim.*
436 A brief discussion follows this line.
437 *Akúp* was corrected to *uukúpk* upon review.
438 This and the following two lines were added upon review. They replace some English discussion of how to translate this passage.
439 A false start is heard here: *'Apénts tsuumpápm—tsuumpáptan kamémk.*
440 Several false starts are heard: *'amáy—'Apénts awíim—'Apénts nyikamáanənyənyts awíim.* Also, *nyiikamáanənyts* was corrected to *nyiikamáanənya* upon review.
441 This line is heard as *'avuuyáats—makyík uu— 'avuuyáats—'avá tiinyáamny nyiiríish a'íim;* it was changed upon review.
442 This line is preceded by several false starts and some discussion.
443 This line was pieced together from several false starts.
444 A false start is heard here: *nyáanyik mawém—mawémtəxá.*
445 This line is heard as *Kuukamnáawk! Kuukamnáawk!* It was changed upon review.
446 A false start is heard here: *nyuutháwk— nyaauutháawk.*
447 This line literally means 'Kumastamxó opened those which were located on the north'.
448 This line literally means 'he did not touch it at all'.
449 Tsakwshányi was corrected to tsakwshánya upon review.
450 Side B of Tape 2 ends here.
451 Each full sentence (delimited by punctuation) of this paragraph (delimited by blank lines) is followed by some discussion.
452 False starts are heard here: *nyáanyənyts—'amátt nyáanyənyts nyiivák athuty—athútya.*
453 This line is followed by some discussion.
454 A false start is heard here: *nyaanyiimánk ava—nyaanyiimánk.*
455 This line is heard as *aatsuumpápəny atáqshəm aváamk;* it was changed upon review. In the discussion which follows this line, Mr. Bryant suggests *'áləsh a'áləsh a'íim, aatsuumpápk aváamk* 'he went bounding along, he did it four times and he got there' as an alternative formulation.
456 This line was first uttered as *'ashént Xalyasmó a'íim amúlyk;* it was corrected at the time of recording.
457 Some discussion takes place here.
458 False starts are heard here: *'atsaayúu—'iisáv 'a'íi—'a'íinya atháwk.*
459 A false start is heard here: *aráaw 'ím viivák— viiváxaym.*
460 A false start is heard here: *eethóo shuukwáal—no, eethóo.* The line is followed by some discussion.
461 A false start is heard there: *'eethóo—'eethóony atháwk nyiitsáatsk a'ét.* This line is followed by some discussion.
462 This line is followed by some discussion.

463 A false start is heard here: *nyáanyi 'eethóo—'eethóony atháwk*.
464 *Taráats* was changed to *taráat* upon review.
465 A false start is heard here: *'ats—'a'áw aatapályək*. This line and the following line are each followed by some discussion.
466 A false start is heard here: *atáqshəsh—atáqshək sanyaayáak*.
467 *Atáqsh* was corrected to *atáqshək* upon review.
468 Several false starts are heard here: *nyaax—kavée—kavéely 'anyaaxáapk*. The word *alyayémt* 'he went away' was added upon review.
469 False starts are heard here: *'Ats'óor uu'ítsnyənyts pa'iipáa avésh nyii—nyiikwanaam—nyiikwanáamts*.
470 A false start is heard here: *'amátt—'amáttnyi tsavóowk*.
471 Mr. Bryant suggests *athúuk a'ét* as a good substitute for *athót* in this line. He points out that in the version of the story he is familiar with, the heart did not become a mountain; instead, grease from the heart dripped onto the mountain making it greasy and giving it its name.
472 False starts are heard here: *'Avíi Kwaxás—Kwa'axás 'ím ooshék—ooshéeyk a'et*.
473 Three lines have been omitted here.
474 A false start is heard here: *Xatalwényənyts iiwáany— kwiiwáanya asóok*.
475 This line is preceded by several false starts.
476 At this point in Harrington (1908), a passage written in Latin describes Coyote mating with the moon. This passage has been omitted here.
477 Some discussion takes place here.
478 A false start is heard here: *Pii—kwa'uukúutstanənyts iiwáanyts 'atsláytstank a'ét*. This line is followed by a brief discussion.
479 A false start is heard here: *Nyáavily—nyáava aalyuuthúutsk*.
480 Some discussion follows this line.
481 A false start is heard here: *Kwatsáan 'iipáany— 'iipáanyənyts xiipúk amíim 'etá*.
482 This line literally means 'that Quechan man cried first, they say'.
483 A false start is heard here: *Xan'aa—Xan'aaváa a'íim amúlyk 'et*. Mr. Bryant corrects *Xan'aaváa* to *Xanaav'váa* in the discussion that follows this line.
484 This line is heard as *malyqé anáw*; it was changed upon review.
485 This line is heard as *malyqé anáw tsapéev*; it was changed upon review.
486 Some discussion takes place here.
487 Some discussion follows this line.
488 A false start is heard here: *matxá—matxányənyts amíim*.
489 A false start is heard here: *Kumast—Kumastamxóts taanáwk tsaqwérək 'ím*.
490 This line is preceded by several false starts.
491 *Nyaalyavíinypátk* was changed to *nyáany lyavíinypatxa* upon review.
492 A false start is heard here: *nyáanyi—nyáany a'ítsapátxá*.
493 *Apúy* was changed to *oopóoyk* upon review.
494 *Apúym* was changed to *oopóoyəm* upon review.
495 A false start is heard here: *pa'iipáa m— pa'iipáa makyípəts 'amáyk matsérəqtəxá*. This line is followed by a comment in English.
496 A false start is heard here: *pa'iipáa tsáaməly ee'ény aakyítt— aatskyítt*. A brief discussion follows this line.
497 A brief discussion follows this line.
498 A false start is heard here: *nyáany pa'iipáa 'ashéntəts— nyáanyts 'ashént-tank*.
499 This line is followed by a brief discussion.
500 This line is preceded by several false starts.

501 Side A of Tape 3 ends here.
502 This line was not recorded but was reconstructed upon review.
503 A false start is heard here: *tsáaməly—* *tsáaməly 'atsaavéshxa.*
504 This line is preceded by several false starts.
505 A false start is heard here: *Iiwáanyts—* *iiwáanyts apúym mashathéevək.* This line is followed by some discussion.
506 A false start is heard here: *taayúushəxa—* *taayúush a'íim.*
507 False starts are heard here: *'Aatsayúu—* *'aayúu atséerqənyts 'aayúu atséerqənyts 'apílyk uuvaxáyk.*
508 A false start is heard here: *nyáanya—* *nyáanya amáam.*
509 Some discussion takes place here.
510 *Aatsuumpáp* was changed to *aatsuumpápk* upon review.
511 This and the following seven lines were inserted upon review. They replace a four-minute discussion of the names of places which Frog encountered on her journey.
512 A false start is heard here: *nyáanyəm—* *nyáanya.*
513 This line literally means 'he turned that Frog into a mountain'.
514 A long discussion takes place here.
515 This line is heard as *aakwíin aa'ashénti athóxats athót.* It was changed upon review.
516 This line is preceded by several false starts.
517 This line is preceded by several false starts.
518 Another lengthy discussion takes place here.
519 A false start is heard here: *Kumastamxóts—* *Kumastamxóts a'íim.*
520 A false start is heard here: *'atsiiráav kaméxa—* *kamétəxá.*
521 A false start is heard here: *Xaanyéts—* *Xaanyé uuwítsəny uutsáawk.* This line is followed by a comment in English.
522 This line is preceded by several false starts.
523 According to Kroeber (1972:5)'s notes on a Mojave version of the creation story, "Aha-'av-'ulypo, 'Water-house-post'" was the site of the first house. He identifies it as "several pinnacles ... some two miles or so from the Colorado River in the flat-bottomed wash up Eldorado Canyon, a tributary arroyo from the west, perhaps 25 miles below Hoover Dam" and notes that "[a]fter [the Creator's] death, Mastamho made the river to wash away his house, ashes, and bones". According to the Maricopa creation story (Spier 1933:352), "[a]fter the culture hero was cremated, the people were thirsty. They thrust a staff into the ground, so that a spring was formed. This is the source of the Colorado River. This was done in the center of their house. The house posts were still standing when the first whites came. They cut them down, but the rocks are still there to show the location. The name of these posts is *axavulpo*, 'water post'.".
524 *'Axalyvoopó* was corrected to *'axaavoolypó* upon review.
525 *Avathím* was changed to *avathikm* upon review.
526 A false start is heard here: *takavé—* *takavék.*
527 Mr. Bryant suggests *avathíi lya'émxa a'ét* as an alternative formulation of this line.
528 A false start is heard here: *'Amáy 'Aavétanya—* *'Aavénya uukanáavəm.*
529 This line literally means 'if he did not hurry and come'.
530 A false start is heard here: *Muuwítsxany—* *muuwíitsxany 'ashoopóowk,"* *a'ítya.*

Notes   203

531 False starts are heard here: *'Amáy 'Aavéts— 'Aavétats xiipúk alyuuváamənya aváamk— aváamxayk.*
532 A brief discussion follows this line.
533 This line literally means 'because they put here things that I would eat'.
534 This line is heard as *'Amáy 'Aavéts 'aványi lyavíik axwíivək 'ét*; it was changed upon review.
535 This line is heard as *máanyts ma'ashéntik*. It was changed upon review.
536 A false start is heard here: *'ayétsa— 'ayétsats aly'oonóoxa.*
537 A false start is heard here: *'avá— 'avá shoopéttəny nyikavátsnya.*
538 A false start is heard here: *pa'iipáats aviithíik— nyiithík lyavíim.*
539 This line literally means 'that which he did was one and he did it'.
540 False starts are heard here: *Kumstamxó— Kumastamxóts tsakwshá kwatsuumpáp— kwatsuumpápənya aakyíttk.*
541 *Nyaakyíttk* was changed to *nyaatskyíttk* upon review.
542 This line is heard as *'Amáy 'Aavétats apúy— Nyaapúyəm*. It was clarified upon review.
543 Mr. Bryant suggests *tsooyóqts viitháwəntík* 'his saliva is there too' as an alternative formulation of this line.
544 A false start is heard here: *'avíi— 'avíi nyiitháwk 'etá.*
545 A false start is heard here: *'Amáy 'Aavétxa— 'Aavéta iimáattənyts nyiuuthíka.*
546 This line is heard as *nyáava 'óor 'axwétt 'ím ashék* 'they named this red gold'. It was changed upon review.
547 This line is followed by a comment in English.
548 This line is followed by a comment in English.
549 A false start is heard here: *Kumastamxó— Kumastamxóts tsakwshá kwatsuumpápəny ashtúum.*
550 A false start is heard here: *Kum— Kumastamxóts a'íim.*
551 *Kwiixáalyts viithíixá xalyavíim* was changed to *kwiitsáalyts viithíi xalyavíim* upon review.
552 A false start is heard here: *'axány— 'axány 'a'íim.*
553 Tape 3B ends here.
554 Mr. Bryant suggests changing *'ata'aanyáaytsəxa* 'we will light it up' to the more literal *'ootanyétsəxa* 'we will cremate it'.
555 This line was inserted upon review.
556 A false start is heard here: *nyaany— nyaa'íim.*
557 This line is preceded by a brief exchange and several false starts.
558 Several false starts are heard here: *vathány— uu'íts vathány awíim avanoo— avoonóok aav'áarxáym*; it was corrected upon review.
559 This line is heard as *pa'iipáats nyiiaatuuqwíirək 'et*; it was changed upon review.
560 A false start is heard here: *nyáanyəm uuthíik— nyáanyik uuthíik.*
561 *Matxávi awíim* was changed to *matxávik awémk* upon review.
562 This line literally means 'he did not touch it'.
563 This line was originally spoken as *nyáava atháwəntik*; it was changed upon review.
564 A false start is heard here: *'any— 'axányənyts viiyáak.*
565 *Uukwaləpalápnya* was corrected to *kwaləpalápnya* at the time of recording.
566 A false start is heard here: *xaak— xáak ayémk aráwk 'et.*
567 This line literally means, 'he intended that the water would go through'.
568 Several false starts precede and occur within this line.

569 At the time of recording, Mr. Bryant suggests several ways to formulate this line. This formulation was preferred upon review.
570 A false start is heard here: *nyáanyi uu— nyaanyiimánk atséwk 'et.*
571 A false start is heard here: *waapóor— waapóorənti atséwk.* Mr. Bryant suggests *waapóor atséwəntik* as an alternative formulation of this line.
572 A false start is heard here: *pa'iipáa kwas'eethéets xam— aa— tsuumpápəm alyatsáam.*
573 A false start is heard here: *Pa'iipáa nyiikwandámənyts— xo— pa'iipáa nyiikamáanənyts.*
574 This and the following two lines were extracted from several minutes of discussion.
575 *'Axá amákəm* 'behind the water' was changed to *'axá maxákəm* 'under the water' upon review.
576 A false start is heard here: *Kaawíts— makyínyts— pa'iipáa tsakyíw 'ím áarək uuváak athúm.*
577 Four minutes of narrative (which duplicates the following material) and discussion are omitted here.
578 For the sake of consistency, *Kwalytátt* was replaced with the preferred form *Kwalyaatátt* upon review.
579 A false start is heard here: *Kumastamxóts Yaavapóoy— Yaavapáay nyiikanáavək.*
580 A false start is heard here: *Yaavapáay nyatsuuváa— nyatsuuváay a'ím.*
581 A false start is heard here: *'Axánya aatsuu— aatsxuukyíts a'íinyək.*
582 A false start is heard here: *'Axám— 'axám áam 'ím aatsuuxáyəmək.*
583 This line is pieced together from a brief discussion.
584 A false start is heard here: *'axá aatsxuukyí— xa— aatsxuukyítsk a'et.*
585 For the sake of consistency, *Kwaruutátt* was replaced with the preferred form *Kwalyaatátt* upon review. A brief discussion takes place here.
586 A brief discussion follows this line.
587 A false start is heard here: *nyáanyi muunóo i— nyáanyi moonóoxá.*
588 *Thomayúuvək* was corrected to *thomayúuvəxá* upon review.
589 *'Anyamátt* was changed to *'anyamátt-ts* upon review.
590 This line is preceded by several false starts.
591 A false start is heard here: *Matta— Mantish Aa'ár uu'ítsənyts.*
592 A false start is heard here: *Kwaatúulyts 'eethóo— 'eethóonya kamíim 'et.*
593 False starts are heard here: *Kumastamxó nyiioo'éeyətsxanya matxá— matxá— matxá 'anyáa s— matxá 'anyáa kwaaxwíir nyiitsáam.*
594 False starts are heard here: *kwas'eethée ku— kwa'uuxúuttnya nyaaxáap— kavéely 'anyáaxáap kwaaxwíirəny nyiitsáantik.*
595 *Koopóoyənyts* was changed to *koopóoʎny* upon review.
596 This is line is pieced together from several attempts and some discussion
597 This line is heard as *makyík matta— mattatháw aly'émxáyk.* *aly'émxáyk* was changed to *aly'ém 'ím* upon review.
598 *aly'émxáyk* was changed to *aly'ém 'ím* upon review.
599 Tape 4A ends here. This line is repeated on Tape 4B.
600 A false start is heard here: *mattáar nyiits— nyiitsatspáatsk 'éta.*
601 A period of silence occurs here, followed by discussion.
602 *nyiitsaayóoyk* was changed to *nyiiaatsooyóoyk* upon review.
603 This line is followed by some discussion.
604 A false start is heard here: *pa'iipáa— Kumstamxóts pa'iipáa kwas'itthítsnya*

'ashíintəm nyiiqáast.
605 Some material is omitted here, and Tape 4B ends. The omitted material is restated on Tape 5A, which begins at this point.
606 A brief discussion takes place here.
607 False starts are heard here: 'avá kwa— 'avá kwatiinyáam alyaakxávəm— m'áshk 'et.
608 A false start is heard here: piipáanyts makyík— makyí uuváam ooyóov aly'émək 'et.
609 Some material is omitted here.
610 A false start is heard here: Nyáanyily uuvám ayúuk 'et— ooyóovək 'et.
611 A false start is heard here: Mar— Marxókavék.
612 A false start is heard here: kaa— shoopóow aly'émtək 'ét.
613 A false start is heard here: nyaawí— nyaathúum.
614 A false start is heard here: 'atsaayúu 'amáyts— 'amáy kwatháwənya.
615 A false start is heard here: 'avá ka— kwatiinyáam alyavák uuvát.
616 Oopóoyəm was changed to oopóoyk upon review.
617 Awéxay was changed to awéxaym upon review.
618 This line literally means 'he thought and he cut them into pieces'.
619 Nyam'aakwíints was changed to nyam'aakwíintsəxá upon review.
620 Mr. Bryant suggests nyáany aauukwíly 'a'íim 'ashéxá 'I will name that the feathered staff' as an alternative formulation of this line.
621 Aauupíly was corrected to aauukwíly upon review.
622 The Kar'úk is an important Quechan mourning ceremony which dates back to this point in the Creation story. For further information on the Kar'úk, see Halpern (1997).
623 Mr. Bryant suggests nyiishúitk as an alternative to nyiishúit.
624 Mr. Bryant suggests 'atsaayúuts makyí atháwəm as an alternative formulation of this line.
625 This and the preceding line literally mean 'things were anywhere, and their unrealized using of them did not exist'.
626 Mr. Bryant suggests iiwáam ootséwəts as an alternative formulation of this line.
627 A comment in English follows this line.
628 A false start is heard here: Kamayáa nyavály ak— aakxávək.
629 Kwa'aapányəny was changed to Kwa'aapányənyts upon review.
630 Maatsuupílyk was changed to maatsuupílyxa upon review.
631 Mathútsxá was changed to muuthúutsəxá upon review.
632 The narrative is briefly interrupted here for a change of microphone battery. The narrative resumes after one false start and some discussion.
633 A false start is heard here: kaawém 'atsana— 'atsawíi nyaa'íim.
634 This line literally means 'your unrealized doing of it properly and going away somewhere would not exist'.
635 Mr. Bryant suggests Xavatsáats 'akútstək athútya as an alternative formulation of this line.
636 Nyashék was changed to 'ashék upon review.
637 To avoid confusion, Xaanyényənyts was changed to Xavatsáatsənyts upon review.
638 nyaaly'íim was changed to nyaalyavíim upon review.
639 A false start is heard here: Piipáa paaxaly— Kwalya'óots nyáany ashék.
640 This line is preceded by several false starts: xamshé kamán — xamshé — 'akwé kamán.

641 'Akwíi was changed to 'Akwíik upon review.
642 A false start is heard here: 'aavé— 'aavé taaxánəny nyaanyiimánk a'íim.
643 Aqásk 'he summoned him' was changed to ashék 'he named him' upon review.
644 Two lines are omitted here.
645 A false start is heard here: Matt'— Matt'á a'ím ashék.
646 This line is heard as talypó uuítsəny 'atsaayúuts. 'atsaayúuts was deleted upon review.
647 A false start is heard here: Nyáanya— nyáanyi kamánk a'ét.
648 Mr. Bryant suggests Pa'iipáa kwanyaméts siiv'óowk nyiiv'óowt as an alternatiave formulation of this line.
649 A false start is heard here: 'Astamuuxán— 'Astamuuxán a'íim ashék. The name is given as 'Ashtamathúun by Harrington; Mr. Bryant is not familiar with either version of the name. Some discussison follows this line.
650 Kumastamxó was changed to Kumastamxóts upon review.
651 A false start is heard here: Eethóony aashkwáaly 'axály— 'axály katsáam.
652 This line is heard as mattáam— mattáam shaaxúukəm 'ten years'. It was corrected upon review.
653 A comment in English follows this line.
654 Viikwathíinyəntinya was changed to viikwathíintinya upon review.
655 A'éxa was changed to ma'éxa upon review.
656 'Ashéntənyts was changed to 'ashéntəntíts upon review.
657 False starts are heard here: 'Anyáats piipáa mootsétsnya Xakshii— Xakshíi ma'ét— 'a'étxa.
658 'Atsxavashúu nyaa'ét was changed to 'atsxavashúuny a'ét upon review.
659 'Throwing the gourd' means playing a gourd rattle. This expression is probably a calque from Quechan 'axnáaly atáp-k 'he throws the gourd (i.e. he plays a gourd rattle)'.
660 A false start is heard here: 'Anyáavik— 'avá 'anyáavik oov'ótsk 'ét.
661 Kayémk was corrected to kaayémk upon review.
662 One line has been omitted here.
663 This line is heard as pa'iipáa avathúuts nyáanyəm kavéely maayémxa; it was changed upon review.
664 A false start is heard here: nyaanyi— nyaanyiimánk.
665 The second word of this line is indecipherable; alynyiimuuthúutsəxa was suggested upon review.
666 This line is heard as makyím manyavá— manyaváyk alymoonóom; it was changed upon review.
667 A false start is heard here: nyáanyi Kumastamxó nyiivoo— nyiivoo'óowənya nyáany oov'ótsapatk.
668 Mr. Bryant suggests vuu'átsk athúulya'émxayk avoonóok nyáany lyavíik as an alternative formulation of this line.
669 'Anyaaxáapk was changed to 'anyáavi upon review.
670 A false start is heard here: 'Avíi Vér— 'Avíi 'Avérá apámk 'et.
671 This is a mountain east of Riverside, California.
672 A false start is heard here: vanyaa— nyaapám.
673 A false start is heard here: 'anyáavi k— kwatsén— kwaatsénənyts.
674 A false stsart is heard here: Kumasta— xoo— Kumastamxóts nya— nyáany áar aly'émk 'eta.
675 Atséw 'et was changed to atséwk 'et upon review.

676 A false start is heard here: *Marxókavék nyáany— nyáany a'tim.*
677 *'Axány* was changed to *'axányi* upon review.
678 A false start is heard here: *'Atsaayú— 'axányənyts aráwtánk 'et.*
679 Mr. Bryant suggests *xiipúktan aatxuukyítsk a'tinyək nyeekwévək 'ét* 'first they tried to cross (but) it was no good, they say' as an alternative formulation of this line.
680 False starts are heard in this line: *pa'iipáa Marx— Marxókavé— Marxókavék apáyk viiwáak 'eta.*
681 This line is heard as *aaxakyéevək- aaxakyíik*. It was changed upon review.
682 Mr. Bryant suggests *'Avíi 'Avuulypó nyaapámk* as an alternative formulation of this line.
683 *Marxókavék* was changed to *Marxókavékts* upon review.
684 A false start is heard here: *Vathány 'amátt— 'iiwáam 'anyamátt-ts athútya.*
685 *Nyáanya* was changed to *nyáanyi* upon review.
686 A false start is heard here: *'Amó Kwata— 'Amó Kwata'órv uu'íts athúuk 'et.*
687 This mountain is also known as *'Avíi Kwata'órv.*
688 This line literally means 'it results from the flames'.
689 A false start is heard here: *nyáany— Marxókavék nyaa'íntik.*
690 A false start is heard here: *Marxók— Marxókavékts aatsooyóoyəm.*
691 A false start is heard here: *'atsaayúu nyiikwantuuwám— nyiik— nyiikwan— nyiikwandam awítsk 'et.*
692 This line literally means 'he really tells them, he finishes it, he does'.
693 A false start is heard here: *'Anyáa— 'anyáa tsuumpápəm vaaydak.*
694 A false start is heard here: *Marxókavékts nyiits— nyii'tik 'eta.*
695 A false start is heard here: *Pa'ii— pa'iipáa kwas'eethéets 'atáyk.*
696 A false start is heard here: *'Amó Kwan— 'Amó Kwata'órəv.*
697 This line was inserted upon review.
698 A false start is heard here: *'Amátt— 'amátt aly'axávxa.*
699 A comment in English follows this line.
700 This line literally means 'it reached his thighs'.
701 A false start is heard here: *nyaa— nyaaxamókəm.*
702 A false start is heard here: *malyxó— malyxóts.*
703 A false start is heard here: *'iimáattnya— 'iimáatt malyxóts.*
704 This line literally means 'he did his wings four times, they say'.
705 *Kwaxamáaly* was corrected to *kwanyíily* upon review.
706 False starts are heard here: *'Ashpáa 'Atsíi Kwats— Kwats— 'Atsíi Kwatssáa.* This line is followed by a comment in English.
707 Mr. Bryant suggests *nyaasiimánk avaathíik* 'they came from there and they came' as an alternative formulation of this line.
708 A false start is heard here: *nyaav— nyaanyiimánk vaathiik athútya.*
709 A false start is heard here: *'axá sa'ílyənyts vi— avathík.* Mr. Bryant suggests *'axá sa'ílyənyts viithík avathík* as an alternative formulation.
710 Mr. Bryant explained that this is a reference to San Francisco Bay.
711 A false start is heard here: *nya— nyáany aamáarək.*
712 Mr. Bryant explained that at this point they headed north to skirt San Francisco Bay.
713 This line is heard as *'avíits shipashípk* 'a mountain was sharp-pointed'; it was changed upon review.
714 This line originally read *nyáany aakwíinək*; it was changed upon review.

715 Literally, 'That Which Carries Fog'. This mountain is also known as San Jacinto Peak.
716 This line is heard as *oonyó nyiitíivək avatíiv*; it was changed upon review.
717 Mr. Bryant suggests *'axóttəm nyooyóovək* (which has the same meaning but uses the plural verb form *nyooyóovək*) as an alternatiave formulation of this line.
718 Mr. Bryant suggests *shaly'áyts mattapéek nyiitháwk 'etá* as an alternative formulation of this line.
719 This refers to the Grand Canyon.
720 Mr. Bryant suggests *piipáats 'atáytank athutyá* as an alternative formulation of this line.
721 This line is heard as *aaíim takyéevək vaathíik 'etəmá*; it was changed upon review.
722 A false start is heard here: *aany— aashmátsk athótk*.
723 They did split up: some (who became the Havasupai) went to the Grand Canyon and some (who became the Hualapai) went to the Kingman area.
724 This refers to the Yuma Valley.
725 Mr. Bryant suggests *uu'íitsk avoonóok a'étəma* as an alternative formulation of this line.
726 *Nyáanya* was changed to *nyáanyəm* upon review.
727 *Kwaatsáan* was changed to *Kwaatsáants* upon review.
728 Mr. Bryant suggests *avaathíinyək nyáavi apák* 'they came and they got here' as an alternative formulation of this line.
729 Mr. Bryant suggests *vaayáanyək* (with same meaning but plural verb form) as an alternative formulation of this line.
730 Mr. Bryant suggests *akúulyəntik 'eta* (with same meaning but plural verb form) as an alternative formulation of this line.
731 A false start followed by a pause precedes this line.
732 A false start is heard here: *mat— matxávik shathómpk vaayáak*.
733 Mr. Bryant suggests *matxávik athúuk a'ét* as an alternative formulation of this line.
734 A false start is heard here: *ats- 'axányts atsénk viithíik*.
735 A false start is heard here: *kaaw— kaawémk avathót*.
736 A false start is heard here: *saa— saayáaxayk*.
737 *Viitháwxáy* was changed to *viitháwxáym* upon review.
738 Mr. Bryant suggests *nyooyóovək* (with same meaning but plural verb form) as an alternative formulation of this line.
739 Literally, 'they have had it as their name'. Ordinarily *shiimúly* means 'to have it as one's clan name', but here it refers to the tribal name.
740 A line is omitted here.
741 This line is heard as *'Axám Kwa— aaxáv 'eta*. It was changed upon review.
742 Two indecipherable syllables are faintly heard at the end of this line. When asked about them, Mr. Bryant suggested that the entire line should read *Xamaakxáv a'ím nyiishúitk* 'they named them Mojave'.
743 Mr. Bryant suggests *nyáany a'íim 'ítya* 'they are called that' as an alternative formulation of this line.
744 They went through water when crossing from Arizona to California.
745 This is a reference to Pai (perhaps Yavapai) people.
746 *'Axám aatsuukúly-k* literally means 'they climb water' but it is used idiomatically to mean 'they went upstream'.

747 'Axáts aráawk literally means 'water was swift'; here it is used idiomatically to refer to rapids.
748 This line is heard as nyáany kwaa'úurnyəm aayáamək; aayáamək (a form otherwise unattested) was changed to aayáak upon review.
749 A false start can be heard here: 'Axály— 'axály oonóok uuthúuts aly'ém.
750 A false start is heard here: aats— 'amáttnyi athúum.
751 The word 'axánya is unclear in the recording; it was clarified upon review.
752 A false start is heard here: kwanyam— kwanyamély apámantík 'etá.
753 A false start is heard here: 'avíits vii— viiyáanyək.
754 A false start is heard here: nyáanyi uuqáarək sii— siivám ooyóovək.
755 Mr. Bryant suggests nyáany kaa'émk ashék a'ím as an alternative formulation of this line.
756 Nyatsuuváayv was changed to nyatsuuváayvək upon review.
757 This line is heard as nyiimúlyəny; it was changed upon review.
758 For the sake of consistency, Xawáalyapáy was changed to Xawáalyapáay here and in the following line.
759 Mr. Bryant suggests tsapéevək avathík kwayúu lyavíit as an alternative formulation of this line.
760 Mr. Bryant suggests 'amáy tan athótk athúm as an alternative formulation of this line.
761 A false start is heard here: aly— kaathomk alyuuváak. Upon review, Mr. Bryant suggests replacing alyuuváak to the plural form vanyoonóok.
762 A false start is heard here: aatsxuukyítsk aats— aakavék athúuk 'ím.
763 Uuváat was changed to the plural form avoonóot upon review.
764 Ayéxaym (apparently based on a stem ayé which is not otherwise attested) was changed to ayáaxaym upon review.
765 Mr. Bryant suggests 'axóttk uuyúu lyavíik a'ím as an alternative formulation of this line.
766 A false start is heard here: 'is 'ii— 'amátt-ts siitháw.
767 A false start is heard here: nyáanyi aax— aapáxm.
768 Mr. Bryant suggests nyáany uuthúutsk a'eta'a 'they did it, they say' as an alternative formulation of this line.
769 Mr. Bryant suggests nyiitháwk as an alternative to avatháwk.
770 Awetá was changed to a'etá upon review.
771 This line literally means 'it was something, they say'.
772 This line actually means 'they saw it in the sky, and as an immediate result'. The loose translation given in the text is based on Mr. Bryant's explanation that the passage describes the way the sky was reflected in the water, making the water appear blue.
773 A false start is heard here: nyáa— 'Axá Xavashúu a'íim.
774 Mr. Bryant suggests uumúulyək a'ík a'ét as an alternative formulation of this line.
775 For the sake of consistency, 'Axá Xavashúupáy was changed to 'Axá Xavashúupáay here. Mr. Bryant suggests 'Axá Xavashúupáay a'íim uumúulyk as an alternative formulation of this line.
776 Nyáanyi was changed to nyáany upon review.
777 Mr. Bryant suggests 'axóttk avatíivək athót as an alternative formulation of this line.
778 Upon review, Mr. Bryant suggested replacing nyiikamáan with the demonstrative- and subject case-marked form nyiikamáanənyts.

779 False starts are heard here: *piipáa maatsawíts soo— soo— soonóom ayúuk*. Mr. Bryant suggests replacing *ayúuk* with *ooyóovək a'eta'á*.
780 Mr. Bryant suggests replacing *kanáavək* with *nyiiuukanáavək*.
781 Mr. Bryant suggests *avathúum athúuk a'étəma* 'it happened, they say' as an alternative formulation of this line.
782 A false start is heard here: *xaa— xáam aatsénk*.
783 This line could also mean 'they came down a different way'.
784 A false start is heard here; *'Axá— Xamakxáavəts a'étk*.
785 For the sake of consistency, *Xawáalyapáy* was changed to *Xawáalyapáay* here and in the following line.

This book does not end here…

At Open Book Publishers, we are changing the nature of the traditional academic book. The title you have just read will not be left on a library shelf, but will be accessed online by hundreds of readers each month across the globe. We make all our books free to read online so that students, researchers and interested readers who can't afford a printed edition can still have access to the same ideas as you.

Our digital publishing model also allows us to produce online supplementary material, including extra chapters, reviews, links and other digital resources. Find *Xiipúktan* on our website to access its online extras. Please check this page regularly for ongoing updates, and join the conversation by leaving your own comments: http://www.openbookpublishers.com/isbn/9781909254404

If you enjoyed this book, and feel that research like this should be available to all readers, regardless of their income, please think about donating to us. Our company is run entirely by academics, and our publishing decisions are based on intellectual merit and public value rather than on commercial viability. We do not operate for profit and all donations, as with all other revenue we generate, will be used to finance new Open Access publications.

For further information about what we do, how to donate to OBP, additional digital material related to our titles or to order our books, please visit our website: http://www.openbookpublishers.com.

The World Oral Literature Project is an urgent global initiative to document and disseminate endangered oral literatures before they disappear without record. Our website houses collections of recordings of oral literature, free-to-download publications of documentation theory and practice, and links to resources and funding for oral tradition fieldwork and archiving: http://www.oralliterature.org

In partnership with Open Book Publishers, the World Oral Literature Project has launched a book series on oral literature. The series preserves and promotes the oral literatures of indigenous people by publishing materials on endangered traditions in innovative ways.

www.ingramcontent.com/pod-product-compliance
Lightning Source LLC
Chambersburg PA
CBHW071842230426
43671CB00012B/2039